The
Voyage
of
Aquarius

The
Voyage
of
Aquarius

Matt Herron
Jeannine Herron
Matthew Herron
and
Melissa Herron

Saturday Review Press | E. P. Dutton & Co., Inc. | 1974

All photographs were taken by the Herrons, except for pp. 4–5 of the photo insert
—Lyle Bongé; and pp. 7, 11, 16–17, and 22–23—Phil Stiles.

LIBRARY OF CONGRESS CATALOGING IN PUBLICATION DATA
Main entry under title:

The Voyage of Aquarius.

1. Aquarius (Ship)   2.   Voyages and travels—
1951-   3.   North Atlantic Ocean.   I. Herron,
Matthew, 1931-
G530.A65V69   910'.41   74–7086

Grateful acknowledgment is tendered to Black Star Publishing Company for its
contribution to the development of this book.

Published simultaneously in Canada by Clarke, Irwin & Company
Limited, Toronto and Vancouver
ISBN: 0–8415–0339–7

Typography by Dorothea von Elbe

For Mat and Ruth, and Jim and Andrée,
Who launched seaworthy vessels.
For Minor, who set a course,
And Mort, who trimmed the sails.

Thanks to Jan Woolley for invaluable help
in preparation and editing of the manuscript.

Contents

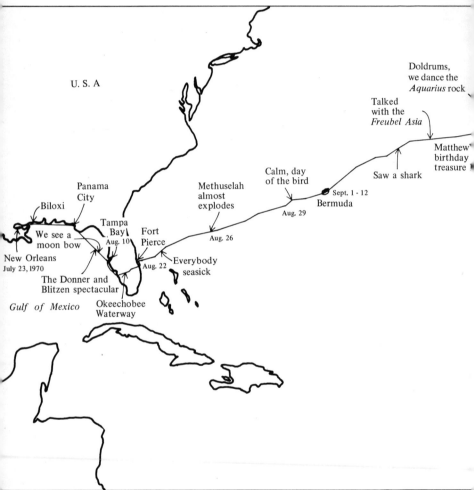

U. S. A

Doldrums,
we dance the
Aquarius rock

Talked
with the
Freubel Asia

Matthew'
birthday
treasure

Saw a shark

Panama
City

Methuselah
almost
explodes

Calm, day
of the bird

Bermuda
Sept. 1 - 12

Biloxi

Tampa
Bay
Aug. 10

Fort
Pierce

Aug. 26

Aug. 29

We see a
moon bow

New Orleans
July 23, 1970

Aug. 22

Everybody
seasick

The Donner and
Blitzen spectacular

Gulf of Mexico

Okeechobee
Waterway

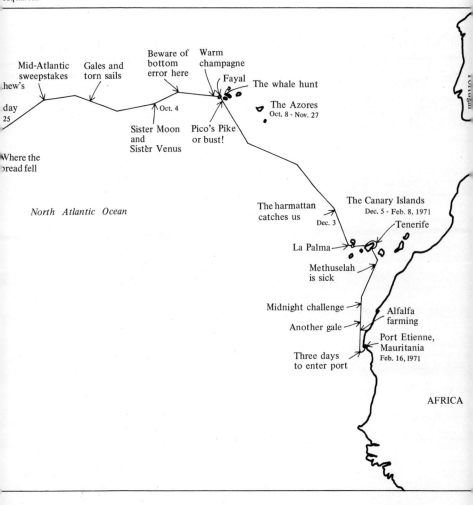

Mid-Atlantic sweepstakes

Gales and torn sails

Beware of bottom error here

Warm champagne

Fayal

The whale hunt

..hew's

day

25

Oct. 4

Sister Moon and Sister Venus

Pico's Pike or bust!

The Azores
Oct. 8 - Nov. 27

Where the bread fell

North Atlantic Ocean

The harmattan catches us

Dec. 3

The Canary Islands
Dec. 5 - Feb. 8, 1971

Tenerife

La Palma

Methuselah is sick

Midnight challenge

Another gale

Three days to enter port

Alfalfa farming

Port Etienne, Mauritania
Feb. 16, 1971

AFRICA

Portugal

Preface

This is the story of a sailing voyage by a family of four persons, two older and two younger—Matt and Jeannine, Matthew and Melissa. It began in the wind of the worst hurricane ever to strike the Gulf shores of the United States; it ended in the sand-flavored wind of a lonely African coast. In between, we learned much about ourselves and each other as we made our way across the North Atlantic; but what we learned was different for each because we are each different people. Thus we have written from four individual points of view. We hope the story is real for you, as it was for us, and that it will tempt you to venture forth from whatever solid ground you now stand upon to try the uncharted waters of a fresh adventure.

Heaven is far from the things of earth,
but it sets them in motion
by means of the wind.

I Ching

The
Voyage
of
Aquarius

1

Hurricane Camille

August 17–18, 1969

MATT: The wind blew straight out of the Mississippi swamps, raking the boatyard with diagonal volleys of rain and bringing the familiar stench of decaying swamp grass, mud and moldering cypress stumps. In the last half hour the tempo had clearly picked up. The gusts came more frequently, the strongest well over forty knots, and above the urgent thrashing of live oaks I could pick out a new rhythm, a ragged timpani from the tin roofs of the boat sheds. Not much time left to me now—no time to appreciate the awesome spectacle of a tropical hurricane closing in on the Mississippi Gulf Coast.

For several days I had followed the adolescent wanderings of tropical storm Camille with more than normal interest, watching her grow up and become a full-fledged hurricane. I had plotted her progress on my sailing chart of the Gulf of Mexico, and waited with increasing concern as she veered toward the mouth of the Mississippi River. Hurricanes are taken seriously along the Gulf Coast but nobody takes them quite so seriously as the sailor with a small boat tied up somewhere. For more than a year I had belonged to that special class of worriers and now on a dark afternoon in August I was trying desperately to prepare for my matriculation exam in a course I never wanted.

In former years hurricanes had meant action for me—excitement and employment, photo assignments from magazine editors in New York, long soggy drives to rural bayous, nights of waiting in small-town police stations, friendly jokes and endless cups of coffee, the howl of the wind and the crash of somebody else's roof tearing loose. I had learned to respect the awful power of hurricanes and had photographed my share of tragedy and mayhem. But it was always somebody else's loss, somebody else's tragedy that moved me. This time it might be different.

In the boatyard I surveyed my vessel: *Aquarius,* thirty-one feet of steel and mahogany, a cruising sailboat with single mast and auxiliary engine, four berths, galley and head—a self-sufficient world afloat and surely one of the world's most winsome vessels. *Aquarius,* apple of my eye. She could hardly have been in a more dangerous position. The previous week I had hauled her out of the bayou for painting and repairs. She stood now in the mud by the edge of a little harbor that gave onto the Pearl River, balanced on her keel by a few props and exposed like a steel Godiva to whatever calamity the coming winds might bring. A boat in the water, well moored in a sheltered anchorage, stands a good chance against a hurricane, but *Aquarius* was not in the water. Her decks stood well above my reach and her deep keel and ample lines presented a disturbing amount of windage to the sullen weather blowing in out of the Gulf. Could she possibly survive? There was no way of knowing, not even time to ponder the question. Around me Jay Eagan and his boatyard crew worked like maniacs to save their tools and equipment. The hoist that might have been used to return *Aquarius* to the safety of the water was now occupied by a large fishing boat. There was no help for me here—no haven anywhere. I must do the best I could with the materials at hand in the few hours remaining.

My problem was not simply to secure the boat against

wind. The major damage from hurricanes usually comes from the combined forces of wind and water. As a storm advances it pushes a great mass of water ahead of it, causing abnormally high tides along the coastline. The water gets up into undefended places and the violent winds churn it into short vicious waves that can pulverize boats, buildings and people in a matter of minutes. Camille was described by the New Orleans Weather Bureau as a small but unusually violent hurricane. Already winds of a hundred and fifty miles an hour had been recorded—twice minimum hurricane force. Even more alarming, tides of twenty to twenty-five feet were predicted along the Gulf Coast. Eagan's boatyard circled a small dredged basin a few feet above the high-tide mark several miles up the Pearl River where it formed the border between Mississippi and Louisiana. A few years ago another hurricane had pumped twelve feet of water up the Pearl and nearly wiped Eagan out. He was determined it wouldn't happen again, and I followed his advice in preparing my boat.

My first job was to make sure she didn't blow over. I dragged a dozen railroad ties through the rain and mud, leaned them against the sides of the hull and chainsawed them to appropriate lengths. I staked the ties in place at the bottom and wedged them tight at the top. With twelve new legs canting out in all directions along her sides, *Aquarius* began to look like a huge mythological spider. I was beginning to feel better. She might stand now against wind, but what about water?

I tried to visualize this boatyard invaded by twelve to twenty feet of the Gulf of Mexico. By opening the hull apertures, the sink drain and the engine water intake, I could convert *Aquarius* into a submarine. The waters would rise around and inside her, and she would probably stay put, sunk in place. Or I could leave her watertight and floating, hoping that anchor lines would save her from being driven off to rust on her side in some swamp twenty miles away. I thought of the salt water rising inside the hull, the ruined interior, the waterlogged engine that would have to be hauled out, torn down and rebuilt. Then I thought of the swamp with the hulks of fishing boats, melancholy relics of the last hurricane, scattered across it. It was not a happy choice: certain water damage against the possibility of losing the boat. I chose to let her float and trust to the ropes. Some part of me rebelled against sinking a boat.

It seemed strange to be so carefully anchoring a land-locked boat, but I broke out lines and anchors and scraped two holes in the clay of the boatyard several hundred feet off the bow and stern where I buried the anchors. I strung the anchor lines aboard and wrapped them with tape to prevent chafing where they came over the rails. I made one line fast around the base of the mast and anchored the other to a large winch on the starboard coaming. I borrowed more line and ran tethers to a telephone pole on one side (would it stand?) and a massive dredge on the other (no problem about *that* baby!). I hauled the mast to high ground and tied it to a tree. The dinghy went also to high ground, odds and ends were piled in my battered van and finally there was nothing left to do.

Around me the boatyard was beginning to look like a battlefield. Its skin of red Mississippi clay and swamp fill had melted under the downpour into a rich viscous mud, churned to gumbo by the procession of trucks, bulldozers and drag-lines which Jay Eagan and his black crew had hauled to high ground. The mud was everywhere, slowing the work. It caked and balled under my tennis shoes until I sloshed along on ridiculous elevator clodhoppers. To the right of me stood the machine shop, a substantial building roughly forty by sixty feet—galvanized tin sheeting over a heavy steel frame-work. Inside the shop preparations for the expected high water were almost complete. Most of the machines and tool benches remained in position but had been jacked and propped up until they were ten or twelve feet off the floor. A giant diesel engine hung from the ridge pole, a hefty eight-inch I-beam. A smaller engine hung from a chain hoist next to it. In the center of the shop a crippled dragline of fifteen or twenty tons had been laboriously jacked up to rest on a Lincoln-Log tower of railroad ties. It was as if the shop had come under the new management of Paul Bunyan who had rearranged everything to a convenient working height. In the small harbor in front of the shop four or five boats lay captive in a spiderweb of mooring lines. They were the invalids and abandoned children of a much larger fleet already moved by various owners to more protected waters. Around the harbor perimeter the boat sheds creaked and rattled in the wind. I did not expect to see them in the morning. The fishing boat in its wheeled cradle hunched incongruously on a hummock next to Eagan's house, and the house itself, a two-story brick structure, was nestled solidly in a grove of live oaks about twelve feet above mean high-tide level.

It was time for us to take shelter there. The wind carried a new note of hysteria, more than a promise of impending violence in the urgent crescendos that swelled every few moments from snigger to shriek. Primal forces ruled the world. Air tore at my clothes, tore barrages of rain from the sullen overcast glowering over the boatyard. Water poured over my body, mixing with mud and sweat. Strangely, I felt exhilarated. Everything done that could be done. Go for broke now. It was the storm's turn and I could only watch and wait.

I couldn't even return to the relative safety of my home in New Orleans. The highway, according to radio reports, was already under several feet of water and Camille was now expected to drive ashore somewhere between the city of Pascagoula seventy miles to the east, and the mouth of the Mississippi to the west. Maybe here. It was going to be quite a night.

I felt like Captain Noah as I took a last careful look at my ark, high and dry but moored as if for a mighty flood. Noah pinned his hopes for survival on God and stout boat. I trusted to luck and strong lines to save my boat, for *Aquarius* represented a kind of survival for me, too. If it perished, a lot of careful plans, a lot of hopes for a different kind of life would go down with it. In a very real sense *Aquarius* was my access to a new medium, a sea change I had searched for to restore balance in a life I felt was going soft with comfort and routine. I hoped, somehow, to replace the secondhand experiences, the emotion-by-proxy that had so deadened the taste of life for me in modern electronic America, to replace it with a series of primary encounters between my family, the sea, and whatever people the sea might bring to us. It was a romantic idea; I realized that. I wanted to explore hardship and tranquility, touch new coastlines, gaze at unfamiliar faces, put out questions in an uncharted world and wait for answers to filter back through the circuits of experience. *Aquarius* was my vessel. I hoped to fill it with life right up to the existential brim, the level where experience tastes strongest. If my vessel broke in the tempest there would be no refreshment for a long time to come. I looked again to the ropes. Would they hold? They *had* to hold!

We gathered in the Eagans' house, those of us who chose or were forced to stay and see this hurricane through. There were twelve altogether: young Jay Eagan, his wife, and their little girl—a blue-eyed three-year-old with Shirley Temple curls—and Jay's father, Dan, who occupied the command post, a captain's chair facing a brace of sliding glass doors that overlooked the boatyard. Dan was a massive man who had abandoned active work in the yard to his son after it gave him an ulcer, and he grew more and more morose as he watched through the night the fruits of ten years' labor ripped to kindling. Mrs. Eagan ministered to us with coffee and unflagging cheerfulness from the axis of her orbit in the kitchen. Jay's older brother, another Dan, down from New Orleans with his fiancée completed the family group. The others were a mixed lot: I, and some neighbors caught by the storm.

With a change of clothes and a mug of hot soup warming my insides I began to feel more optimistic about our prospects. Solid walls considerably diminished the impact of the howling wind and thrashing trees outside. In a corner of the darkened living room, the still functioning television glowed a cathode blue, bringing the banality of a rerun Western through the wild ether to reassure us that all was still right with the world. Even the telephone continued working after a fashion although it could not be forced to conjure up my family in New Orleans. A few hours later it quietly expired along with the electric power.

We refugees gathered comfortably around a small transistor radio to hear latest reports of the storm's progress. Camille was now expected to miss New Orleans entirely and cross the coastline somewhere east of us. New Orleans D.J.s chattered knowingly about local damage—blown-out billboards and flooded streets—but from Pass Christian twenty-five miles to our east a citizen telephoned in an awesome description of the fury of the approaching storm as he faced it on the beachfront. I would have preferred to think of that coastline as entirely evacuated but now I began to wonder about the fate of those who stayed to see the storm through. It did not occur to me to put ourselves in the same category.

As the hours passed the radio brought less and less information. The chatter from New Orleans only emphasized the ominous silence from the Mississippi Gulf Coast where Camille was beginning to deliver her most damaging blows. Our only guide to what was happening around us was the state of our barometer and the direction of the wind outside. At ten P.M. the wind continued to blow out of the east, indicating Camille's eye was still offshore, but the cosy little knotty-pine barometer on the kitchen wall hovered near the absolute bottom of its scale and I was horrified to see the needle suddenly dip visibly lower. It was a quiet little movement but I had never known the pressure to drop so fast you could actually *see* the barometer fall, and it brought home to me the full gravity of our situation.

Outside everything was darkness and chaos although I could still see, dimly and intermittently through sheets of rain, some of the principal features of the boatyard. I opened a door and trained the beams of two powerful torches so they converged in the vicinity of *Aquarius* somewhere off in the holocaust. She was completely invisible but I could just make out the shape of one of the railroad ties slanting dimly against her side. That was enough. The tie was like a battle flag and so long as it remained in position I knew the fort was secure. I returned with the torches time and again to seek it out.

It was strange to haul open a door and stand at the threshold of the storm. The noise was overpowering. I had always thought wind "whistled" or maybe "screamed," but this sound had no music, no character, no individual notes to it, just a steady, deafening, monotonous roar—a never-ending avalanche of noise like a thousand jets at takeoff. At first I expected to be knocked flat, but the threshold seemed to be an enchanted barrier which the wind never crossed with more than a buffet of air or a few drops of water. It was as if the hurricane knew its place and we left the sliding glass doors slightly ajar all night to protect them from being shattered by sudden changes of pressure. It was out of the question to step across that magic line, however. The world outside was peopled with lethal sheets of flying tin and shreds of airborne timber. I could hear the crashes as obscure missiles wrapped themselves around trees or collided with buildings. To stagger out into that demented universe was to invite decapitation. I had begun to think our sanctuary possessed some magic immunity though, when suddenly a crash sent us running upstairs. A bedroom window had collapsed and the storm was pouring its wet violence into the room. We spiked a sheet of plywood up to stop the breech.

At midnight the storm was still increasing. The barometer had dropped completely off its scale and we could no longer judge the intensity of the wind. Beyond "too much" there was a sameness that defied analysis. (Later I learned from the Weather Bureau that Camille's winds had exceeded two hundred miles an hour before blowing the anemometer clean off its mast. This was the highest velocity ever recorded for a hurricane anywhere. At our location the wind must easily have topped a hundred and fifty.) The night outside was punctuated now by loud indefinite crashes that gave evidence the boatyard was beginning to come apart. We never heard the sequential departures of the various boat sheds, nor did we receive news of the death of several modern apartments overlooking the tiny harbor, but events nearer home made themselves known. In front of us a tool shed shucked its tin roof to the wind, sheet by sheet, like palm leaves peeling off a thatch. And from deeper in the night came a great ominous explosion like an artillery barrage. We rushed to the windows. A crash that big had to signal a major change in the geography of the boatyard, but for minutes our probing torches illuminated nothing. When at last we worked it out, the change was not a new feature but a great empty void. The workshop, that huge steel building, had simple vanished into the night. There was no sign of wreckage, no trace of all the tools and equipment it contained, nothing but a murky emptiness where the shop once stood. The giant diesel that hung from the roof beam must have whipped off into the swamp like a rubber ball on a string. We were stunned by the loss—we looked at each other in simple disbelief. And then a deep gloom began to settle over us and with it the conviction that this hurricane, so infinitely more awful than any we had ever known, would grind on and on, like an immense angry machine until everything around us was sucked to destruction.

A sick dread settled in my stomach, a sense of helpless impotence. The storm no longer seemed merely threatening. It was monstrous, it would destroy us and everything we owned. How could *Aquarius* stand up to such a wind? It didn't seem possible and I went, reluctantly now, to probe the night once more for the railroad tie that was my only sign of the boat's existence. I swept and reswept the darkness with my lights, looking for the tie's diagonal slant. I paused again and again, misinterpreting a slash of rain or settling hopefully on some obscure tumble of debris, but nothing in all that angry murk would resolve itself into a prop against a steel hull. Finally, facing away from the storm, I faced with certainty the awful truth. The tie was gone and with it, beyond any doubt, my *Aquarius.*

For a moment I felt nothing. And then, flooding in with the realization of loss came an understanding of what *Aquarius* had meant, how much more it had been to me than simply a boat, how inextricably it had become involved in our hopes and plans for the future, how different life would seem without it.

I remembered that grand moment two years ago when I first took the helm, nine months of searching behind me and all the frantic weeks of negotiation and purchase, hauling and painting, stocking and fitting out for the voyage from Miami home to New Orleans. I was not at the helm as we eased away from the dock at Dinner Key Marina and out into Biscayne Bay. I was much too frightened for that. Lyle Bongé, a friend and veteran yachtsmen from Biloxi, was there to help me, and as the steady breeze filled the sails Lyle turned to me: "Here. It's your boat."

My boat? I could hardly comprehend that idea yet. I was still numb with the sin of purchase, my Puritan conscience reeling from the shock of pouring all my savings into this yacht of pleasure, this rich man's thing, this wild and extravagant indulgence. I touched the tiller tentatively, felt life in the wood, the energy of the wind transmitting through the sails, translating kinetically to the hull pressing through the water—that force coming back alive to me through the oak shaft, through my arm, my body, my brain. I looked forward along the lines of it, this lovely machine that needed only wind to move it. It seemed huge to me. I could feel its bulk, the momentum of seven tons of steel pressing through the bright water. I gave the helm a tentative push and *Aquarius* responded, heeling a little, picking up a touch of speed, moving coherently between the bay and the sky only because I held the helm. A light burned my eyes, a heat surged along my spine. Salt air stuffed my lungs till I couldn't release them. We sailed on and on into the gathering dusk, a pact and a promise growing between myself and this lovely boat. New life here. Something growing. I want more of it.

Now, the promise dead, my mind moved again, back to a golden California afternoon, Jeannine and I climbing into the hills behind Berkeley. The hilltops were just beginning to lose their lamb fuzz of winter green and we pushed exuberantly up through the bracken and the brambles. We had something exciting to talk about and we needed a place to let our talk expand, a space big enough for it. Jeannine had just been offered a research job down the bay near Stanford, a job very close to her major interest, the organization of language in the brain. The job would not be available for two years, but the offer fitted our needs perfectly. After four graduate years of dissecting cadavers, memorizing nerve pathways, preparing specimens for the electron microscope, and then rushing home to cook for a hungry family and pour over anatomy books far into the night, Jeannine was more than ready for a change. She had been splitting herself between two worlds, accepting the buffets of preparing for a professional career in the neurosciences, and agonizing over whether she was being mother enough to her children. What she needed, what we both needed, was breathing space. Time away from our careers, time to reflect on our lives, and something new and completely different to absorb us.

There was no question what we wanted to do. *Aquarius* had been waiting almost two years for a major cruise. We had talked a lot about exploring the coral reefs off the coast of British Honduras. We'd even submitted proposals for an underwater film on marine biology using our two kids as actors. The film idea got nowhere but we could certainly scrape up enough other assignments to pay for some kind of trip. But somehow Honduras didn't feel ambitious enough. We sat back-to-back in the sun letting our minds stretch out for other ideas. Something was gnawing at the edge of my awareness. It surfaced suddenly in a single word. *"Africa!*

Africa," I breathed. "Jeannine, could we do it? *Could we sail to Africa?*" We looked at each other tensely. Sail to Africa? What a frightening, far-out, fantastic idea!

Since our marriage twelve years ago we'd been talking about visiting Africa as if it were some kind of mythological garden. Africa, nursery of the human race, natural habitat of the largest wild animal herds left on earth, home of a complexity of modern and ancient societies, revolutionary breeding place of third-world nations. Yet somehow our plans had never materialized—we couldn't be satisfied with a superficial tour and we hadn't the means for an extended visit. Maybe we could do it now by sailboat, carrying our home with us, teaching Matthew, thirteen, and Melissa, eleven, from textbooks, living simply and spending almost nothing for transportation or lodging.

It was one of those ideas that teetered at the brink of wild improbability yet maintained enough of a bare clawhold in the realm of possibility that we had to take it seriously. We circled it warily, this unknown and possibly dangerous beast. We poked at it from odd angles, testing it, half afraid it would vanish or explode wrathfully in our faces. But it did neither. It got a hold on us from the start.

Could we do it? We had never really been to sea before. We knew almost nothing of navigation, heavy weather sailing, or any of the thousand seaman's skills that made an ocean passage so different from a weekend cruise. Yet I felt we could manage all that. Could *Aquarius* do it? I knew that boats her size and smaller had crossed the Atlantic without mishap every season, and I felt with careful preparation *Aquarius* would manage the voyage in style. Where would we get the money? From picture assignments? Maybe my agency, Black Star, would put up some money. Maybe we could sell a book. Maybe we could rob a bank or peddle the Brooklyn Bridge. I had a hunch if we could pull the project together we'd find the money somewhere. There were a thousand questions to consider. Some would take months to answer, some we couldn't even formulate, but the idea, the voyage, gleamed clear in our minds and we carried it triumphantly home.

That idea was dead now. I returned to the Eagans' candle-lit living room and announced my loss. There was hardly a response. Too much had gone in the storm, too much for anyone to care about one boat. The disasters of the night had numbed our spirits like morphine. We sat nodding in corners, dozing on the floor, junkies of the hurricane. And outside the giant machine ground on. The wind swung from east through north to northwest as the eye of the hurricane passed inland somewhere to the east of us. Almost imperceptibly the wind began to diminish. Sharp announcements of mayhem came less frequently out of the night—perhaps there was nothing left to lose—but we did have one more general alarm.

About three I went to the door for a quick look outside. Water was invading our world. A strange cabin cruiser floated quietly in the back yard, and the river stood a few feet from the doorway ready to push into the house. I planted a stick in the mud at the water's edge and watched the brown foam creep forward and surround it. In minutes the water would be inside. We gathered hurriedly in the kitchen to make preparations for a siege. Drinking water was bottled and carried upstairs. Food, first aid equipment, torches and clothing followed. Jay waded into the back yard, captured the wandering cruiser and tethered it to the house. If the rising water became a flood this would serve well enough as our ark. I followed my first marker stick with a thin procession of sticks to chart the water's rise. The last stood at the doorstep with water lapping its feet. But three minutes later the stick still held its ground, and in five the water had retreated leaving the stick a soggy foothold three inches above the flood. A reprieve of sorts. The hurricane winds, which had driven the Gulf waters up the Pearl to the edge of our doorstep, were backing to the west now, urging the flood back to sea.

I do not remember many expressions of thanksgiving.

Like somnambulists we filed back into the living room and dropped into our individual positions of slumber. None of us looked forward to the unveiling that dawn would bring and I was the only one awake when the first gray tentacles of light began to sift through our shattered world. The wind had almost stopped and I fumbled blindly out into the light, an irradiated mole surfacing in postatomic rubble.

It was hard to take in such extravagant destruction all at once. The house, the only generally undamaged object I could see, squatted solidly at the hub of a vast wheel of havoc, a fringe of shredded awnings hanging limply from its sides like a grass skirt plucked to shreds by impatient rapists. Gathered around the house like amputees, the live oaks thrust their shattered and denuded stumps of branches toward the sullen sky. The discarded limbs formed a vast undulating sea of foliage which covered the ground all around to a depth of six or seven feet. Here and there an automobile thrust a despairing aerial above the waves.

I gave the landward side of the house only a glance and turned my wondering eyes to the west where water still covered the marina and shops with a gray, debris-strewn scum. There among the wrecks of motor launches and drunken hulks of houseboats stood a single undamaged boat, an apparition that looked remarkably like *Aquarius*. I blinked and focused again as one would check an uncertain image at night through lightning flashes; and even as the hot waves of relief washed over me I grappled with the crazy, capricious, inexplicable phenomenon of her survival—for *Aquarius* appeared to have endured only by divine providence or magical charm.

She stood in her original position quite upright and stately with water around her ankles. The flood had risen almost to her waterline and then fallen away. All the railroad ties that once spiderlegged along her sides had vanished, washed away in the night. A piece of tin roofing sagged limply against her rudder. The four ropes intended to hold her in place all hung slack at her sides. There was no visible agent to keep her upright and yet upright she stood, all seven tons of her: balanced, inexplicably *balanced* on the six-inch width of her keel! It defied all logic, all laws of man and nature. Somehow she had stood like this without props against the pressures of the wind that had brought down in ruins all the works of the boatyard around her. I could not explain it, I could not even imagine a possible explanation, and like a simple superstitious creature I began to feel a conviction growing in me that I had witnessed some kind of Sign. We would prevail together, the Sign suggested, ourselves and this boat which had defied the windy bitch, Camille. We had prevailed here and would prevail many times more against the ocean and all the unforseeable dangers of the voyage to Africa. Together we would make it.

2

"Dear Mom and Dad"

JEANNINE:

September 15, 1969

Dear Mom and Dad,

Thanks for your thoughtful letter. We understand your concerns about our trip and I will try to reply the best I can. It's natural to be worried when those you love are contemplating what seems to be a risky venture. I won't deny that there are certain risks in undertaking this trip—risks to our finances, risks to our health, perhaps even our lives. But there are steps we can take to minimize these risks and in the end they may be no greater than the risks of living in a large American city or driving an automobile on American highways.

Actually a well-supplied and well-sailed boat is quite safe at sea. People cross oceans in small sailboats without mishap all the time. Of course there are dangers, but there's something important in learning how to evaluate danger and deal with it. During Hurricane Camille last month, thirty-six people gathered in a motel near the beach not far from Gulfport, Mississippi to have a "hurricane party." They were all killed when the building was leveled! It is incredible to me that anyone chose to stay near the beach after the Weather Bureau predicted winds of over one hundred fifty miles per hour and tides exceeding twenty feet. What happened to their basic animal instinct for self-preservation? What disastrous failure of nature or society prompted those thirty-six to party in the face of a hurricane? Had they been so sheltered all their lives that they didn't recognize real danger when it finally presented itself? Were they too used to depending on others? Policeman? Mother? Insurance Agent? God? Just plain Luck?

There is a difficult lesson to learn, relearn, and pass on somehow to our children: it is the imperative to persist with a whole skin (and a whole soul) to *challenge* any attack on that wholeness, to know when that integrity is threatened (and equally important, when it's not), and to meet each threat with effective and responsible action. We want our children to be prepared for any danger—the obvious physical ones like Camille and especially the sneaky slow ones that quietly steal the zest and joy out of life and leave you wondering where they went.

You are worried about "finances" and "security." We have different thoughts about security, partly because we have lived in a different age from you. To those who went through the crisis of the depression, security means money in the bank, a good steady job, and a nice safe home. But thanks to our parents, we have been fortunate enough never to have experienced the kind of insecurity the depression caused. So we are freed to search for other kinds of security —an inner security if you will, that doesn't depend on economics, but reflects the talents, capabilities and wisdom we have stored away in our own neurological banks. We both feel confident that we have the ability to make a comfortable living for our family no matter what happens, and this frees us to a certain extent from the necessity of accumulating goods for the future. The idea of having to "start all over again" if we spend all we have on this voyage is not frightening to us because there really is no "start" and no "finish"

—there is just LIFE, to be lived as fully as possible. We don't regard the last twelve years as an accumulation of anything but experience—and we can't lose that very easily.

We will put aside some money in the bank in case of emergencies on our trip and leave Matt's mother with the "power of attorney" for our affairs. The cost of the trip should not be great unless we run into unforseen emergencies or repairs. We will simply make our way across the Atlantic via Bermuda and the Azores to Africa, and then proceed slowly down the west coast. We're not going to make hard and fast plans right now, but decide things as we go along. We might sail the boat home, have it shipped back, find somebody else to sail it home, or even sell it. Whatever we do we probably won't lose money. The boat is ours and with the tremendous number of improvements we are making she will be worth much more if we do decide to sell her. Other costs will be modest. We will have no rent, no automobiles to keep up, no insurance, utilities, or services. Our life will be simple and groceries inexpensive. Matt will send photographs to Black Star and handle assignments for them in Africa, and we both will be writing. During the struggle to keep my head above water in graduate school I have had little time for reading (other than textbooks), or for writing or thinking, strange as that may seem. Now I will have a chance to sort out some ideas and try them out on paper.

Mom and Dad, in your letter you sounded so worried and sad! I hope I can explain what this trip means to us. There are times when people feel an instinct to reach out and move to the frontiers of their experience. To some this instinct seems like God's whisper, or a special destiny; to us it is just a strong feeling that this is a right thing to do, and that now is the right time to do it. Throughout a lifetime there are many moments of decision like this—times when you can choose between staying home and sowing your crops, or taking a risk and jumping into the unknown. We happen to think there is a high price to always choosing the safe way. When life becomes routine and predictable, you have stopped testing yourself, and you stop growing. I think Thoreau was feeling this when he moved to Walden:

> I went to the woods because I wished to live deliberately, to front only the essential facts of life and see if I could not learn what it had to teach, and not, when I came to die, discover that I had not lived.

Perhaps sailing away for a year is the equivalent of Walden for us. Certainly there are many negative things about American society that warrant stepping aside and taking a fresh look at our life here. We love our country and have tried to be responsible citizens, but the end of the civil rights movement left us with many questions. Are we contributing to a positive change in this society? Is there any way to be politically relevant, short of violence at this moment in history? And what can we do about schools? For the most part children are being smothered in American schools. They are led, pushed, and ordered, without humor, into lives of boredom and conformity. They learn life by rote. The more they watch TV, the more they will depend on the vicarious rather than the real. We have a gut feeling, Matt and I—like the mother cat who stalks and pounces on her tiny offspring, teaching them how to survive in a cat's world —that somehow we must provide Matthew and Melissa with experiences that will teach them to survive to their fullest potential in a world that seems every day more treacherous. Then there is the problem of meaningful learning. Children go through our school systems and emerge with no real resources because they have spent all that time pursuing work someone else wanted them to do. Learning new facts isn't enough. They never have a chance to *produce* anything really useful, or to learn in a way that's related to the world outside school.

I know it is difficult for you to understand, but we do not regret taking our children out of school for a year. Some people are horrified when we say this, of course, and their immediate question is, "What will you do about their *education?*" Actually, the more I think about what their "education" is going to be like, the more excited I get.

Matt and I know as little about Africa as the children, so we will all learn together. Some subjects we will have to learn in order to get by—coastline characteristics, climate, geography, even politics. Other subjects we will pursue for pleasure as we stop in various ports—art, history, music, crafts, religion, anthropology, and things we haven't even thought of yet! A lot of intangible learning will take place as we shop in strange market places, exchange money and make new friends.

In some ways our education has already begun. In preparation for the trip we have made a large map of Africa tacked onto a piece of plywood. We throw darts at it, and each player gains points when his dart lands, by being able to identify the country, the capital, and other pertinent information. (Someone told Melissa that Arabian horses are bred in Senegal so that's always her contribution for Senegal.)

At sea we all will be involved in the everyday business of sailing the boat. We will need each other for every operation —standing watches at the helm, predicting the weather, navigating, cooking, and preparing the log. What better reason to learn meteorology, astronomy, physics or mathematics? The ship's log traditionally contains the technical data of a journey's progress, but we hope that ours will also be a record of our thoughts and feelings as we go along—a depository of poems, stories, songs and dreams.

We're going to take lots of books to fill the long TV-less days. We'll read to each other and perhaps even revive the ancient art of storytelling. Matthew never reads for pleasure now, but maybe he will start enjoying reading on the boat. We have always made music together as a family, but there may be time for more of it on the boat. We are taking instruments for all of us. I think learning French will become very important to us if we want to be able to communicate in West Africa, and I intend to use our first aid drills as a way of teaching some basic anatomy and physiology.

Actually, for me the best part of the trip is that we are going to be living for a year as close to sunshine, rain, clouds and stars as you can be. And there's just the excitement of the thing—the idea of pitting yourself against the unknown —the game of stretching the ego, always asking a little more of it—the thrill of confronting physical hardship and danger and coming out on top. We need that excitement, that spark. You can immobilize yourself pretty thoroughly in your environment. You can deaden your senses so nothing is too threatening, too sad, or even too joyful. And the self continues to exist—not robust, barely alive. But cut off that spark of excitement, that primitive impulse to learn and explore, and that's when the process of dying begins.

My mind can't even imagine what it must feel like to make landfall after a month of sailing across empty ocean. But I think we'll remember it for a long time.

This letter has gotten lengthy but I want you to understand that our plan is not flippant; we are very serious about it. I hope I have succeeded in resolving some of your many worries. We love you and want you to enjoy our adventure too.

Love,
Jeannine

3

Nuts and Boats

July 15, 1970

MATT: *Aquarius* is what naval architects call a mast-head sloop, that is, she carries two sails, a main and a jib, and the forestay on which the jib is strung runs to the head of the mast. She is thirty-one feet in length at deck level, twenty-four on the waterline, and was built in 1960 by a French-Canadian shipwright, Jerry St. Jacques, at a boatyard in Port Credit near Toronto. Jerry built three boats like *Aquarius* at the same time, sold two of them to finance his own and moved aboard it with his bride of two months. He named his nuptial ship *Atria* after one of the fifty-seven navigational stars in the *Nautical Almanac.* When I met Jerry eight years later in Miami, he was still living aboard, his family now augmented by a little girl. The *Atria* was obviously his pride and joy, as immaculate and sound as the day he laid the last weld, but Jerry was beginning to feel cramped for space and was happy to reach a financial agreement which allowed him to complete work on a larger boat, and me to go to sea for the first time.

Jerry was a fiercely self-sufficient fellow with a crafts-man's pride in careful workmanship and a French-Canadian's instinct for the value of a dollar. The *Atria* re-flected these qualities in every plate and frame member. She was designed by Al Mason, a protégé of the famous yacht designer, F. Francis Herreschoff, and the plans for *Intrepid,* her prototype, appeared in the March 1946 issue of *Rudder* magazine, along with ads for war surplus diesel engines and articles on how to live with gas rationing by converting your gasoline auxiliary to kerosene. I suppose Jerry chose those particular plans partly because he could have them for the price of the magazine, but he must also have been impressed by the sound design and sturdy welded-steel construction. He didn't hesitate to change the plans where it suited him. He drew out the hull lines at the stern into a graceful sawn-off counter, and he extended the jibstay to the masthead. It is interesting that when Mason himself redesigned and modernized the original plans sixteen years later (*Intrepid* had proven an able boat) he made the exact same changes.

Atria was a pretty boat to look at. The carpentry work was superb, every detail solidly made and meticulously finished. Jerry lavished mahogany on the interior and the boat had an elegance not usually associated with steel. The welding, so a marine surveyor informed me, was solid and plenty strong although not handsome enough to please a master welder. Fair enough. Jerry was a carpenter, not a steel worker—but he built to last. Other features of the boat reflected Jerry's penchant for stretching a dollar, sometimes successfully, sometimes not. The hefty winches in the cockpit were homemade. Jerry himself cast them of silicone bronze and they worked quite nicely. But the electrical system was an unmitigated horror: a tangle of household extension cord twisted together and wrapped casually with electrical tape, not a fuse in the boat. Most of the wiring lay in the bilge along with the storage batteries, ready to be drowned by the first influx of water. In a steel boat this is an invitation to disaster. Any leakage of current into the hull can set up electrolytic action between the salt water and the steel that will eat a hole through the skin faster than you can say, "Where's my boat?" Jerry acquired the gasoline auxiliary, a four-cylinder Greymarine, as a collection of parts in a cardboard carton. I traced the serial number and found the engine was *thirty-three years old*—a genuine antique! I promptly dubbed it *Methuselah*. It proved a game old fellow though sometimes cranky with age. *Atria* was lacking in one other important respect. She had spent most of her days idling at dockside and carried only the minimum gear for cruising—and almost nothing for an ocean crossing.

The task of fitting this beautiful but somewhat impoverished maiden for a sea voyage meant correcting her few fundamental defects and adding quantities of new and vitally important equipment to her trousseau. But how could such rank beginners as ourselves learn what the lady required? By practical experience, obviously. We renamed her *Aquarius* and began a sailing courtship with her that lasted the better part of two seasons in the waters around New Orleans. We took our knocks together, and endured a thousand minor misadventures which, if they didn't make sailors of us, at least took the edge off our rawness, and certainly exposed the flaws of our boat. We ran aground so frequently I lost count; we suffered engine failure in the most inconvenient places; we plowed inexpertly into docks; tore sails; misjudged channel buoys; experienced obscure electrical failures; and were bereaved by the steady disappearance overboard of all untethered possessions. A typical lesson: one idyllic afternoon as the ship's company took their Renaissance ease in the cockpit with wine and guitars, I struggled with a balky seacock deep in the bilge. A sudden pressure on a pipe wrench snapped a plastic hull fitting clean off. I gazed in fascination and horror directly through the hole in the hull at the sparkling sand below while a geyser of salty water washed my face and threatened to sink us. Today all hull fittings are welded steel collars. By such steps we advanced to a new intimacy with our boat.

But our cruising experience was inadequate when it came to equipping *Aquarius* for a major ocean voyage. We turned first to books, particularly Eric Hiscock's *Cruising under Sail*, and his masterful *Voyaging under Sail*, and I collected a shelfload of marine catalogues and yachting magazines. But our sea-wise friends were our best resource. We consulted three of them almost continually.

In Biloxi lived the remarkable Lyle Bongé—photographer, banker, tree surgeon, horticulturalist, raconteur, bon vivant, slumlord and yachtsman. We made some memorable excursions to offshore islands of the Mississippi Sound aboard Lyle's twenty-seven-foot cutter *Loon,* and he helped me sail *Aquarius* home from Miami. Lyle insisted that life at sea should be lived with sensuality, taste and style: good company in the cockpit, good wine in the locker, afternoon tea with rum or crème de menthe *in a glass,* time out to appreciate a sunset or the sounds and smells of an early morning sea. Our debt to Lyle is vast.

Bill Osterholdt, a naval architect and yachtsman, supplied us with information of a different sort. How much water does one person consume in a day at sea? (Half a gallon.) What is the minimum quantity the boat should carry? (Seventy to ninety gallons.) What gauge of stainless steel wire should I use for rigging; how many square feet to my twin staysails; what quality of rope for anchor line? Bill had answers for all these questions and a hundred more. He owns a handsome fifty-foot schooner, *Windsong,* which he is refitting from stem to stern, a process that never seems to end. Every chainplate and carpet tack in *Windsong* is the strongest, most enduring known to naval science, and the advice Bill gave me was of the same quality. But occasionally his specifications exceeded the limits of practicality, patience or my pocketbook, and I found it useful to check them against the practical judgment of another very special friend, Bill Seemann.

Bill owned no boats but knew more about them than any person I ever met. He was part yacht architect, part boatbuilder, part engineer, and he possessed an abundance of that native American talent for invention and practical innovation. Bill ran his own company, a shoestring enterprise that made fiberglass parts for industry, and he also built Rube

Goldbergian machines for spraying polyurethane foam. The machines were his own design and so was a new material he called C-Flex, a kind of flexible fiberglass plank with properties so unique it seems likely to revolutionize the way custom fiberglass boats are built. Bill was no armchair engineer. He liked to get his hands dirty and whenever I dropped by his shop with another question I usually found him waist deep in tools and materials. He must have been informal engineering adviser to at least a hundred people. He had unlimited patience and if you came to him with a particularly knotty problem he took it to heart, pondered it in his spare time, consulted manuals, looked up specifications, talked to specialists, and days later would come back to you with a carefully reasoned and often brilliant answer. Most people couldn't buy the advice that Bill gave away for nothing.

I often wondered why we had become such fast friends. I think Bill saw in our voyage an unrealized ambition—an adventure he'd always wanted for himself. It became almost as important to him as it was for us, and he respected our intentions at a time when most of our friends regarded us as slightly demented. Beyond this, Bill and I were drawn together by a common affliction. We both suffered from philomachinia—we *loved* machines, were fascinated by their workings and needs, found it important to our self-esteem to understand and master them. For this reason rebuilding *Aquarius* never became a chore; indeed, solving her many problems built a special bond between Bill and myself. I guess under the skin we were like those kids who spend all their hours under the hoods of hot rods. If we believed at all in the mystique of blood brotherhood it would be grease, not blood we'd pinprick into each other's veins.

Bill's advice began to really count when I started working seriously on *Aquarius* in early September 1969, about a month after Hurricane Camille. Eagan's boatyard was in ruins. There was no electricity, no running water, and no assistance available. I was on my own for welding, spray painting, wiring, rigging—everything. I began to spend every day I could spare from photojournalism at the boatyard, putting in a full day of work and driving the eighty miles to and from New Orleans. Sometimes Jeannine and the children would come along to help but mostly I worked alone. Our photographic Christmas card that year reflected our condition quite accurately. It pictured a family scene aboard *Aquarius,* myself at the helm, Jeannine hauling on a jib sheet, the children fishing. The card was folded under at the bottom margin along the boat's waterline, and when unfolded revealed that *Aquarius* was standing high and dry in the clutter of the boatyard. How we longed to be in the water!

It happened, finally, in February 1970, and by then I had crossed off my list the following jobs: enlarge and replace cockpit drains; replace all plastic through-hull connections with welded steel collars; fit strainer on engine water intake; replace undersized bilge pump; cut down rudder; weld steel reinforcement under rudder gudgeon; weld plate over crack in keel; pour cement in inaccessible well in bilge where water collects; lay epoxy faring over rough spots in hull; spray hull with five-coat vinyl paint system; fiberglass both hatch covers and masthead; install depth sounder; cut down propeller; rewire engine and entire boat; convert electrical system from six to twelve volts; install engine alternator; build case for heavy-duty batteries and weld to hull; install floodlights on spreaders; build fuse box with (1) circuit breakers on all circuits, (2) voltmeter to check battery condition, (3) power converter to charge batteries from shore, (4) double-throw knife switch so either or both batteries could be used for ship's lighting system and engine-starting; rebuild marine toilet; scrape and paint mast and boom; replace galvanized rigging with stainless steel; rebuild masthead fitting; service all fire extinguishers.

I set a certain standard for all these repairs. *Aquarius* must be strong enough to withstand any forseeable disaster at sea. The mast and rigging must stand up to winds of at least hurricane force; the cockpit drains, hatches and other fittings must be such that the boat could survive a 360-degree roll-over and come up, if not unscathed, at least floating and intact. The battery case, for example, was built strong enough to keep the heavy batteries from shifting or breaking free in a storm, or from dropping out if the boat rolled over. I didn't really expect to encounter any of these nightmare conditions, but I wanted to be ready for them. I felt we were resourceful enough as a family to handle any normal emergency but I didn't want to expose us to needless dangers caused by equipment failure or lack of preparation.

In March we moved *Aquarius* to the guest pier at the posh Southern Yacht Club in New Orleans where we could work on her more readily. With the commencement of this last phase of preparation my doubts about attempting the voyage began to ease somewhat, but my personal psychology of commitment has always been very complex. After the first flush of a new idea began to fade, a smog of self-doubt and underconfidence would usually settle over me. I regarded any project like the voyage as being hopelessly beyond my powers of organization and endurance. But I learned long ago that if there was a pathway to success it passed through the fragrant gardens of self-deception. I'm not making a *commitment* to this enterprise, I would reason with my fearful self, I'm merely trying parts of it on for size. No use worrying about all the time, money, energy, work, fuss and confusion that might lie ahead, just pick an obvious place and start working. And so I would begin, mercifully screened from the terrifying vistas of the great forest by the comforting shade of all those individual trees; and in the end the awful moment of Total Commitment would usually creep up quietly enough, and maybe pass unrecognized. By then it would be too late for panic.

In this spirit I avoided, at the beginning anyway, laying out money for the expensive items of equipment we would need solely for the ocean voyage: the inflatable life raft, the radio direction finder, the charts and nautical books, the self-steering device. Secretly I didn't feel sure enough of our venture to spend the money. I also hesitated talking about it to skeptical strangers. Only among friends did I speak with any confidence, although between us, Jeannine and I maintained the fiction of assurance because it was the only practical atmosphere in which to go forward. Occasionally though, our fears and doubts would wash over us, and then we tried to face them honestly. Quite often these confrontations would recharge us with genuine confidence and move me closer to a real conviction. And my conviction did continue to grow—with every hour of sweat invested in the boat, every fitting made fast, every idea that miraculously solidified into wood and steel.

As April shaded into May the work in New Orleans began to move more rapidly. Pressure was mounting. Our list of tasks was still formidable but our schedule was fixed by the inflexible verities of meteorology. June is the beginning of hurricane season in the Gulf of Mexico, a time when small boats are well advised to limit their open-water passages to a few days, to maintain a vigilant radio weather watch and keep a pretty fair estimate of how many hours to the nearest safe harbor. The frequency of hurricanes rises rapidly in August and September as the storms move out of the Gulf of Mexico and lower Carribean area into what is known as "Hurricane Alley," roughly the path of the Gulf Stream north between the Atlantic seaboard and Bermuda. Originally we had planned to leave New Orleans by June first, before hurricanes became frequent and in time to reach Bermuda by early July for a July-August crossing. But even our most careful estimates failed to account for the myriad details and molasses-like progress of fitting out the boat. Before we knew it July was approaching rapidly with no real end to the work in sight. True, *Aquarius* looked more fit and able every day but still our lists kept multiplying like bacteria in broth.

September is the last possible month one can take a small sailboat across the North Atlantic in safety. Bill Seemann impressed this upon me very strongly. By October the fall and winter storms are beginning to set in, and later into the

season massive low-pressure systems build up that may foul
the entire ocean area between the Atlantic seaboard and the
European continent with gales and storms. The worst mid-
winter storms can develop winds of hurricane force over
periods of eight to ten days or more. Large merchant ships
have a very hard time of it in such weather and the majority
of yacht disasters occur then. We had absolutely no desire to
try our luck with them, and since we had to allow a month
to reach Bermuda and another month for the Atlantic crossing, we must set off from New Orleans by the first of August
at the latest or abandon the voyage altogether.

Into the few weeks remaining we crammed the following
tasks (Readers dreaming of a similar venture are warned to
pass over these lists. Had we known all that was involved
from the beginning, we might have passed over the entire
voyage.):

    make grab rails for interior and exterior of cabin top
    build self-draining forward hatch
    build cover over aft hatch
    build and install life lines and pulpits
    install radio-telephone and aerial
    clean and paint fuel tank
    install fuel line cut-off valve
    install engine ventilation system and blower
    install two fifteen-gallon plastic water tanks
    paint engine
    design and order storm jib and twin staysails
    make extra spinnaker pole
    build compass binnacle
    install self-steering gear
    attach cleat to foredeck for anchor line
    build icebox
    build shelves in galley, hanging locker and head
    build cockpit locker
    partition lazarette
    build main cabin table
    build liners against hull for canned goods
    sew sail cover, cockpit cushions, bimini cover, flags for all

West African nations, wind sail and canvass bunk retainers

make tang for substay

And we purchased the following gear:

ropes, blocks and deck tackle
chronometer (two $25.00 Timex electric watches)
handbearing compass
sextant
charts
Inflatable dinghy-life raft, the *Zodiac*
safety lights and flares
gasoline-powered emergency pump
radio direction finder
shortwave radio
spare anchor and 500 feet of anchor line
binoculars
stopwatch
scuba diving equipment
spare engine parts
life jackets
hand tools
foul-weather gear: boots, slickers, wool pants, etc.
boat hook
hand signal light

And then, Lord, the things we left undone—to complete in other ports:

make bosun's chair (Biloxi)
install depth sounder (Biloxi)
make reefing gear for main sail (Panama City)
make baggy wrinkle (Panama City to Azores)
calibrate compass (Panama City)
make chip log (Panama City)
make frame on cabin top for storing fuel cans (Fort Pierce)
install screens (Okeechobee Waterway)
make engine crank (Bermuda)
install automatic bilge pump (Tenerife)
make boarding ladder (never, never, never)

We also completed registration of the boat as a U.S. documented vessel, and we applied for passports and visas and got health inoculations. I made a quick trip to New York to promote magazine assignments in Africa.

As the last weeks slipped by, our horizons narrowed to the work at the Southern Yacht Club pier and to the characters and events of dock life. My favorite dockside character was *Rosemary,* a cabin cruiser of doubtful vintage and undistinguished origin—maybe twenty-five feet overall. *Rosemary* was an invalid, forgotten by her owner and despised or ignored by the gung-ho yachtsmen who quartered their immaculate fiberglass steeds in other slips along the pier. She was ugly in an unselfconscious way—no style to her but a kind of honest homeliness that made me like her in spite of having higher standards for what a boat ought to be. She lay by herself at dockside, an old lady dying of neglect, listing to port a little more each day as a fatal leak hidden somewhere down in her innards admitted a thin but unrelenting trickle of water. About twice a week when *Rosemary*'s condition became critical, Paul, the night watchman and the only marina employee who gave a damn for her, would put a pump aboard and save *Rosemary* once again from drowning. But no friends visited her; nobody tried to fix the leak.

Gradually and almost imperceptibly *Aquarius* began to show the fruits of our labors—every day a little more beautiful, a little more ready for sea. As she improved, my pride in her grew, and with it, my distress and affection for *Rosemary.* She gave me a guilty twinge as I greeted her every morning, another as I bade her "Good evening" at the end of a long hard day. It was like passing a nursing home and seeing a cast-off lying there. You could do something for her, but you knew you wouldn't, and her obvious need and the contrast with your own health made you feel angry and a little guilty.

Early July was blistering hot in New Orleans. By ten in the morning the sun was already sucking away at our energy and resolve. By midday the process was almost complete. We moved in a semi-torpor, our minds glazed and almost inert —unable to cope with the simplest problem. Every job took three times as long. To survive and to get more work done, we began working nights and sleeping during the hottest part of the day. About two o'clock one morning I passed *Rosemary* on my way to begin my working day, and noticed immediately that her illness had become terminal. Water covered her stern nameplate and had risen at the bow far beyond a certain rivet I had marked weeks ago as the signal for summoning grieving friends and relatives to her bedside. But there were no grieving friends and relatives, not even Paul to pump her out. The watchman who relieved him seemed to view his responsibility as ending with the punching of a time clock.

"*Rosemary* is sinking," I informed him.

"Izat so. Maybe I'd better call the owner."

"If you wait to call the owner there won't be any *Rosemary.* Why not try to pump?"

"Don't have any pumps around here," he replied, "and besides, if I set foot on the boat I might be responsible."

Eventually I located the only pump available, a miserable garden hose siphon, and hooked it to *Rosemary,* but it was like administering aspirin for a severed artery. As I watched her settle lower in the water I realized there was nothing I could do to save her.

I went back to my work, but it was impossible to keep my mind occupied. I returned to the dock every few minutes to gauge *Rosemary*'s progress toward the bottom. She took several hours to die.

It's dreadful to watch even an unloved boat go under. I could guess how much human energy had gone into polishing every inch of her fading woodwork; how many loving curses had been lavished on each balky fitting. I wondered how many couples had lain in her tidy bunks, what touches they exchanged, what feelings were shared. I imagined her on a quiet evening out in the Gulf, rocking gently in a perfectly peaceful sea, surrounded by an unbroken sea horizon, with only the slap of a hungry fish and the slow fading of light.

Water reached *Rosemary*'s deck, coming fast. Through an open window I could see a shower curtain drowning, a toothbrush awash. The water climbed silently toward a cabin window, reached it, rushed in: a choking gurgle in *Rosemary*'s throat. It crept onto the cabin roof. I stood numb on the dock. I wanted to throw a rope to her—to hold her up with my bare hands. Slowly and peacefully, with hardly a murmur the water closed over her and she drifted to the bottom.

There was a hard lump in my stomach. I thought of all the times Paul had saved her from sinking, of how unbelievably simple it would have been in the beginning to step aboard and plug that little hole. It came to me that death by sinking, through indifference, drunkenness, stupidity, disaster at sea or just plain age is the eventual fate of almost every boat, even mine, and it sent a cold chill through me.

I returned to *Aquarius* in a kind of frenzy. Make every hull fitting doubly secure. Triple-test every shroud and stay. Lay in spares for every vulnerable engine part. Don't let the water in.

4

"It Does Not Further One to Cross the Great Water"

July 18

JEANNINE: Back in early January we paused in our headlong preparations to consult an ancient oracle, a Chinese book of prophecy, the *I Ching*. We should have stuck with contemporary sailing authorities and left the fortune-telling to gypsies—our encounter with the *I Ching* almost threw us into an uncontrolled tailspin.

The *I Ching* is a collection of philosophy and practical advice that is over two thousand years old. The book contains sixty-four hexagrams, patterns of six parallel lines, some solid, some broken, which refer to discrete pieces of wisdom that are applied to particular situations and circumstances. The person seeking counsel throws three coins six times, noting the arrangement of heads and tails each time. These configurations are translated into a pattern of complete and broken lines, the inquirer's own hexagram, which is matched against the hexagrams in the book and, when the corresponding prophecy is read, is interpreted by a chapter of advice. Matt's mentor in photography, Minor White, first taught us to appreciate the *I Ching* and its possibilities. In Minor's house, a period of meditation usually preceded the opening of the book. It was a reflective ceremony during which the coins were thrown with care. The oracle was consulted for guidance only a few times a year when there were serious questions to be answered.

Overtly, I viewed the procedure with a cautious western skepticism. Inwardly, that skepticism had been shaken several times when the wisdom offered by the book had been uncannily and specifically apt. It seemed to speak directly to the question that had been posed! When the question concerned marriage, the designated hexagram discussed marriage; when Matt asked about his work, he was advised about creativity and production. Once we consulted the *I Ching* with a friend who was about to spend time in prison: Phil Stiles, who lived with us for a period while he was studying photography with Matt. He was opposed to the war in Vietnam and refused to be drafted. Eventually his case went all the way to the Supreme Court before he lost it. We expected him to go to Canada rather than spend two years in prison, but one day he walked into the darkroom saying he'd decided to stay and go to jail. He never really explained why; Phil was an inward person. Perhaps he was too proud to run, or perhaps he felt it was better to settle the score than to face a long period of exile.

His decision moved us greatly. Matt had become a conscientious objector during the Korean War, had cooperated with his draft board and performed two years of alternative service as a teacher in the Middle East. Yet he always wondered whether prison wasn't the only honest way to resist conscription. When we sat down that night to throw the coins for Phil, he had already made his decision; the *I Ching* couldn't change that. But he wanted some guidance about the events that were about to take place in his life.

The name of the hexagram we threw was *K'un,* which means Oppression. It said:

> In times of adversity it is important to be strong within and sparing of words. The superior man stakes his life on following his will. In such times there is nothing a man can do but acquiesce in his fate and remain true to himself. This concerns

the deepest stratum of his being, for this alone is superior to all external fate.

What more could have been said? The words were profound and reassuring. Phil left for New York the next day to settle his affairs. Little did we know that two years later we would all be crossing the Atlantic together.

These experiences with the *I Ching* remained quite vividly in our minds; and when Matt and I finally came to consult it about our voyage we brought to the ceremony a certain amount of awe and trepidation.

We lit some candles and sat together quietly before we threw the coins. As they fell, Matt noted their sequence on a piece of paper. They gave the hexagram *Sung,* which means Conflict. He began to read:

> Conflict; you are sincere
> And are being obstructed.
> A cautious halt halfway brings good fortune.
> Going through to the end brings misfortune.
> It furthers one to see the great man.
> It does not further one to cross the great water.

> In times of strife, crossing the great water is to be avoided, that is, dangerous enterprises are not to be begun, because in order to be successful they require concerted unity of forces. Conflict within weakens the power to conquer danger without.

We were stunned. The words sank coldly to my stomach. "IT DOES NOT FURTHER ONE TO CROSS THE GREAT WATER"! Chilling words! How could its reply be so specific? We had asked a lifeless batch of paper and ink, "Shall we cross the ocean?" and it had replied: "No! Don't cross the ocean!" What could it mean? Should we give up the idea of going altogether? "GOING THROUGH TO THE END BRINGS MISFORTUNE." That was the last thing we wanted to hear! I felt suddenly paralyzed with depression. All the doubts came back.

Matt looked grave. "Wait a minute," he said, "there's more. Let's not panic until we read the whole thing."

> The image indicates that the causes of conflict are latent. . . . To avoid conflict, everything must be taken carefully into consideration in the very beginning. If rights and duties are exactly defined or if, in a group the spiritual trends of the individuals harmonize, the cause of the conflict is removed in advance.

"I'm confused," I said. "I don't understand what the 'conflict' is about. I don't feel any conflict, do you?"

"No, we're in accord—at least I think we are," Matt replied. "Maybe that changes the prophecy. Maybe it's saying that it's okay to go if the individuals are in harmony. Let's keep reading":

> Danger. In the end good fortune comes.

> Only that which has been honestly acquired through merit remains a permanent possession. It can happen that such a possession may be contested, but since it is really one's own, one cannot be robbed of it. Whatever a man possess through the strength of his own nature cannot be lost.

"Well, that's true enough," I said. "That's like what I was saying to my parents about storing experience in neurological banks instead of laying away money in savings accounts. But I still feel depressed! It's too close for comfort! How did the *I Ching* know we were going to cross the great water? Maybe we are crazy to be setting off on a voyage like this when we don't really know what we are getting into."

Matt was studying the hexagram pattern. "You know, this is a Book of *Changes*. It predicts directions—tendencies rather than fixed states of fortune. There are certain casts of the coins which indicate one hexagram changing into another, and the way I threw the hexagram *Sung* (Conflict) shows it changing to the hexagram *Kou,* which means Coming to Meet."

"Well, read it! Maybe it will be a little more optimistic!" By this time I was feeling decidedly bleak.

> Of its own accord the female principle comes to meet the male. It is an unfavorable and dangerous situation and we must understand and promptly prevent the possible consequences.
>
> Although as a general rule the weak should not come to meet the strong, there are times when this has great significance. When heaven and earth come to meet each other, all creatures prosper.

"That sounds promising," I said. "Maybe that will take care of the conflict, whatever that is all about. Does it say anything else?"

"Yes! The image of this hexagram is very interesting! The top three lines represent Heaven and the bottom three lines represent the Wind. Listen to what it says!

> Under heaven, wind
> The image of Coming to Meet
> Heaven is far from the things of earth, but it sets them in motion by means of the wind.

"By means of the wind, Jeannine. By means of the wind! We're going to be set in motion by means of the wind! You know, I feel we've allowed ourselves to become bottled up this past year, and the idea of this voyage has really got us moving again." He closed the book and put his arms around me. "Don't be depressed! I don't completely understand what the *I Ching* is trying to say to us, but I *believe* this voyage is right for us. Come on, let's go to bed."

I let him steer me away from my morbid thoughts, but I was still uneasy. After all, perhaps it *was* some kind of warning. And in spite of Matt's reassurances, I could tell that he was tense too. We went to bed still disturbed and doubtful.

In the days that followed I tried to shake off my preoccupation with the prophecy. I couldn't afford to dwell on it—I had to prepare myself for my Comprehensive Ph.D. Examinations in April. I pushed feelings of foreboding aside and buried myself in textbooks, studying late into the night until my brain was crammed like a supersaturated solution of chemicals—then I would sleep and all the goodies would precipitate out. In the morning I couldn't remember anything.

Exam day came, a day of torture, suspense, and finally relief. I emerged scathed and daunted, but *finished,* by God! I had passed and I could forget about school for a while. I launched myself at last into full-time preparation for the trip.

Provisions were my first consideration. I discovered the railroad salvage yard, a Home for Lost and Damaged Articles. Items (anything from refrigerators to Froot Loops) slightly dented, bashed or otherwise offended, wound up there to be sold at prices marvelously lower than those at the cheapest neighborhood supermarket. Making periodic pilgrimages, I picked my way between slightly floury cases of cake mixes, smashed catsup bottles and asymmetrical pork and beans. Sometimes there was only one damaged item in a whole case; often I couldn't detect any flaws at all. The choicest and least damaged things disappeared quickly so I timed my visits to coincide with the morning peak of delivery, which was often frantic. Loading machines scuttled along the rows among the boxes—backing and stacking. Just behind me one day there was a small collision between two loaders which resulted in the total wipeout of four cases of vinegar. The sharp smell diffused through the huge shed in seconds and followed me out into the sunshine with my purchases like a tenacious ghost, entering the car and establishing a semi-permanent residence.

On a good day I arrived home triumphantly with whole cases of wheat germ, canned pears, corned beef hash, raisins and honey. Other days sometimes I found only the same old relics, the familiar cracked mustard in the corner, that unknown brand of sauerkraut, the torn Trend boxes and those damp toilet-paper rolls that soon turned decidedly moldy. Our garage became lined with cartons of paper towels, canned fruit and juices, meats and vegetables, and dried products of all kinds—fruit, milk, potatoes, beans and multitudes of soups. I surveyed it with pride and dismay. I had no idea whether it would fit in the boat!

Matthew and Melissa marked the contents of the cans on the lids with felt-tip pens (the non-water-soluble variety) and then dipped the entire cans in varnish or melted paraffin. I didn't want to open the bilge to select a dinner after several weeks at sea and encounter an anonymous crowd of rusty cans. (The method worked well. We lost very few cans even among those that were periodically drenched with bilge water, and we were still opening faithful "mush soup" all the way to Accra.)

In the midst of all the marking and dipping, I received a shipment I had ordered from an organic farm in Pennsylvania—several hundred pounds of whole wheat flour, brown rice and health cereals. Some I shared with friends, but most we packed away in the big plastic mayonnaise jars I had begged from the Medical School cafeteria. Tucking a walnut-sized piece of dry ice in the top of each jar, we closed the lid and then dipped the entire top in warm paraffin. (The dry ice did its work of preservation. Later on the high seas and as far as Senegal and Gambia we would draw up repulsive abominations from the bilge, plastic jars coated with the grease and ick of ten months of voyaging and, after scrubbing the outside we would find the contents as fresh and delicious as the day it was packed. The wheat flour, which has a high oil content and usually spoils more quickly than white flour, was never rancid and we never found weevils.) The indispensable jars also received freshly laid eggs, lovingly smeared with vaseline and nested down in a cushion of rock salt. I was told by experienced friends that they would keep fresh for three or four months this way, and they did. We created a place in the bilge for cans, and laid them in rows up the sides of the hull right against the skin, and Matt nailed stringers between each row so the cans would stay in place when the boat pitched. It was a clever utilization of otherwise useless space. We could easily lift a floorboard and retrieve a can from the bottom of a row. As one tin was removed another rolled down to take its place.

My concern lessened considerably as the last can was stowed. They all fit! And we had food enough for four or five months—if we wanted to eat a lot of brown rice. We made a map of the bilge and plotted all the treasures. This we filed carefully away somewhere with a general inventory of all our supplies. Unfortunately, no one ever could remember where we filed the file.

We needed food for the head as well as the stomach. I dawdled in bookstores whenever I could, collecting pocket books for each of us. When Matt scolded me and declared flat out that there was no room for all those books, I calmly replied that I would find room, and continued to buy books. I had no notion of where I might put them but after carefully examining the whole boat I settled on the head. (After sitting there a moment I saw the obvious solution.) The walls on each side of the toilet were bare! My father and I made some small unobtrusive shelves which held about eighty books. When the shelves were stocked, the children delighted in startling visitors by saying, "Excuse me please, I have to go to the library."

All in all I tucked away about one hundred fifty books not counting the twenty enormous volumes of navigation and sailing lore which Matt bought: Bowditch, Mixter, Hiscock, and various U.S. Hydrographic Office publications. They resided on the "folio" shelf above the hanging locker.

I bought multitudes of science fiction (Heinlein, Clarke, H. G. Wells, Jules Verne), adventures (Mark Twain, Jack London, Conrad, Tolkien, Robert Louis Stevenson, Melville), mysteries and horse stories for Melissa, the Penguin

African Library for us. The resource books had to be stowed wherever I could find a spot. Some fitted on shelves in the main cabin: *Book of Games, Handicrafts, String Figures, How Things Work,* the dictionaries (English, French and Portuguese), a thesaurus and *The Joy of Cooking.* Larger books like *Living Invertebrates of the World* and *How to Macramé* had to be slipped under the children's mattresses.

Like a squirrel with a mouthful of autumn pecans, I hid away tempting caches of books, comic books (for critically listless days), new games, models, art supplies, and assorted surprises from bubble gum to Silly Putty. Facing storms was much less intimidating than dealing with bored children.

Matt's mother contributed "Grandma's bag of tricks," a fantastic assortment of supplies for weaving, embroidery, macramé, crocheting and knitting. My father gave us carving tools, various sorts and sizes of wood, some linoleum blocks and whittling knives, the sharpness of which led me to consider medical problems.

I decided it would be prudent to be ready for just about any emergency, from wounds to broken bones, malaria to sunburn, fungus infections to constipation. I made up a list of supplies from two books which I found very helpful: *First Aid Afloat* by Paul B. Sheldon, M.D. and *How to Travel the World and Stay Healthy* by Drs. Doyle and Banta. A friend from my medical school gave me a copy of *Merck's Manual* (a masterpiece of malicious maladies) and wrote the prescriptions for me, filling out a whole Rx pad: plaster bandages, hypodermics, novocaine, sutures, penicillin, sedatives, antibiotics, even adrenalin. I took the pad to the best cut-rate drugstore in New Orleans and shoved it casually across the counter to the pharmacist who flipped through it, his eyes widening at each page.

"You're kidding aren't you?" he asked.

"Nope," I said, "I really want all those things!"

He whistled. "This has got to be some kind of a record!"

It must have been. It cost $140.00! He delivered the bulky parcel to our door himself that night armed with an afternoon's accumulation of questions. We invited him to visit the site of our chaotic preparations to verify our unlikely replies.

Those days of preparation followed each other in hazy, happy confusion. The sawing, fitting, sanding, grinding, caulking, painting, polishing proceeded steadily. Unfortunately one's balance of pride is measured not by the amount of labor invested but by the visible proof of work completed. Sometimes at the end of a day there was no tangible evidence of our effort and we left the marina feeling vaguely empty. Another time, a week's accumulation of cogitating, designing, cutting and bending pipe, brazing, fitting and adjusting resulted suddenly in a glorious climax—pulpit, afterrail and life lines! The whole aspect of *Aquarius* was transformed. She looked larger, sexier, more self-assertive (and safer). With each job we were storing up potential energy in wood and steel to be reclaimed and reabsorbed in some future flash of recognition as we clipped ourselves confidently into a well-sewn safety harness on a rough night at sea, or braced against a steady pulpit to take a noon sight, or caught onto a smoothly varnished handrail while groping our way forward along a slippery deck.

At night our bodies fell into bed murderously weary. Muscles complained with each additional task demanded of them like lifting up a foot to take off a pair of pants. Hands, horny with keratin and stubborn paint, smarted with un-healed cuts. Skin prickled with the maddening slivers of fiberglass which tenaciously resisted the most dedicated showers. Nevertheless they were still bodies. Not too weary to appreciate the feel of cool sheets, not too tired to make contact and touch—a vivid touch, catalyzed by the quick circulation of an active body and a satisfied mind, tapping a well of emotion abundantly filled during a day of working together: I cranked, he went up the mast; I varnished, he sanded; I measured, he fitted. I held, he hammered. I quiv-ered, he entered. I received, he thrust. We came.

One by one we burned our bridges before we were ready for the crossing. Our landlady found new tenants in June so we gave up our well-loved apartment and hastily stored the few things we wanted to keep in Matt's darkroom in the cellar: rugs woven by Matt's mother, the harpsichord he built, myrtle and redwood lamps handmade by my father. We had to find homes quickly for nine fuzzy puppies—a going-away present from our collie, Boo, who was going to stay with our landlady until our return. Our cat, Muggles (they were both very turned-on animals), was miffed at being upstaged, and delivered four kittens the weekend before departure. And Kaa, a five-foot diamond-back watersnake, went to live with the boy across the street (the landlady definitely didn't want *him*).

We sold or gave away the rest of our household things. Goodbye to the canoe that we portaged through the Canadian wilderness one summer. Goodbye to bicycles and the train set and the Ping-Pong table. Goodbye to the dear old army surplus bunk beds. They had wandered with us almost from our beginnings. When they joined us in Philadelphia in 1962, delivered ostentatiously by Salvation Army truck, they immediately received a bright coat of red paint. They followed faithfully behind us in a succession of U-HAUL trailers as civil rights activities drew us back and forth across the South: Jackson, Atlanta, Jackson again, Mt. Beulah, New Orleans. I clung to them with a whimsical maternal notion that the children should have something familiar to fall asleep in. We would miss them.

In a massive garage sale we finished off old records, clothing, toys and books—Pound and Joyce from Matt's English Lit days at Princeton, books on the Middle East from his graduate work at Ann Arbor and our years in Jordan, a complete set of Gandhi's writings on non-violence. We advertised our Ford van and sold it to the first buyer. Friends arrived from Mobile to drive our car west to be used by parents. Suddenly we had no vehicle—with a million errands still to do. There was no doubt about it. We were going to have to leave.

Bereft and homeless, we were gathered in to shelter,

affection and food by the grace of lovely Holley, our friend and neighbor, who patiently tolerated all our midnight peregrinations. At Holley's I went into a tailspin of sewing, co-opting the children for assistance whenever I could. In the last two weeks the three of us made seat covers for the cockpit cushions and two large bimini covers (awnings) from waterproof vinyl. When laced together they covered the cabin and cockpit from mast to backstay. From canvas we sewed weather cloths to keep the cockpit dry and bunk stretchers to keep us in our beds. Nylon webbing from an army surplus store became safety harnesses, which we fitted individually to each member of the family. We had to borrow a shoemaker's sewing machine to penetrate the heavy webbing and we prayed with each probe of the needle that it wouldn't break because we had only one. Matthew cut up an old spinnaker and made a windsail to funnel air down the forward hatch and circulate a cool breeze through the cabin.

In our "free" moments we made the flags. A little research: maps, books of sailing etiquette, encyclopedias. But where in the world do you buy flag material? Let your fingers do the walking . . . AWNING SUPPLIES.

"Eighteen yards of flag bunting please, four each of red, yellow, green, and white, and two of black."

"Going to make a few flags, are you? What are they for?"

"Well, we're going to sail a little boat to Africa and visit the countries along the West Coast. We need to fly the flag of each country as we arrive. It's courtesy."

Disbelief. (Had my tone lacked conviction?) Oh well, the pharmacist believed me.

Matthew did most of the sewing and grommeting. Melissa cut and ironed in hems. They were beautiful flags.

At times, life on the dock attained a surrealistic momentum. Propelled by the urgency of the work and locked into our capsule of compulsion, we glanced out at the world only on occasion. Sometimes people popped in and out of our consciousness like actors in a play. Once a bevy of ladies was exiting from a Yacht Club tea as I was carrying lumber from the parking lot. I had a long plank over one shoulder and some smaller boards under the other arm. I was maneuvering carefully, trying to avoid the sharper stones with my bare feet, but quickly because the ground was hot. It had been a full day and I was a little the worse for wear. My hair had fallen down and was blowing in the wind. My orange bikini was permanently scarred where I had leaned against some fresh paint. The same mistake was evident on my thigh. And I was pretty dirty.

I didn't notice the woman until she was about ten feet away, but she had obviously been looking me over rather thoroughly as she walked toward me to get to her car. She was tall and aged, though probably not much over sixty, and she carried herself with a southern elegance that suggested the Methodist Women's Society and the Magnolia Garden Club. She was wearing a violet suit with matching silk hat, bag and shoes in a darker shade of purple. A small veil dangled aimlessly over her blued hair, and in her hand were the inevitable impeccably white gloves. Her eyes were reproachful and as I came closer, her facial muscles gathered themselves familiarly into an expression of distaste.

Engrossed in our instant prejudices, we advanced. On impulse I decided to try to communicate with the woman behind the freeze. I lifted my chin a little and smiled.

"You're a mess!" she hissed, and rustled by.

Later I was thinking about her as I worked on the wharf. Was she a happy woman, I wondered? I was using a power sander on a long, newly finished spinnaker pole which was braced between my legs. The sander roared up and down as I bent to the task and suddenly my thoughts precipitously shifted to the vibrating pole. No, Jeannine, not here in broad daylight right beside the Yacht Club! A brazen delight crept over me and I began to laugh as I devotedly moved the sander against the wood.

A few minutes later I turned off the machine and sank weakly to sit on an overturned paint box. "You're a mess," I grinned wickedly to myself, "a real mess!"

Occasionally as I worked I found my mind fantasizing, trying to foresee the wilderness of unknowns that lay ahead. What was it like to be totally alone in the middle of the ocean? How would it feel to be tossed around by thirty-foot waves? What would we do if *Aquarius* were disabled, or if one of us were lost overboard? There was no way for me to tell how many anxieties bubbled below the surface of my consciousness. I didn't feel at all anxious. But every once in a while I would find myself engrossed in some incredible private daydream, imagining the solution to some unforseeable emergency. Usually they had happy endings, but not always. The purpose of these mental maneuvers, it seems to me, was to protect against the eventuality of a shock so great the mind couldn't cope with it.

A few times I went through the agony of losing someone at sea and the terror of searching, searching, searching through empty water and endless waves. I suppose I faced the death of each member of my family at least once in my imaginings. But I never contemplated my own. Was it because of some impetuous conceit that I was invulnerable? Or was it simply because there is no point in preparing for your own death? You're not around afterward to cope with the shock of it.

Whatever else these little exercises might have accomplished they made me laugh sometimes. In one of the more absurd episodes an enormous octopus was climbing over the back of the boat, approaching Melissa in a nightmarish attack. The monster was far too powerful to deal with physically. In panic I looked around for a weapon, grabbed the fire extinguisher from the galley and sprayed foaming carbon dioxide into his eyes. He seemed to shrink visibly at the contact, then slowly oozed himself back into the sea. What a victory! What a glorious and heroic solution! I will certainly know exactly what to do if we are ever attacked by an octopus!

The radio-telephone figured in some of these daring mental rescues. Disabled or sinking, we would send a desperate

SOS. At the last moment a freighter would appear on the horizon and save us. Usually I managed to have *Aquarius* saved as well. It was comforting to know that a radio would be there if we ever needed it.

One evening we were fitting the insulation into the icebox and I was enumerating the tasks for the next day.

"Matt, when are you going to find the radio-telephone?"

"I've decided not to get a radio. The range is so limited. It would be too expensive for what we'd get out of it. Everybody I've talked to who has a radio says he never uses it."

I was stunned. "But you said we were going to get one! We discussed it so many times! I thought we agreed that it was going to be expensive but we would get one anyway!" Suddenly without realizing it I was close to tears. The strain and pressure of the last weeks closed in on me and my reason collapsed. There was no conclusive argument on one side or the other. It was probably more sensible to spend the money on other things. All I knew was that I *wanted* a radio. I wanted that fragile link with *some* other human being, tenuous though it might be. If all our resources were not good enough, if someone were injured or one of the children had an appendicitis attack there would be at least a chance we could call for help. Even if that chance were small I wanted that last resort. Matt had decided unilaterally. He had announced it so casually as if it weren't an important matter at all! I was furious.

"You don't give a damn! You knew I felt strongly about a radio but you didn't care. And I don't believe we're ever going to be ready! You won't hurry! And you won't hire a carpenter or anyone to help so we can get finished and leave. You're just going to piddle along doing everything your way and insisting on doing everything yourself until the middle of hurricane season. Then when everything is perfect you're going to sail the boat out into the teeth of a tropical depression and send us all to the bottom! Well, if it's going to be like that I'm not going. I'm tired of the whole thing!"

I stormed off the boat and went out into the dark at the

end of the wharf and sat down. Everything was sour. The
balloon was punctured. I was no longer interested in the trip.
We had worked so hard! I cried bitterly for all that had been
lost in those few minutes. The black water and the lights
dancing on it didn't care. The boats nodding in their slips
didn't care. I didn't care. Anymore. I was empty.

I thought back to the prophecy of the *I Ching*. Here was
the conflict! It had been there for weeks bubbling below the
surface stirred by my anxiety to leave before the dangerous
weather began.

> In times of strife, crossing the great water is to be avoided.
> Conflict within weakens the power to conquer danger without.

Matt came and sat down beside me. "I didn't realize it
was so important to you. We'll see what we can do about a
radio. I'll talk to Bill again tomorrow. And we *are* close to
leaving, we really are."

It wasn't what he said. There was something new and
strong in his voice, some latent element that had emerged out
of the crisis. He wasn't apologetic or conciliatory. It was as
if he had reached inside many layers to his most intimate self
and pulled out his essence, naked and vulnerable, to offer me.

"I can do it, Jeannine, I have no doubts. And I want to
do it more than anything I have ever done."

I wasn't breathing. How very much I loved him! My
diaphragm let go and the surge of emotion came flooding
from my depths, jamming briefly at my throat and eyes until
the ache melted and let the tears flow. I looked at him.
Nothing else existed at the end of this dark wharf, in the
harbor, in the world, in the universe except our eyes and the
energy locked between them.

From that vast continuum of moments that is a human
life span, some moments separate themselves. They gather
uncommon significance and burn themselves a place among
ordinary memories like Sirius among the stars. It is as if from

a great pool of water one drop might jump up and cry, "I am! I am unique!"

The intensity of our communion was absolute. For that instant our love transcended all loves. Suddenly I was serene, with a confidence I had not allowed myself before. I knew quite clearly that I would go anywhere with him, as he would go anywhere with me.

> . . . the female principle comes to meet the male. There are times when this has great significance. When heaven and earth come to meet each other, all creatures prosper.

We walked back to the boat and took up our tools.

5

Champagne
and Goodbye

July 23

MATT: The day dawned like almost any morning in that long last frenzy of preparation. It was hot before the sun was up—muggy hot, with the promise of a blistering noonday bombardment that always left me half-paralyzed and gasping like a bug in a pressure cooker.

Jeannine and I lay on our bed at Holley's, sweating a gentle dawn sweat and trying to plan the day. In these last weeks the effort to complete work on the boat and wind up our affairs had taken on the urgency, if not the precision of a military operation. Unfortunately it often appeared that the Mad Hatter was commander-in-chief. Our lists had a kind of Alice-in-Wonderland quality too. But this morning we could no longer afford the luxury of lists for it was our last morning in New Orleans. Until this perilous moment we had never had the courage to give "departure" an exact time and place. To our friends we had always said, "Maybe this weekend," or "Probably around Wednesday," or "As soon as we finish the rigging." But we had come to realize that if we didn't leave soon, in fact within a few days, we would have to give up all thoughts of leaving for at least another year. The logistics of weather and time were beginning to close us in.

Thus we found ourselves this morning committed to depart the same afternoon for a year and a half of voyaging in strange waters, a terrifying prospect, and it was fortunate we had no time for terror. Our immediate concern was to shed the patina of lists that had grown like scales over our lives. We searched among the scraps of flag material, snap shackles and miscellaneous marine gear that cluttered the bedroom, collecting all the odd bits of paper we could find. Spread out across the bed, they formed a reasonable history of our lives during the past few months. It was astonishing how much work we had actually completed, but it was manifestly impossible to finish even a fraction of the uncompleted items by five that afternoon, so our principle of selection became very simple: no job that could possibly be done at sea or in another port would occupy even thirty seconds of our time today.

Out went such items as "install depth sounder, paint vane gear, fix tachometer." We ended with a list that could easily be completed in a week's time, and we had almost a whole day for the job. By our present standards it seemed reasonable enough: clean out office and darkroom, pack photographic equipment, sort and pack clothing, organize files, wind up business affairs, close out bank account, pack boat, buy ice and champagne. *Buy champagne?* At five we planned to gather on the dock with our friends, drink to the success of the voyage and say farewell.

We set off in separate borrowed vehicles with synchronized watches and carefully arranged rendezvous at crucial junctures of the day. By two o'clock the interior of the boat was piled so high with gear that we couldn't move around. No time for cleanup. We left Matthew to rationalize the mess as best he could and clean the boat.

At three-thirty we were plowing through our basement darkroom, picking up these papers, throwing out those. Close the files of notes on the anterior triangle of the neck, the Kreb's cycle, and the olfactory pathways. Tuck away the electron micrographs of rat mammary tissue. Lock the files of negatives and proof sheets: the voter registration pictures, the Birmingham church bombing, mass meetings, Mississippi cops, Neshoba County, Dallas, Lee Harvey Oswald, Malcom X's funeral, Memphis—murder of M. L. King. Close the door on an era of lacerating political education, passionate fraternity, turbulent living, and ambitious purpose.

We had just time enough to get to the marina. We threw more ice on the champagne, loaded Bill's truck, picked up Melissa, who had been transferring our favorite recordings to the tape recorder Holley had given us, and sped to the party.

As we drove into the parking lot we caught a glimpse over the backs of the cars of our mast and a bright flurry of color running all the way up the backstay. Our flags! A flutter of confidence and promise engulfed us, a surge of adolescent team spirit. We wanted to cheer, wave a pompom, leap in the air. After months of scrimmage—the Big Game!

It was a happy group that gathered to celebrate our departure. *Aquarius* rode splendidly at her warps, clean and lovely. Matthew had saved the day. Salvos of champagne corks rose to the masthead and if there were any tears they irrigated smiles. Matthew and Melissa and their friends, too busy for sentimentality, were chasing champagne corks with a net. Every few minutes the dockside chatter was interrupted by the energetic arrival of a new delegation of friends. Holley, realizing that we had not taken a moment to consider what we might eat for supper, brought a succulent stew. Carolina made a love gift of chocolate cake and a jug of freshly squeezed orange juice, "To keep you from getting scurvy." Dennis, apparently anticipating those endless days between the pitiless sun and the cruel sea, presented us with a copy of *War and Peace*.

The press attended. A photographer and reporter from the *Times-Picayune* politely refused a glass of bubbly ("the paper doesn't allow drinking on the job") and asked us to pose without ours. It seemed a queer touch of puritanism for wicked old New Orleans, but we complied. I ducked below with Roy Reed, a friend and the local New York Timesman, who wanted to probe our motives for undertaking the voyage. It was not the best moment for summing up one's philosophy of life and I must have replied somewhat incoherently.

As I talked to Roy my eyes roved the forepeak with increasing horror. The secret of Matthew's miracle mop-up was there. He had stuffed all our last-minute accumulations into the forepeak, so many that they threatened to engulf the whole boat. There were sea bags of clothing, cardboard cartons filled with business papers and income tax receipts, suitcases, bags of shoes, games in fragile boxes holding thousands of elusive pieces. Impossible even to enter the forepeak let alone bed down there. My mind boggled at what would happen when the boat heeled over. Smorgasbord of family possessions served up with bilge water and a topping of whipped pillow feathers.

Back on the dock all the champagne bottles were empty. There followed a tender exchange of embraces. Everyone was hugging each other: solid male bodies, soft female bodies, energetic child bodies—all of them so variously interwoven in our lives, so attached in ways we could never chart. How hard at this last moment to think of leaving all of them, to amputate so decisively this complex intermingling social part of us that had been so satisfying.

An expectant hush fell over the dockside celebrants. I waited expectantly with the others. Why was everyone looking at me? My God! Were they waiting for us to embark? I looked at *Aquarius*. She hadn't left the dock for more than a month. Did I remember how to sail her? Couldn't mess up now. Whole world watching. If I fell in the water or crunched the dock who would believe we'd make it to Africa? How many believed it anyway? Where's the wind? Off the dock, fortunately. Can't use the engine, poor form. Must sail away somehow. Too much champagne.

I stumbled aboard, shouted to Matthew to raise the jib, Jeannine to cast off the lines, Melissa to fend off the dock. Slowly, even majestically, *Aquarius* stood away from the dock with the wind filling her jib. Fingers touched across the gap and broke apart. *Aquarius* picked up speed. No stopping now. Carolina at the end of the dock ululating like a Mexican market woman. Holley crying. Jeannine crying. Captain suddenly very busy with his boat. Goodbye New Orleans. Don't want to leave you. Maybe we could just sail around Lake Pontchartrain and quietly sneak back. No good. No one would ever speak to us. Ready or not, we're off, off to Africa. Christ! *We're off to Africa!*

We got the main up, the jib polled out, and soon we were running wing and wing along the shore of Lake Pontchartrain, our colors flying. Supercharged, supergratifying day. Beautiful stew, beautiful sunset, beautiful people. What next? Blearily, we contemplated the evening ahead. Psychic engines losing torque. Run all night to Biloxi? Absurd. The object of this day was to *leave,* right? We have just accomplished that in style, right? We never promised more.

New Orleans out of sight? Okay, we have *left.* Sails came down, anchor snuggled into the mud. The forepeak was stuffed like a Thanksgiving turkey and the kids had already dropped on our beds in the cabin. Jeannine and I nested down in the folds of the jib on the foredeck, the only unencumbered space, smiled briefly at the stars, and fell asleep.

6
Deep-Blue Revolution

July 24

MATT: Sunday morning. End of the beginning—beginning of everything. We lay on our improvised bed, a folded jib on the foredeck (the "humping jib," Lyle once dubbed it) and watched the lake get light. Our first sleep aboard had been uneventful, the night dead calm, no mosquitoes, nothing to mar the serenity of our repose. The dawn light played glissandi across the lightly ruffled water. Piers and pilings and suburban rooftops of Slidell punctuated the faraway horizon very faintly. To our right the horizon line thickened into a railway causeway under which we would soon pass—and thereby pass finally from the influence of New Orleans.

And beyond that? The future yawned blankly ahead, unmarked by any predictable events—an unknown into which we sailed with unknown consequences. On any other day the thought of that existential chasm might disturb me, but not today. Nothing could mar the giddy euphoria of this marvelous sunny Sunday morning. I sat up slowly into the new world, aware of an unexpected weightlessness. What was it? Missing baggage? Of course, the lists! First morning in months with no urgent list of vital tasks to hassle my breakfast coffee. The only duty written on the blank pages of this virgin day was the entirely pleasurable one of sailing us down the coast to Biloxi. I poked Jeannine and she awoke, stretching and giggling at the same time. We lay together a few minutes longer watching the sun gather its forces, intoxicated by the completeness of our escape, smug Dillingers preparing to rob a new world of its experiences.

Then practicalities: Jeannine in the galley brewing coffee, repairing the chaos of departure; myself on deck performing the same rites, hauling up the anchor, raising sails like matins to the morning breeze. *Aquarius* underway. The voyage underway. We negotiated the railway bridge before the children were awake in their bunks.

The morning waxed. With the wind behind us *Aquarius* danced along the sparkling waterways as we made our way through the winding courses of the Rigolets, the channel connecting Lake Pontchartrain to the Gulf of Mexico. Melissa settled on the foredeck with a new Nancy Drew mystery. We would not hear from her this day. Matthew played with the portable radio recently purchased to bring us weather reports, shortwave news, and navigational time signals. Amid the clatter of a D.J. program came an unexpected news account of the Sailing Family Herron which, according to the newscaster, had departed that day from New Orleans to escape the Evils of Television and explore the west coast of Africa. We listened in mounting astonishment to this rapid-fire caricature of ourselves and our voyage. It was repeated hour after hour with added details. (In one version Matthew was delighted to discover himself magically matured as our eighteen-year-old son.) For the span of an afternoon the Voyage of *Aquarius* got higher billing than Vietnam and all the world's litany of woes. It was hard to believe. Had we touched some responsive chord, some secret urge lurking among the citizenry to chuck it all and run away to sea; or were we simply welcome relief on a dull and newsless Sunday afternoon? I couldn't tell but those news blurbs ruffled the tranquility of the voyage's first hours with their suggestion that our venture was somehow important to friends and strangers sitting now at home.

It rankled me to have the purposes of our voyage reduced to a simplistic comment made in the confusion of departure about escaping television. In truth our reasons were complex, their roots so intertwined with ten years of our political and social activity that it would be hard for us to explain the voyage to ourselves, let alone to an inquiring reporter.

"Jeannine, I've been thinking about that letter you wrote to your parents last spring. Remember? When they wanted us to give up the whole trip. It's true enough—all that stuff you wrote about adventure and Thoreau and the children's education, but that's only part of the story. Let's face it, one of the big reasons we're leaving is that we're frustrated politically—fed up with all those years of trying to bring about social change in this country and not getting anywhere. We've come to feel stifled by our government—by political policies that promote war and social policies that do nothing to lessen poverty or racism. It's that old-fashioned idea that people in a democracy should be *responsible* for their government. We've been trapped by that idea and you could say we're getting away in order to find a fresh perspective, to start breathing again. It's not only our lives we need to take a fresh look at, we ought to look at our politics too."

"Yes, I agree. Responsibility may be an old-fashioned idea but I still believe in it. The only problem is I can't see a way of implementing it any more. It's as if we've been surrounded by walls, Matt. Walls that stopped us from achieving our political goals or hindered society from growing in ways we thought were positive. You know, if you run up against a wall there are only a few things you can do. One is to accept it, change your plans, sit down where you are. I think that describes a lot of people we know, people who've lost their dreams, who've gotten locked into lives of compromise and routine. Sometimes they pretend they don't see the walls at all. They float around within their little enclosure, pretending they're roaming a huge field, but being very careful to draw back just before they hit the fence. I don't think that's us, though. Our walls are different, and our response has been to try to break them down. Sometimes it seems to work, the walls crumble and you change the shape of things. Other times you can't find the right wrecking tool or the wall is simply too big or there are too few of you. When that happens you begin to feel impotent, and that's intolerable. Isn't that how we felt in Philadelphia? We called that particular wall 'Militarism,' and we thought if we were sincere enough and steadfast in our non-violence, militarism would begin to crumble."

"Yeah, Gandhi's way. But we weren't as tough as Gandhi, or as politically sophisticated. We weren't prepared to die for our beliefs or even to suffer very much, and so nothing came of all those demonstrations and vigils and marches. I'll never forget those days. Sometimes it seemed to me the missiles were going to go off any minute. It was so mournful and depressing. I remember sitting in our sunny kitchen in that Philadelphia carriage house, watching Matthew and Melissa splash happily about in their cereal. Suddenly I was overcome by the awful thought: *I've got to make these moments as happy as possible for them. Time is so short. They'll never grow up to be adults. Someone is going to push the button.* Sitting here in this cockpit eight years later with the bright sunlight all around, those thoughts seem morbid and extreme. But they were real enough to me at the time. Nuclear annihilation seemed very possible, and there wasn't a damn thing I could do to stop it. That was a wall for sure!"

Jeannine was lying on the cabin top, soaking up the sun. She sat up and tried to scratch the middle of her back but the itch eluded her and her eyes invited me to take over the job. Her skin was hot. I noticed the old terry-cloth bikini was still holding its shape quite nicely in spite of the paint. "Ahhh, that's better. No. A little higher. Now to the right. Yes! Ahhh! Right there. Mmmmmmmmmmmmmmm!"

"Got any more itches? My treatment is very special."

"Stick to business. We were talking about walls and how frustrating all that peace activity was. But we did find a kind of way around it, Matt. I think that's what the civil rights movement meant to us, that's why it attracted us in the first place—it had such energy and we knew the peace movement was up against a dead end. God! I'll never forget hearing about SNCC and the sit-ins in the South for the first time. It scared me, but I felt as if the movement was drawing us south like a magnet. Those kids were willing to die for their freedom and that made Southerners really *care* about the demonstrations in a way people in Philadelphia never did about ours. They proved it with guns and clubs. How innocent we were then! And what an incredible education we got. Remember how shocked we were that policemen could be racist? Or that Methodists and Baptists and Presbyterians would block their church doorways to keep Negroes from coming in? I'd never been afraid before and suddenly I was afraid most of the time."

"*You* were afraid! It took me years after we'd left Mississippi to stop checking my rearview mirror in traffic to see who was following me."

"Well, if those two years in Mississippi didn't accomplish everything we hoped for, Matt, at least we learned a lot. What I remember most are not the bad times but the spirit that was there: the depth of commitment everyone felt, the excitement of trying to establish a really democratic society from the roots up. Every time Fannie Lou Hamer sang, 'This Little Light of Mine,' every time someone registered to vote or got out of jail something happened to my insides. I remember thinking in the middle of the really hopeful times: *The trouble with older people is they stop believing they can change the world.* I hoped that would never happen to me because I felt so intensely close to all those people who wanted to change it with me. Such a feeling of strength and satisfaction and love!"

"The sad thing is what happened to all that power."

"Yes, those old walls again. That love seemed like the strongest force I'd ever experienced but it slipped away in such a tiny fragment of time. One moment there was the hope and the momentum of thousands of voices singing, 'We

Shall Overcome,' and the next moment it was all strangled in a war that wouldn't end, in those monumental collisions with political corruption, in that divisive new cry: Black Power! We'll probably never go through a period as intense or beautiful in our lives again—or one as tragic."

"I won't argue with that, Jeannine. Mississippi was certainly special. Almost everything that happened there was so vivid just talking about it brings me back. It all seems larger than life now, simpler, more like a film than a slice of experience. And it certainly couldn't be more different than the murky business I got involved with afterward—the whole Kennedy assassination thing. What a change! All those plots and subplots, those conspiracies and counterconspiracies, the CIA and the FBI, the Warren Commission and Jim Garrison—it was like a script for an espionage thriller written by committee. Yet I think through all those frustrating years of trying to find out what really happened in Dallas I was moved by the same concern that brought us to Mississippi. When you consider it, the assassination was one more example of the machinery of democracy breaking down, not because Kennedy was killed, but because there was so much strong evidence of conspiracy which the government tried to cover up. My own involvement, working to get articles in magazines and helping Garrison, was just as political as what we did in Mississippi only the weapons were different: trying to publish pieces of the truth instead of registering voters or marching in front of courthouses."

"Well, if Garrison had convicted Clay Shaw you probably wouldn't be leaving New Orleans today—you'd still be involved, doing magazine stories and helping with the next stage of the investigation."

"Yes, you're probably right, but losing the trial doesn't change the facts, it just makes them politically irrelevant. I'm sure someday enough will be known so we can piece the whole story together—it's too big and too messy to hide indefinitely. By then probably it won't make any difference except as history, and that's not enough for me. Closing the

Shaw trial was like closing another wall around five years of my life. It made it easy to think about leaving New Orleans."

A sprightly fiberglass auxiliary passed us going upwind under power, probably heading back to New Orleans after a weekend on the Gulf Coast. Two couples lounged in the cockpit, drinks in hand. They waved. We waved. *Are they real? Are we real? How absurd! Are we actually setting off for Africa on this pleasant Sunday afternoon, or just loafing down the coast for a few days of fun? What if they knew? Would they believe us? Do I believe us? If I don't, how in hell are we going to make it?*

"Jeannine, I've been wondering what gets me into all these battles. Whatever it is, I'm sure glad we're trying something different for a while. I woke up this morning feeling just great to have all the preparations behind. I felt really free and unhindered—that's so rare for me. I guess I've spent most of my life feeling hedged in, bound by duties and obligations to some unknown higher authority that had the right to define how I used my time and what I did with my life. In practice it usually worked out that some institution held the authority: school, college, draft board, employer. Personal freedom was an issue that simply never came up. Any freedom I had came in around the edges—in vacations, sexual adventures, or the time I spent in the woods or on bicycle trips—but always I had the sense of a monolith of institutions hunched over me ready to take over my life when I returned to business. I didn't really understand how coercive it was at the time, but I can remember how tense I used to feel, how hard it was to relax. Toward the end of high school I began to develop a permanent lump in my throat. It would get bigger and bigger as the school year progressed, and by vacation time I'd have to get away for a few weeks in the woods just to unwind. Usually I had a job in the summer, but I knew I couldn't go back to school until I'd taken some time by myself to get rid of that lump."

"How does the vane gear work, Dad?" Matthew's question drew me abruptly back to the present. *Aquarius* was well

out into the shallow waters of the Mississippi Sound, following the dredged channel of the Intercoastal Waterway.
Ahead a line of red-nun buoys danced away to the horizon,
vanishing and reappearing in the glare of the late afternoon
light. Matthew was bored by the radio, probably looking for
a new problem to occupy his mind. I wondered how bored
he'd be with the voyage after he'd dismantled, explored and
comprehended every gadget on the boat.

"So far as I know, Matthew, the damn vane doesn't work
at all. At least I haven't been able to make it work. Try for
yourself if you want." The vane gear had been a big letdown.
In the final month of preparations, with most of the money
gone, I realized I'd made no provision for automatic steering.
I thought about building a self-steering wind vane from
scratch, but the experience of friends who'd tried made me
cautious. I ended by ordering one untried from the pages of
a magazine. It was fairly cheap, but I could never get it to
work and Bill Seemann was unsuccessful at modifying it. So
we just sailed off into the blue with the useless vane gear
attached to the afterdeck like an appendix. I didn't know
what we'd do for self-steering; maybe the vane would become
Matthew's favorite anti-boredom machine.

"Matt, you were just getting interesting. You were talking about lumps and freedom—and institutions."

"Well, I took some lumps from the biggest institution of
them all, the government. But it took me a while to recognize
it. I only saw it in the guise of its most visible representative:
my friendly local draft board. The board gave me a number
and required me to register my name and report where I was
living and when I intended to travel, and where. There was
always the threat that someday it would *really* restrict my
freedom by throwing me in the army, and maybe doing me
out of my life in the bargain. I couldn't articulate much of
this at the time, but I was beginning to get the message about
selective service and to recognize I would have to stand up
to it. I couldn't oppose it for taking away my personal freedom, I still wasn't sure that I had a *right* to that kind of

freedom, but I knew it was asking me to perform immoral acts, killing for example, and I started with that.

"I remember when I finally made the decision to become a conscientious objector. It was a fairly rare position to take in the early fifties. There were only two conscientious objectors I knew of at Princeton—myself and a grad student. I had the scary feeling of standing at the junction of a very tangible crossroad. One road led in the direction a lot of my classmates took, the way my father certainly wanted me to go, toward regular jobs, respectability, an accepted niche within the system. I couldn't tell exactly where the other road led, but I knew it would change my life and that I'd never be able to go back to that conventional road again. I guess that's when my political education really got started. I had to work out the implications of what I was doing so I wouldn't be traveling down that road completely blind. I began then to understand what freedom was all about, and to realize that most of us move in lockstep all our lives without ever sensing the chains, you only feel the coercion when you try to step out of line.

"One of the most frightening acts of my whole life was quitting that job in Philadelphia to begin freelancing. The unstructured time was more than I could take at first; it was like stepping out of a suit of clothes and suddenly deciding never to wear clothes again. I had the overpowering feeling I was doing something wrong and it really terrified me, but I couldn't identify what the new rules were. I half expected to wake up some morning and find a man in a dark suit standing by my bed saying: 'Well, you've had your fling. Now we're putting you back to work.'

"When you look at this voyage in terms of freedom, Jeannine, it's the most radical thing we've ever done. We're really kicking loose from all those institutions, those silent obligations. We're saying, let's spend the next two years exactly as *we* please. It's a radical move on our children's behalf, too. Taking them away from schools, the place where institutionalization first gets started."

"Yes, when you think of it that way, *leaving, itself,* becomes a positive action. I hope I'm not just rationalizing. Anyway, we know what we're leaving behind—and it's more than TV. But it still seems a little selfish to me. Maybe we're copping out, leaving others to be responsible. Maybe we didn't search hard enough for new ways of getting involved."

"Like what, Jeannine? Bombing banks? The civil rights movement as we knew it is dead and there's nothing else happening politically right now that fits our style. Don't you think this is one of those times when it's better to lie back and flow with the rhythm of things until we feel the rightness of something new? Maybe that will happen. How do we know? Maybe we need to go in and out of this society like we go back and forth from cities to woods. You have to step back from political struggles in order to look at them from a different perspective."

"You're right. My God! We can't let them become our whole life. If all the causes were to disappear overnight, would there be anything left of us? I certainly hope so. People can't depend on opposing wars and racism and injustice for their sense of purpose and community. That's too much like what keeps the military industries going. I can't resign myself, as Daniel Berrigan suggests, to a lifetime of resistance. I can't say 'No' constantly. There have to be moments when I am creating something positive, when I experience for myself the kind of freedom and peacefulness I am trying to achieve for society. Otherwise how can I know it is good?"

"I'm *tired* of feeling guilty for someone else's wars, Matt. I'm tired of feeling responsible for someone else's racism. Can't we resist without being burdened down by all that? Look at it this way. I have several roles: in the family I am a wife, a mother and a daughter; in the society I am a friend, an associate, an American, a human; in my personal life I am a woman, a writer, a scientist, a gardener, a cook. 'American' is just another category. I'm not going to let it run my life!"

"Yea! The second Declaration of Independence!"

"Seriously, Matt. There are so many other things we

contribute to society that are intrinsically ours, not a part of any 'movement.' Our *work* is relevant to the community, and we continue to grow as persons, that's relevant. And maybe the most important of all are our *kids* and our love for each other. We're taking all these on our voyage. If the political movements are in hibernation then maybe it's a time to step out into the sun ourselves."

"You're right! Abolish guilt! Down with duty! Actually, I think this whole heavy conversation has been just an elaborate justification for going off and having a good time. We've been battling the same old bear over and over again—old crochety Puritan Ethic himself. Goodbye, Bear! We're off on the deep-blue revolution! We're off across the great water! ... You know something, Jeannine? I love your mind almost as much as I love your body."

"You know something, Matt? You're full of garbage. Let's have some tea."

7

Shakedown

July 24,

MATT: The shoreline features had retreated into complete darkness by the time we picked out the four-second occulting flash of the Biloxi lighthouse from the hurdygurdy jumble of shore lights. I eased the sheets and nudged the helm over, pointing *Aquarius* toward the channel-entrance buoy and the reassuring pulse ashore. We were putting in at Biloxi, only a day's sail from New Orleans. In our present condition even moderate rolling in a seaway would turn the melange of clothing, games, books and miscellaneous gear that packed the forepeak from cabin sole to deckbeams into a mighty unsavory claptrap stew. We had to simplify, sort out, throw out, and digest the ingredients of that stew before proceeding any further. We could do this most pleasantly at the gracious Biloxi digs of our old friend Lyle Bongé. And while we worked, Lyle would fill our heads with tall tales and entertain our stomachs with masterful preparations from his redoubtable skillet. It was a hard combination to beat. It fitted right in with our brave new resolution that from today onward the voyage must yield pleasure at least in equal measure with the work.

The wind had freshened steadily with the fading light, and Matthew and I now doused the mainsail, but *Aquarius* fairly careened down the narrow channel under working jib alone. As the channel markers bore swiftly down on us I reflected that Biloxi wasn't the same homey haven I had entered so many times past in Lyle's little cutter, *Loon.* I hadn't seen the waterfront since Hurricane Camille's cataclysmic visit almost a year ago and I was certain all the landmarks I usually depended on to keep off the numerous mud shoals would be altered beyond recognition. The shoals themselves must have been pushed into entirely new configurations. We reached the marker where the channel makes a dogleg, rounded up, dropped the flogging jib, fired up Methuselah and motored irresolutely onward into the gloom. The remains of Biloxi's venerable yacht club might be any one of those clusters of broken pilings that loomed so obscurely out of the darkness, but *which* one? Nothing was recognizable. I could sense the suck of those mudbanks possibly only a few inches under our keel, and I wished for the depth sounder I'd been too busy to hook up. At last I spotted a temporary dock with several husky shrimp boats tied alongside. Boats that size seemed to promise deep water and I powered confidently in their direction. Of course we drove straight onto a formidable mudbank. Methuselah churned furiously in reverse but we were stuck solid, apparently fated to end the first brave day of our voyage ingloriously marooned in Biloxi mud.

And so, near midnight I stood half-naked in the plush lobby of a waterfront nightclub dripping harbor water on the terrazzo and pleading with the startled hatcheck girl for the use of a telephone. Fifteen minutes later Lyle clattered onto the wharf in his battered jeep. He surveyed our plight quite philosophically.

"For chrissake, find a boat and haul us off," I pleaded. "The tide is falling. If we don't move fast we'll be stuck here forever."

"Well now, you don't look too badly grounded to me," Lyle ventured. "Why don't some of you women and children maunder out on the foredeck and jig around a little." Jean-

nine and the kids jigged while I horsed Methuselah hard
astern. With the added foredeck weight loading her bow,
Aquarius raised her tail a touch. I wagged it judiciously with
the rudder and she backed ponderously off the mudbank.
(Why couldn't I have figured that out for myself?) Under the
yellow beams of Lyle's ancient headlights we tied to pilings
he showed us where the water was deep, tidied up the boat
and clambered ashore for a night of untroubled sleep.

But our untroubled night turned into a troubled week.
The morning news brought reports of Hurricane Becky, the
second windy lady of the season. She was wandering around
the Gulf and threatening to come ashore near Biloxi. We
moved *Aquarius* to the sheltered waters of Biloxi's back bay
to wait Becky out. That evening over plates of rock shrimp
and stuffed mushrooms in Lyle's kitchen we began to piece
our plans together.

"I don't understand what we're doing," Jeannine complained. "I don't know about you, but I feel completely
unready to sail to Africa. If we struck out so easily on a
Biloxi mudbank how are we going to make it across the
Atlantic? And that's only part of our problem. Look at the
boat. In spite of all the sweat we've put into her, nothing
really works properly, and we're not working properly ourselves. I don't even remember how to reef the mainsail. But
our real problem is time. I know you'd like to sit right here
and get all the mechanical quirks ironed out but we can't
afford even these few days. We were already six weeks behind
schedule when we left New Orleans. If we don't keep moving
we'll never make Bermuda in time for a safe crossing. As for
stowage—I don't even want to *think* about that!"

There was a moment of silence while Lyle refilled the
wine glasses. "Okay," I said, "we've got some problems but
we solved the biggest problem of all when we sailed away
from the Southern Yacht Club pier. Now let's take the others
one by one and figure out what to do."

As we talked a kind of plan emerged. The goals of the
first weeks were clear enough. We must proceed to Bermuda

as quickly as was consistent with prudence and safety. At the same time this first leg would have to serve as a shakedown cruise. We must crowd into it as much testing of the boat and her equipment as a cruising family might normally accomplish in a whole season before even considering an ocean crossing. Besides modifying gear and rigging, we badly needed to polish up our rusty seamanship, and what little navigation we had learned from our only blue-water sailing experience, a three-day passage from Tampa Bay to Apalachicola two years ago. Finally, our psychic baggage was as jumbled and disorganized as that tangible tangle in the forepeak. The duress of getting ready had hardly given us time to prepare for the actual physical and emotional consequences of living at sea.

Bill Seemann and others had impressed upon us the importance of this proving period. Bill had even suggested (ever so gingerly) that the practical experience of shakedown might induce us to give up the voyage to Africa altogether. Privately I felt that giving up now would be the worst shakedown of all, an extortion of the hopes and dreams that had brought us along this far.

Becky procrastinated in mid-Gulf. We applied her week of indecision to paring down our gear, tuning the depth sounder and curing the first of an apparently endless series of Methuselan infirmities. We submitted to our third newspaper interview. We consumed quantities of Bongé cooking and gave over long evenings to Bongé wine and talk. We fidgeted. We listened to weather bulletins and wondered if this was what sailing to Africa was all about.

July 29

JEANNINE: Becky passed and we left Biloxi with firm resolutions to be serious about our shakedown. But truthfully, it was so nice to bask in the sun that our days were not totally devoted to purposeful work. We did go through a few drills with the "crew" until satisfied that any of us alone could handle the boat well enough to reach the nearest land.

We also practiced "man overboard" drills. Matt would suddenly throw the lifebuoy over and shout, "Hey! I just fell overboard! Melissa! Rescue me!" Whoever he named would have to leap up from a nap, book, or dinner, and grab the helm, jibbing the boat around and coming up into the wind for a rescue. To equalize things (no tyranny on this ship) the children and I made Matt rescue us a few times too.

It was hard to settle down to writing in the log, but that was one thing we hoped to be consistent about throughout the voyage. That part of the experiment had to work or our log wouldn't really represent a family's sailing experience, nor would Matthew and Melissa develop their writing skills, something we considered a vital part of our alternative school-style.

Matthew is left-handed and dislikes writing because it is difficult for him. I have a professional interest in the learning problems of left-handers and I have never met one who doesn't have painful memories about the whole process of learning to write. Spelling, to put it kindly, does not come naturally for Matthew either. But I didn't want his self-expression to get bogged down in technicalities so I decided not to make any fuss about spelling, penmanship or punctuation. It was a good decision, although his early log entries are practically illegible. The most confusing problem was a consistent and alarming lack of punctuation marks, particularly periods and capital letters. However, words spelled phonetically could, with inspiration, be translated: "On ocation we said the plej of alegenc." Later when he saw how often I had to ask him to "interpret" what he had written, Matthew began to take time to lay down a few dots and squiggles in the proper places. At one point in the voyage he asked me to teach him how to write and print "properly," and he spent several weeks experimenting with different script styles, new positions for his hand and slants for his paper.

His greatest boon, however, was the typewriter. It was fast, it was neat, and it was a *machine*. Matthew immediately loved typing as he loved using any practical machine. He and Melissa both started working through a self-teaching typing book. One of the first assignments I gave them was to write down some of their recollections of school, so that later we could compare "Aquarius School" with "Real School." Matthew wrote the following (only spelling and punctuation have been changed to protect the innocent):

MATTHEW: The school I went to in New Orleans was bossy and boring. No one liked it. The teachers were always threatening the students with two hour detentions and a thousand lines—"I must not talk out of turn. I must not talk out of turn," etc. Sometimes the students threatened the students. No sensible kid would go into the bathroom alone. What happens was that you got trapped in that little room and then some big tough guy would come in and say "Gimme a nickel!" What could you do? Scream for help? No. The guy would cream you after school.

I didn't have to worry too much about getting caught in the bathroom because it was almost impossible to get there. First you must get permission from the teacher which is the hardest. Then you must get her or him to write you out a little blue slip that says that you have permission to go to the bathroom and indicates the exact time that you left the classroom. If a teacher stops you in the hall you show your little blue slip to him and he goes away. Next you go to the office and wait in line to get your slip stamped with the school's new time clock. This gives you exactly three minutes to go down to the basement floor, show your slip to the person on duty down there, use the bathroom, go up to the office and get the slip stamped again to show that you have or haven't done all that in three minutes, and then go up to your class and give your teacher the blue slip so that she can put it in a little pile just for that purpose. That's the way it is if everything goes well.

My history teacher was very nice and she knew how to

teach well, but sixty percent of the class were students who didn't care. I had three different teachers for science during the year. The first was teaching well and being nice about it but she had to leave for some reason. Our next science teacher was fun and we all liked him but he just couldn't seem to teach. He was doing all the right things but nothing happened. About the middle of the year he got drafted and the whole class was trying to find a way to have him stay. He left and was replaced by a dictator of a teacher who had a little black book. Everytime a student misbehaved he would quietly put a little zero by the student's name. If you got more than three he was supposed to call your mother, but he never did and, believe me, almost everyone in the class had at least three.

One day the news got around very quickly that someone had stolen his little black book that he used sort of like his security blanket. Oh boy! We laughed and laughed and he tried to laugh with us but he couldn't.

My English teacher was bossy but friendly. Sometimes she lost her temper and I wished I could hold my ears. When she assigned a composition to be written she would say, "Stop fooling around!" when you were thinking about what to write. After English I had to rush to Math class because if I walked I wouldn't get there in the five minutes I was supposed to. The punishment was less for running than for being late. I think my Math teacher was the best and I think Math is the hardest to teach.

My next class I dreaded. It was Reading. Not that I didn't know how to read, but that the teacher was horrible. She was about fifty years old and not married. I can understand that because she was very ugly. She wore a red wig and once at the end of a school year a boy tied a string around it and pulled it off. Then he ran and ran all the way home. She was very very strict. She would not let us use spiral notebook paper to write on because she claimed there were little "smidgens" of paper all over the floor. When it was time to leave she made us look around for the "smidgens." If she found any that we hadn't found she would get very angry.

She was the sort of teacher who never liked to be wrong. We had lots of arguments in class but she won most of them. Once we got her back. There was a big argument over where the stays and shrouds went on a boat. A friend and I were saying that the stays went in the front and back of the mast and the shrouds on the sides. She didn't agree. Finally we settled it by looking it up in a huge encyclopedia. She had it for just such occasions. When she found out that we were right, she flew into a rage and said in a very nasty tone, "You think you're so smart! I ought to send you to the office for talking back!" I was almost busting with laughter. She was like a bomb with a hair trigger—almost anything would set her off.

My P.E. teacher was an ex-sergeant in the army. There was a rumor going around that his wife drove him to school every morning and took the car away to make it look like he jogged to school, and also to protect his car from all the poor kids who wanted to get revenge on him. He thought that just because he was in the army, we should have to be too. Since we were not old enough, he made his own little one for us. Almost every morning we had "inspection" of our gym outfit and he would call out our names and we would answer, "Here, SIR!" He thought it was important to teach "respect."

If he came into the gym to find the whole class talking he would make us stand "at ease" for the whole one-hour period. Then he would keep the people who were talking and goofing off after school for about two hours. Once we were standing "at ease" and one of the boys just collapsed and hit his head on a chair. The coach gave him permission to sit down. Pretty soon whenever we got punished this way a boy or two would faint. Then they would revive very quickly and get permission to sit down also. It was easy at first but it didn't last long.

JEANNINE: We didn't know whether our "Aquarius School" would be a valid or useful replacement for formal school. A New Orleans reporter, antagonized by our criticisms of TV and school systems, wrote of our departure, "One is tempted to ask about a parent's responsibilities toward his children."

Well, perhaps we *were* being irresponsible. Our parents certainly thought so; the *Times-Picayune* evidently thought so. But we would never really know unless we tested our beliefs. We had lots of ideas about what Matthew and Melissa might learn from the trip, but whether they actually *would* learn and would *enjoy* it were still matters of conjecture.

Melissa's log was very different from Matthew's. She took pride in her penmanship and spelling, which came easily, but had trouble thinking of something to say. She told me once that she believed she had no imagination. (Looking back on my own early years I remember believing the same of myself.) Her description of school read, "I liked school. My teachers were very nice. I miss everybody at school." She worked hard to please her teachers and was proud of her good grades, but most of the work was a passive kind of rote learning. She was rarely required to be original, and when she was it made her uncomfortable. She wasn't really interested in working or playing at something long enough to develop a real skill; it was easier to curl up with a horse story or watch television.

Sometimes I was afraid Melissa would leave high school with no real passions, no satisfying skills, and find herself terribly bored in a society of bored teenagers. I looked at her friends. From these influential peers she would develop her concept of womanhood. For the most part they were pretty and bland, like a lot of women I had met in Mississippi and Louisiana. (The white South has traditionally admired women who are classically beautiful and essentially helpless, gracious complements to chivalrous and superior men.) I hoped Melissa would learn to value courage, wisdom and strength of spirit as *human* qualities, not sex-linked traits. And I hoped she would recognize these qualities in herself as she became more and more competent in dealing with the world.

There's a struggle ahead, my daughter, my love, as women take their place in the world. And the fiercest struggle for most women is bridging that dichotomy—closing that terrible and tantalizing gap between an intellect which says, "There is no reason I shouldn't be equal," and an ego which has learned, oh so well, to say, "I am really not as good." There is no way to believe yourself into being equal; you must learn step-by-successful-step that you are.

Step-by-successful-step. Just what every ego needs. The steps can be steady advances, inch by inch, or great but infrequent leaps of faith. Our preparation for the voyage had inched successfully along and we felt good about it—so far. Now we were at the verge of the first big leap and we needed to be sensitive to the fact that our shakedown was testing subtle human capabilities. How good would we be at piloting through conflicts, predicting emotional storms, self-steering on the happiest courses?

Melissa had the biggest problems with self-steering, literally and metaphorically. On the literal side, she was hampered by her tentative and usually pessimistic relationship to all things mechanical. Trying to adjust the trim of the boat or the angle of the vane gear was no ego-trip for her when she couldn't get it to work well. Her watches were frustrating unless conditions were ideal. Impatience catalyzed by mild seasickness sometimes became resentment and even rage.

Figuratively speaking, Melissa hadn't really steered herself into this sailing voyage in the first place. Whereas the rest of us were enthusiastically motivated and ready to endure discomfort for the sake of the trip, Melissa, if given a real choice, would probably have preferred to stay put in a dry non-pitching house, near her friends' dry non-pitching houses. She came along because she was ten years old and her family was going off on a sailboat; she left behind her friends, the TV, her flute teacher, the swim team, her dog, and the chance to ride horses. What's more, she was not at all sure we were going to make it across the Atlantic!

At one point she wrote:

> In the beginning of the voyage I didn't like it. I thought we would never make it. I really didn't want to go but I did want to stay with Mom and Dad. I told them we would never make it. But they wouldn't believe me. I thought they were absolutely crazy. Then I decided we might be safe because we had a life boat.
>
> I guess Matthew and I don't fight so much on the boat but that's because I'm getting used to his teasing and the boat is really too small to fight in. But I have to admit that sometimes I just feel like beating everyone up.

We encouraged her participation judiciously. We didn't want her completely turned off before the voyage had really begun. On the other hand, we couldn't let Melissa intimidate us with the stomping and wailing that accompanied her occasional watches. Her anger at *Aquarius* for moving off course usually resulted in a jerk at the tiller and a gross overcorrection which in turn was overcorrected with another emphatic jerk. Matt spent long hours showing her how to respond patiently to the helm. We all tried to communicate that we needed her. It was true, we did. But above all, we wanted her to be happy, and when she balked at participating we were torn. On the one hand, she had a right to choose a passive kind of existence if that's what she wanted. What right did we have to force our kind of adventure on her if she didn't dig it? On the other hand, we did have a responsibility for her future happiness, a happiness that would depend in part on her own sense of self-confidence in a variety of every-day situations. It didn't take a barometer to predict a few emotional storms ahead with Melissa. We hoped we all would weather them fairly and gracefully.

August 2

JEANNINE: We pondered these things, Matt and I, one evening as *Aquarius* whispered past distant resort lights along Florida's panhandle. The moon would not be up for several hours, but as the night grew darker, our wake became lighter! Fired by the energy of a million tiny bioluminescent bodies, a lustrous beam foamed out behind us like the exhaust of a mighty rocket. Through the front hatch I called Matthew and Melissa up to watch. We were leaning over the bow pulpit, mesmerized by graceful phosphorescent curls below us when my eye was caught by a large glowing area dead ahead! In alarm I called to Matt at the helm.

"Hey Matt! What's that ahead? The water is agitating around something!"

"I don't know. It looks like shoals, but there should be deep water out here."

Before we could make any sensible judgment we sailed into the luminous patch, our hearts pounding. Looking down into it from the foredeck we saw thousands of wriggling black forms boiling the water into an explosion of candlepower—it was a huge school of mullet, doing strange circular mullet rituals. We passed through them and continued onward, watching eagerly for other ghostly manifestations. A school of smaller somethings sped across our bow with a large fishy ghost in pursuit. It was as if all undersea life had suddenly become visible by virtue of its motion.

We were still wrapped around the pulpit discussing whether or not the big guy had caught his supper when we heard a loud splash just under the bow, so close it startled us. The splash was followed by a small afterglow, and that by a comet with a tail of light streaming behind it. Then, just ahead of us, another splash, a Roman candle spinning through watery space. Dolphins!

There were three of them playing with us, their bodies clearly outlined by magical golden halos. We watched their movements like blips on a radar screen. Because of the re-

markable phosphorescence we could see the whole sequence
of their movements, not just a brief glimpse when they broke
the surface. Their game was relatively consistent. First they
wheeled in a holding pattern about two hundred feet off the
starboard beam, circling there until some common signal
sent them flashing for the boat like three glowing torpedoes,
their heads aimed for a leap at our bow. Then came a sudden
vertical thrust toward the surface and they disappeared upward, dark in the air except for a few sparkles caught in the
drops clinging to their bodies. The next sight of them was the
bright flash of their re-entry.

Again and again they repeated their dance of light, to our
increasing pleasure. As they wheeled and teased we tried to
predict exactly when they would break pattern and sprint for
the boat. Did they somehow perceive our joy? The appreciation and love I felt for this unique performance was so ultimate and satisfying that I knew, when they finally left us, if
there were never again any dolphins in my experience, these
dolphins would have been enough.

The following morning the radio brought reports of serious weather with the beguiling name of Celia, and we scuttled in to Panama City, Florida, for what we hoped would
be a brief wait.

As soon as docking lines were secured, Melissa, our resi-
dent anthropologist, set off on a series of exploratory field
trips. Gathering her independence around her, she wandered
the dock area, making friends and collecting intelligence on
all sorts of matters. The boat across the dock from us was
a fishing boat, she reported. They bait-fished for snapper and
other bottom fish for a week or two and then came home to
port for a few days. The fishermen taught her to play a funny
card game and we could hear them laughing uproariously
from their afterdeck.

She also made friends with the myriad people who came
down to the harbor to catch crabs: black mothers in straw
hats encircled by platoons of buckets, crab nets, and small
children; retired gents in Harry Truman sport shirts; teenage

boys and girls using their crablines as a good excuse to sit in the warm sun and hold hands; old salts who came at dusk to pull in "a couple of good ones."

The harbor water was incredibly clean. Looking over the side of the boat we could see flickers of movement on the bottom—crabs, schools of fish, all kinds of sea-life to be had for the catching. Melissa begged some fish heads from her fishermen friends and set out seriously to catch some crabs. She fished all day long with a passion quite new to her. Every once in a while she would come back to report excitedly the latest count, then be off again, happily singing. Toward late afternoon, having completely forgotten lunch, she climbed aboard with a bucketful of wriggling crabs.

"Thirty-four!" she announced proudly.

"That calls for a ceremony."

"Let's have a feast!"

It took a couple of hours to prepare the banquet but it was worth it! We laid out a red-checkered tablecloth in the middle of the dock and sat cross-legged around it, eating sweet Crab Louis with lettuce and hard-boiled eggs. Wild flowers from a nearby field garnished our "table," and we shared our salad and cool white wine with smiling passersby.

Melissa went to sleep at seven o'clock, but she was already out crabbing for the next salad by the time we woke in the morning.

August 5

MATT: Life itself was a salad on the docks of Panama City—a salad in which all manner of diverse personalities were tossed randomly together. It may be true that one can live years in a city apartment and never meet a neighbor, but on the dock conviviality requires no volition. People come by, they are curious, they want to talk, and before you know it you find yourself part of a community. The process began almost before our docking lines were ashore.

One of the delights of cruising is entering a strange harbor after many days of isolation and recognizing the sheer line of a familiar boat. The first friendly sheer we saw in Panama City belonged to *Misty,* a thirty-eight-foot sloop from Chicago that we had known in New Orleans, where she was fitting out for a voyage to the Panama Canal and unspecified points beyond. *Misty* was of steel, lovingly and beautifully welded together by her owner in six years of hard labor. Free at last, he cherished no plan in the world save to live at his ease and cruise quietly in the Pacific. But Hurricane Becky had a different plan for him. Not being inclined to keep a radio weather watch, he sailed from New Orleans straight into her energetic arms, and she clasped him in a strenuous embrace through two terrifying days. *Misty* survived to shelter in Panama City, all her sails but a working jib blown out and the hefty framework supporting her self-steering gear twisted into a fanciful stainless-steel pretzel. If I needed yet another lesson in hurricane caution, *Misty* provided it. During our six days in Panama City (hosted by Hurricane Celia, who arrived on the heels of her sister), *Misty*'s skipper could be seen at any hour sitting cross-legged on the foredeck, a can of beer beside him, industriously restitching his sails. There was always a beer for me when I passed his way and we spent many a pleasant hour in conversation until Jeannine would come to summon me back to duty.

Other visitors came to relieve the endless round of repairs and alterations that occupied me. Between machining a new drive shaft for the water pump and rebalancing the vane gear, we met Rex, a truck-driving cowboy from the arid vastness of West Texas. Rex was so distressed by the watery instability of our home that he adamantly refused to be lured aboard despite overpowering curiosity. He would squat on the dock in his cowboy boots as I worked, disposing of three or four beers and telling wonderful stories.

Rex claimed to be a simple tourist in Panama City, but he was really searching for a former love. When he found her and brought her to meet us, we enticed them aboard for a scallop hunt. We sailed across St. Andrew Bay to the scallop beds and anchored off a small island in about fifteen feet of water. While Rex and his amour stayed safe, dry, and boozy in the cockpit, we dived. It was lovely prospecting among the underwater crustaceans, and Jeannine wrote a poem about it:

Stalking the Blue-Eyed Scallop

The sea imposed a slowness on our movements;
We absorbed its modulating rhythm, kicking silently along a
    sandy bottom,
Punctuated here and there with tufts of grass.
Morning light diffused down through the moving liquid;
Probing pseudopodia of yellow dancing on the bottom
Picked out hidden bumps anonymously camouflaged with
    sand.
Sometimes a crescent row of tiny bright blue eyes
Reflecting back a beady shaft, betrayed the luckless mollusk
    to our grasp.
Or else he sensed us as we made our slow invasion
Of his semilunar field of view,
(With what strabismic gaze he must perceive the world!) and,
Clicking audibly, his two shells pumping desperately together,
He jetted off in awkward backward jerks to freedom,
And to glorious escape.

We returned to the dock with a sack of scallops, but Rex and his lady collected a treasure too. While we were submerged they decided to get spliced.

The day before leaving Panama City we found a letter bearing the stamp of the federal prison at Danbury, Connecticut, waiting for us in General Delivery. It was from Phil Stiles, our old friend who'd gone to prison on a draft charge eighteen months before. I had been corresponding with Phil in Danbury, and had visited him once. When our voyage to Africa became a certainty and we realized our departure would coincide more or less with Phil's release, I wrote him suggesting he might like to join us for all or part of the voyage. The idea suited him. He changed plans and arranged to meet us in Bermuda for the passage to the Azores. The Panama City letter was his last from prison:

I'm reading *Across the Western Ocean,* the story of a trans-Atlantic cruise on a forty-seven-foot yawl. It gives me an idea of what's involved, much discomfort, many unique satisfactions. (Do you know that because of the floodlights here I haven't really seen the stars for eighteen months?)

I imagine you can dig them from a small boat in the ocean quite well. In any event the trip seems as much challenge and adventure as I can imagine. I wonder how cold it will be. Won't it be hot that far south in August? Do we go through the Sargasso Sea? I'm really freaking on the whole idea of the trip and how different it is from the scene here. At one time this was my only reality. Now this place recedes. The light at the end of the tunnel gets bigger and bigger. I'll be able to take pictures! Make love! Eat good food and enjoy solitude and silence! The expansion of mind and world after release seems to be on the order of rebirth. . . . There is more on my mind than I can get out now. Talk later. Rendezvous in Bermuda!

Love,
Phil

8

Rainbeams
and Moonbows

August 6

MATT: It was early afternoon before we slipped our mooring lines and chugged out of the yacht basin at Panama City. A brisk northerly breeze ruffled St. Andrew Bay. Once clear of the dock we spread our wings, main to starboard, genny to port. *Aquarius* picked up speed like she was turbocharged. We plowed across the bay and out through the channel into the Gulf of Mexico. It was great to be putting out again, the first open-water leg of the voyage before us.

The weather was promising. Hurricane Celia had moved inland to harass the citrus growers of Florida and no infant tropical depressions bloomed in the Caribbean to disturb our 230-mile passage from Cape San Blas to Egmont Key Light at the head of Tampa Bay on Florida's west coast. I needed all the help I could get. My first trial as a fledging navigator was beginning and I could hardly flap my wings let alone find the proper flight path. I felt more confident of the boat though, and for the first time I had all the navigational gear in good working order.

During our sojourn in Panama City I had improvised a chip log from a length of line and a piece of wood, using a formula extracted from Bowditch's *American Practical Navigator.* The chip log is a very simple and ancient device for measuring boat speed, and hence, the distance traveled through the water. It came into general use around the time of Columbus and has not changed in any important respect since. A line is knotted at regular intervals according to a formula and a small wooden board, or "chip," attached to one end and weighted so it will float upright. The board is thrown out behind the moving boat and the line allowed to run out freely for a measured length of time. The number of knots that pass through the navigator's hand will equal the boat's speed in "knots," supplying useful information and another word for the language. I hadn't the money for a "patent" log but my chip log was just as accurate, if slightly more cumbersome to use.

We repaired another deficiency before leaving Panama City—but not without tribulation. From the day we left New Orleans our compass had been seriously bemused by the quantities of iron and mild steel surrounding it. The fickle needle would swing off course in search of attractive ferrous masses at the slightest provocation—a serious matter on a steel boat. Between Biloxi and Panama City I calculated the error at more than thirty degrees on some headings.

There is a procedure called "swinging compass" for correcting deviation errors that involves placing small magnets around the compass case. It might more accurately be called "swinging the yacht," since it requires turning the boat around reciprocal headings while comparing compass readings against a sundial marked in 360 degrees. We began under a blazing August sun with *Aquarius* centered in a web of lines leading to four pilings. By hauling on some lines and slacking others we hoped we could revolve her at will. At will? The exercise proved fraught with emotional and physical complexities.

The first step was to point *Aquarius* due west by the compass. "Okay, Matthew, you uncleat that line and bring it aft while Jeannine and I hold fast here. Good. Now, Melissa, you bring your line forward. Damn it! We're swinging the wrong way. Sorry, my fault. I miscalculated. Melissa, bring your line back here again. Good. Now, Jeannine, you sing out when the lubber line of the compass is exactly on west while I try to set this little sundial thing on one hundred eighty degrees. Too far? Why the hell didn't you sing out? Sorry. I'm not really angry, I just *sound* angry. Okay, Matthew, pull more on your line. Not so hard. Not so HARD! You're pulling me off the boat. I'm running out of line! Hell, there it goes. Matthew, see if you can reach that line with a boat hook. Out of reach? Okay, get the dinghy. . . .

"Now, let's all try again. Listen carefully, everyone. We're going to swing the *bow* to *starboard*. Melissa, why are you crying? Baby, there's no reason in the world for you to be crying. Damnit. Just stop that right now and pull on your line! Melissa! . . . ." They say professional compass swingers charge only twenty dollars an hour. They must love their art to perform for such a pittance.

With an accurate compass (yes, we managed eventually), an effective system for measuring boat speed, a sextant, a reliable watch and a radio for receiving time checks, I had in my hands for the first time all the tools necessary to find our position at sea. I only had to learn to use them. I had intended studying navigation before we left New Orleans, but the demands of fitting out were immediate and pressing, the duties of navigation remote and theoretical. Somehow I never got beyond opening my books a few times and I was far too busy to worry about the deficiency. But with the shoreline dropping rapidly away and almost three days of open water before us, it was a different matter. Fortunately I wasn't a total stranger to Greenwich Hour Angles and altitude correction tables. On the voyage from Florida two years before Lyle had given me a "short" course in navigation consisting of fifteen minutes' earnest conversation, a page of written instructions and a nautical almanac. So armed, I was able to approximate noon positions; and whether by accident or design, we made our landfall along the Gulf Coast withing a few miles of our estimated position. As we prepared to retrace the same path I knew I could always fall back on those simple methods or, if all else failed, steer a compass course for the west coast of Florida. I could hardly avoid striking it somewhere. But fair weather tricks wouldn't guide us across the Atlantic.

I was fortified with George Mixter's masterful *Primer of Navigation,* a businesslike and inspired effort by a yachtsman and veteran of many Bermuda races. Mixter has a knack for graphic metaphor and lucid description that somehow pulls together the complexities of navigational theory into a picture that can be grasped even by a mathematical numbskull like myself. Nevertheless, my first hours with Mixter produced a monumental vertigo and the first unmistakable signs of seasickness of the voyage. I pressed bravely on, with frequent time-out to lie flat on the deck breathing heavily while Circles of Equal Altitude, Celestial Equators, and Bearings of Bodies reeled through my head. By noon the following day some of it had sunk in and I emerged into the sunlight, blinking and clenching the sextant in my trembling hand, to try for my first sight. I was fortified by a vague but definite feeling that all those numberless bodies out there, each moving through space at its own speed in its own direction, were all of them attached to me by an invisible but measurable web of chords, arcs and tangents; and that I really *could* find that precise point on the terrestrial sphere where I stood trapped in the intersections of their many angles. It was weeks before I mastered the details of navigation, but the feel came the first day.

I'll never forget trying to work that first sight, braced in the port bunk against the roll of the boat, pouring over my workbooks, searching for elusive numbers among the columns in the tables, plunging back into Mixter for reassurance, copying and refiguring Greenwich Mean Times and Local Hour Angles until the numbers spun before my eyes and the sweat of the cabin settled in my stomach. The sight required two hours in the working (later reduced to five minutes), but the position I obtained seemed to agree with my dead reckoning. Even if it didn't, any answer at all that didn't put us square in the middle of Antarctica was a clear triumph. I was satisfied.

August 8

JEANNINE: We were two days from land, taking our ease at the helm and feeling cocky and loose as we watched on the afternoon screen of our horizon a re-run of a show we'd seen a couple of times before: "Squall," starring that inevitable Hollywood duo, Donner and Blitzen, in a highly charged spectacular.

We were getting pretty good reception (except for a lot of flicker) and it seemed only natural, caught up in the plot as we were, that the two protagonists should become more and more intimate, only seconds apart. Time out for taking down the sails hardly broke our hypnotic trance; it was less distracting than a commercial. The pace quickened. What a drama! Hero and heroine were almost in each other's arms when, with a clap (it happened in such a flash we were practically electrified) Donner blew his cool and Blitzen bolted almost simultaneously. I was so shocked I jumped up and flipped around the dial—N, E, S, W,—all I got was static. Static all over the sky!

The trance was broken. We were smack in the middle of a spectacular summer thunderstorm which, being from California, I was definitely unused to. I did have the instinctive notion that I was supposed to avoid staying under anything very high. Oh Mother! A sudden crack looked like it hit the water about a mile away. In its flash I took in the fact that the world around me was flat, totally flat except for that bright white spar high above me. I sat down quickly and lifted my feet from the wet cockpit floor.

"Steel's safer than wood," Matt laughed. "We won't sizzle! If lightning strikes the mast it will run right down the stays and through the hull to the water. No problem. With a wooden boat we'd have to rig a conductor into the water."

I knew he was right, but alarm had already made several

zippy trips around my circulatory system. There seemed to be some kind of epileptic focal point right above our heads: an aura, the blast of an explosion, then the convulsion. Great gold cracks spread across the black sky in a massive celestial seizure. The wind was already piping and we waited, sails down, for the storm to open up on us.

We were probably overcautious, but we knew that squalls could knock a boat over in the first blast. Ever since last Fourth of July when a freaky squall in Lake Pontchartrain had driven more than forty boats ashore, we had established the principle: if a squall looks nasty, drop all sail. It's easy enough to raise them again after you get a feel of the storm's punch. So we waited but there was no big wallop. Even after the rain began the wind continued heavy but not serious.

Melissa called up from below and asked if we needed help. Then before our wondering eyes she appeared, in her yellow oilskins!

"I want to help!" she declared.

"Great! We need you!" Matt replied. "Jeannine and I are going to get the jib up and reef the main and we'll need someone to handle the boat. Can you do it?"

Since we were very unpracticed, reefing was a long and tedious process. Melissa found extra ropes for us, handled the helm, eased the sheets, and was generally indispensable.

"How come you're so cheerful and helpful all of a sudden?" I asked.

"I dunno. Just feel good, that's all."

Strange phenomenon. She fussed about doing petty things during mild weather, but here she was, with the boat pounding over choppy seas and rain pouring down, as gracious and pleasant as she could be!

"We'll have to call you our foul-weather girl!" Matt said when we had finished our maneuvers.

"Okay, I guess that's what I am, all right. Is there anything else you want me to do?"

"Nope. I don't think we'll have any trouble now, thanks. I'm not sure we could have on it without you!"

"That's okay. Call me when we have the next storm!" And she disappeared down the hatch.

We came to the edge of the clouds about an hour later; the moon was full and dazzling ahead of us; the rain dwindled to a drizzle and then was left behind. We chanced to look back at it and were astonished by a rare sight, in fact one which we never saw before or since: delicately arching across the sky, pale but absolutely distinct—a moonbow!

August 11

MATTHEW: The best thing about the storm was that we got the vane gear really to work. We hadn't been able to get it to do well in light airs, maybe because it wasn't balanced well enough. The principle of it is simple. You set the vane so the edge points into the wind when you are on course. The vane is on a pivot so it can flop over in either direction. When it flops over it tightens one rope and loosens the other like a muscle. The lines are run to the tiller so when the boat goes off course the wind catches the vane and throws it over. This pulls the tiller over and corrects the course.

I don't know whether it was Dad's navigation or the vane gear, but somehow we came in to Egmont Key right on the button. I remember I dimly heard some clattering in the night and the next morning when I woke up we were riding peacefully at anchor and everyone was asleep.

We crossed Florida on the Intercoastal Canal and Okeechobee Waterway. On some parts of the waterway it looked like we were deep in the swamps, but we never saw any alligators or snakes. We saw great white herons with wings about two feet long that flew right over our boat. And we saw lots of anhingas fishing. Dad was taking pictures of all the different wildlife and I was steering the boat and Mom and Melissa were getting sunburned. Sometimes I worked on some balsa wood my grandfather gave me. I was carving a ball within a cage. He sent directions how to do it.

It was a little spooky in the canals at night. We tried to find very wide places to anchor so we wouldn't be run down by some big barge. One night we kept going after dark because we were trying to find a wide place. The edges of the canal were pretty clear because the trees stood out against the sky, but the middle was dark and murky. Dad sent me and Melissa to the foredeck to watch out for obstructions while he stood at the helm trying to see.

Suddenly he threw the tiller over and we swerved sharply to starboard. We just skimmed by a houseboat anchored almost out in the middle of the channel! I don't know how Dad saw it. I didn't see anything until we were right beside it. Then I noticed a light, about as bright as a firefly, flickering from a little lantern at the stern of the boat. Whew! Close shave!

We had to use mosquito nets at night for the first time. We had made pliable ones out of plastic screening and then sewed Velcro strips to the edges of the screen and glued the other Velcro around the hatches. When we needed to put up screen all we had to do was press the screen against the hatch and zip! we were mosquito-proof. Unfortunately Florida has bugs called No-See-Ems and they can come right through the screen sometimes! There were other bugs that didn't bother us. Once in the middle of Lake Okeechobee we were surrounded by a swarm of bugs just outside the companionway. They were so thick we could hardly see out the hatch. They didn't bite so Mom went out in the cockpit and Dad took her picture holding up a tourist folder that said "Florida, a Nice Place to Visit." We could just see her dimly through the bugs.

On our way in to Fort Pierce a boat called *Seaducer* offered to lead us into the marina. She led us aground seven times in one hour! We never followed another *Seaducer* again!

August 20

MATT: We have paused in the pleasant Pelican Marina in Fort Pierce for nine days now. I can't believe how quickly the time has passed. Our current repairs and alterations seem especially important because we are leaving the sheltered waterways for good.

The vane gear finally earned my respect by agreeing to function so I agreed to paint it. I also built a rack to hold jerry cans in the space on the cabin top just behind the mast. All items better stowed outside like gasoline, the life raft, or anything miscellaneous and cantankerous gets stuffed into this new territory. We call it our "pig pen."

Yesterday a new set of sails arrived from Biloxi by Greyhound—twin staysails to be flown like angel wings from the forestay when we are running before the wind. Also a storm jib which I hope I'll never have to use. My sail locker is now full.

We have entered into friendly relations with the Coast Guard. Once a day we make a ritual visit to their radio room to check the current status of tropical depressions. For more than a week the Caribbean weather has been unsettled—no full-fledged storms but a series of dyspeptic low-pressure systems that could easily blow up into something nasty once we're fully committed to the 860-mile passage to Bermuda. Last night for the first time the weather appeared to be stabilizing, and I went immediately to a phone and called Bill Seemann in New Orleans. Bill had agreed to make the run to Bermuda with us, for fun and for our own protection, provided he could leave his work. He's arriving tomorrow and already I feel much better about that hurricane-prone passage. With luck we'll be off day after tomorrow.

9

Hurricane Alley

August 22

MATT: *Aquarius* is at sea! Wow! We left the Pelican Marina in Fort Pierce at about 1500 hours with a squall towering above us in the southern sky. As soon as we passed the breakwater the wind and seas began to hit us. Billy raised the working jib, I got the main up and immediately *Aquarius* stopped wallowing in the seaway, lay over to port, and began to move in harmony with the waves. I went forward to furl docking lines and remove the last reminders of our ten days tethered to a dock. The sun was strong on my back and every few moments the boat would rise to a sea and part of it would wash over the foredeck. In seconds I was drenched in lovely salt water. Wind and spray moving together and salt air in my lungs. Wow! The pulse of life beating strongly.

How much people miss who never go to sea! How can you explain the feeling of wind on your skin, of being really alive again without sounding corny or romantic? It's pure John Masefield, yet I'm sure it is this gift of the sea—this sheer animal aliveness—that has compelled men for centuries to put to sea in boats, to endure the most harrowing conditions, to serve the cruelest of masters and yet count the hours ashore as deadness and wait only to put out to sea again.

August 23

JEANNINE: Left Fort Pierce around three P.M. yesterday and the last sea buoy of the channel at three-thirty. Good stout wind from the south and heavy waves. Two or three squalls visible, a few young pretentious thunderclouds with ambitions of becoming a storm. The motion of the boat becomes endless—a never ceasing, never ceasable up and down. To my great disappointment the seasick pills are ineffective. My body begs for stillness. Fleetingly I consider how peaceful it must be beneath the waves. No need to mention the first few days at sea. For me they are miserable. I haven't the slightest inclination to write, so I don't.

August 25

MATT: Apparently the first lesson Mother Ocean has in mind for us is a class in hard knocks. The wind has been blowing from the southeast at force six (25 to 31 mph) almost constantly since we left Fort Pierce. Everything and everyone is wet. The waves are running about six to eight feet high but very short and choppy, the influence of the Gulf Stream perhaps. Every big wave is built irregularly from a lot of small ill-shaped ones. The effect is of sliding diagonally through a very sloppy, giant bean patch indifferently hilled by a sloppy giant. The motion is rough and irregular and about as violent as a carnival ride—if you can imagine a four-day carnival ride. If you are unfortunate enough to be on watch, you sit in the cockpit braced into the windward seat, an arm hooked over the coaming. From this position it is sometimes possible by judging the shape of the oncoming waves to predict which ones will pass under the boat and which will slop aboard. Sometimes. Mostly the waves behave themselves, but only for the purpose of lulling you into unwariness. The moment your eyes glaze and your attention wanders, SPLAT! A spastic wave strikes the topsides full force exactly at your elbow, rewarding your inattention with another faceful of salt water. "Uncomfortable" is the only word for our passage so far. All our romantic illusions about the beauty and poetry of making an ocean passage are being rapidly drowned in salt water. Bill Seemann is a very good antidote for whatever illusions remain. When I asked him how long we could expect this extraordinary weather to continue, he explained that force-six wind is pretty normal at sea. Bill regards voyaging as difficult, uncomfortable work that no one would willingly choose except for the necessary purpose of moving a boat from place to place. I am beginning to understand him.

Naturally all of us have been seasick but with each the malady takes a different form. Jeannine is the most seriously stricken. Her face is white and drawn. There is a faraway look in her eyes. Her attention is withdrawn from this external world of wind and sails, focused on her own internal, unstable, and supremely untrustworthy gastro-intestinal world. Eating is a special balancing act of internal chemistry. What little she puts down is consumed reflectively and she lies down immediately afterward—or suddenly in the middle of eating. She frequently returns to the sea everything she has taken in. Jeannine never complains but I feel like an ogre for subjecting her to this torture. I worry about her well-being and about the future of the trip. If she is sick all the way to Bermuda it will be strong evidence that she is one of those rare individuals who *never* accommodate to motion. If so it would be dangerous for her to continue (people *die* from chronic seasickness) and the voyage of *Aquarius* will come to a sudden end almost before it has begun.

The others do not suffer so badly. Matthew has been very quiet these first few days; he was sick a few times and kept stoically to his bunk. Melissa has complained a great deal about the discomfort but was sick only once and seems completely recovered. I've no doubt in a real emergency Melissa would revert instantly to her normal state of cheerfulness-in-adversity. Bill joked away his few bouts of sickness, working it out by keeping very busy around the boat. I've felt hardly any queasiness, but a great lethargy did settle on me once we left Fort Pierce and none of the projects I so energetically planned for our first days at sea got done. I'm beginning to recognize this as my own personal brand of seasickness.

I guess we're beginning to get our sea legs now, but I wish the sea would hurry up and get its land legs.

August 26

MATT: It's a great comfort having Bill with us. His experience gives us all confidence. Our greatest worry is being overtaken by a hurricane as we crawl our way across hurricane alley. (I feel like an ant traversing an expressway.) We listen with rapt attention to weather bulletins several times each day but so far there have been no tropical storms reported and I think we may reach Bermuda unscathed. If we do get a blow, having Bill along gives me confidence we can weather it.

It's interesting to watch him work. Every job is done quickly and cleanly, in well-controlled bursts of energy. Most of his offshore sailing experience has been ocean racing, and it shows. I know our general sloppiness bothers him but he never gives a sign except to laugh sometimes at the contrast between our cruising habits and those of his ocean-racing friends. He shows the same tactfulness in what I might call "problems of command." When Bill sees the need for a repair or a change in the trim of a sail he will call it to my attention but always in the form of a suggestion—as if addressing the "captain." I appreciate this. He knows more about boats than I ever will, but this is *my* boat and *my* responsibility. We both recognize it. Bill is teaching us a great deal by never playing "teacher." I like the attitudes he is helping to establish and I hope we'll carry them on after he leaves us in Bermuda.

August 26

JEANNINE: Melissa is angry. It shows in almost everything she does. Her voice is angry and so is her body. She didn't really want to come on the trip and she hates the boat when she is feeling black. Last night she came to me and said she was homesick. I realized suddenly what a big jolt it had been to drag her away from everything familiar. She was missing her friends. Even though during the day she had said, "Ha! Ha! All my friends are starting school in New Orleans today," I could tell that she really wished she were starting school with them. I put my arms around her and she let go and really sobbed for a minute. Then, strangely enough, for the rest of the evening she was her sweet old self. She and Matthew and I sat up late in the cockpit learning Morse Code and sending each other messages. Later she snuggled up in my lap and fell asleep.

August 27

JEANNINE: At last I am myself! The seas are calmer and I can move about on the boat without the fear that my stomach will lose its precarious equilibrium. But yesterday was a heavy day.

In the afternoon Matt tried to start Methuselah for our daily battery charging. No luck. After messing with it for thirty minutes he discovered that there was a considerable amount of water in the gas tank; evidently it had leaked in around the deck filler cap during the rough weather. For three hours Matt and Bill worked to flush out the system and clean the carburetor and fuel pump. I have a constant admiration for these two men. They are very much alike where machines are concerned. When something fails they plunge into the puzzle with zest, analyzing, taking apart, cleaning, putting together, testing, taking apart again. I watch them jealously, reflecting on my own outstanding inability to deal with malfunctioning mechanisms. My typical response is anger and strong feelings of betrayal.

By six o'clock the fuel system had been cleaned and reassembled and the engine was ready for a try. Unfortu-

nately by the time they identified the difficulty as fuel con-
tamination, Bill and Matt had run Methuselah's batteries
down to almost nothing with repeated starting attempts.
Matt calculated we had juice enough left in the batteries for
about two tries at starting the engine. If we failed on the
second attempt, that was it. We had neglected to provide
Methuselah with a hand starting crank and that meant no
recharging batteries, no cabin lights, no running lights to
make us visible to other ships at night, no power for the
radio, and no Methuselah to save us from danger or to help
negotiate the unfamiliar channel into St. George, Bermuda,
where we might face contrary tides and flukey winds.

As they prepared for the final try, tension was high. Matt
connected a twelve-volt dry cell to the ignition coil to prevent
the starter motor from hogging the few remaining electrons
in the system. On the second, and absolutely final, attempt
Methuselah coughed twice and began running. Lovely old
beast.

Outside the weather was getting rougher and with the
approach of night the boat needed our immediate attention.
We decided it would be best to reef the main, but as we
lowered the sail, all the slides started coming off the sail track
at one point high on the mast. Someone would have to go up
in a bosun's chair and repair the track before we could set
the reef. Bill volunteered and went below to pad his body
with spare clothing against the beating he would take from
the wildly gyrating mast. By now the night was black and the
seas were fairly high. As we hauled Bill up and Matt cleated
down the halyard that was holding him aloft, a stricken look
crossed his face.

"Watch Bill!" he said, "I've gotta go take care of that
engine!" He fairly ran aft, while I took a brief recess to lose
my lunch over the rail. Bill was high above my head, describing wide arcs back and forth with the roll of the boat as he
tried to cling to the mast and repair the track.

When Bill was safely down, and the main raised, and we
were all trembling quietly in the cockpit, Matt revealed the

worst danger of all. He had forgotten to connect the some-thing to the something when he put the engine back together and gasoline had been spurting out of this line into the bilge all the time the engine had been running. Thank God I hadn't had the motivation to light the fire for supper. Gaso-line vapor, being heavier than air, collects in the bottom of bilges. A half pint of gasoline vaporized there is equivalent in explosive force to fifty sticks of dynamite should a stray spark reach it. We estimated we had lost at least several quarts of gasoline into the bilge, enough to blow us all the way to Bermuda. We flushed out the bilge with detergent and water again and again and again. Then Matt and Bill fell into their bunks without eating.

I took the watch. Within an hour I was sick again, heav-ing great dry retches, crying finally in fatigue, hating the sea now for stealing my strength and my self-esteem.

I suppose there have to be doubts. That's why we came on the trip, after all, to see if we could take it. Maybe at the end of the voyage I will look back at these pages and laugh. At least I can say that I haven't considered turning back.

August 28

MATT: The setting sun put on a spectacular show for us at dusk yesterday, painting the sky with a lavish palette and transforming himself into a glowing ruby egg for his final curtain call at the fringe of the western horizon. His perfor-mance was a genuine "sailors' delight" and true to the old adage he bequeathed us a spell of good weather. By the time he reappeared benignly in the east this morning the wind had moderated to a pleasant force four (about 15 mph) and the waves had dropped to about half their former size. We changed to the Genoa jib and with less interference from the waves, footed along as handsomely as ever—on half the wind.

Our progress has been encouraging. Although Gulf Stream chop held us to an average of 75 miles the first two days, we ticked off 110, 130, and 125 miles on each of the next three. Today our run dropped to 100 miles with the moderating wind but no one is complaining. Bermuda is drawing closer.

Our A.M. radio, which gradually stifled the disc jockeys of Florida a few days ago, is returning to life now with sounds of Bermuda. Fast-talking Calypso D.J.s with Oxford accents are reporting the latest cricket scores, the fatal collision between a motor bike and a taxi, the hit tunes of the Caribbean. Truly, it is a different world we are sailing toward, and I am becoming impatient to sample it.

Bill and I have been hard at work honing our navigation with a dozen sights or more each day. We understand the theory pretty well by now; it's in the practical application that we fall down. We begin around ten each morning with a sun sight. We cross the line of position thus obtained with a noon sight for latitude, and advance that position to the new one suggested by a three P.M. sun sight. We often follow with a round of stars at twilight. If we're not saturated by then, we sometimes attempt another triangle of stars at dawn or shoot Polaris for a second latitude position sometime during the night.

We take our sights at the same time and work them separately using different tables. Then we compare results and check each other's work for errors. I was chagrined to discover that most of my errors are stupid ones—reading the time incorrectly from the chronometer, copying the wrong figures out of the *Nautical Almanac,* consulting the wrong column in my Sight Reduction Tables. It was slow going at first, but we've been gratified lately to see our X's and lines of position falling on top of each other on the plotting sheet. By the time we lay our warps ashore at St. George, I believe we'll be able to work a sight in five minutes and depend on its accuracy.

No discussion of navigation would be complete without a tribute to the weightiest tome on my nautical bookshelf:

Nathaniel Bowditch's *American Practical Navigator.* Noble Bowditch! If there are problems of navigation not encompassed within its literate and well-ordered covers, I don't know of them: Marine Navigation, Submarine Navigation, Polar Navigation, Lifeboat Navigation, Ocean Currents, Weather Observation, Sound in the Sea, Hydrographic Surveying are but a few of the chapter titles. And the tables include everything from "Distance of an Object by Two Bearings" to "Correction of Amplitude as Observed on the Visible Horizon." From 1802 when Bowditch, a New England sea captain, brought out his first volume, through the seventy intervening editions, the aim has always been to present principles of navigation and related information thoroughly, but in language as easily understood by the average seaman as by the mathematician-astronomer. Bowditch by itself is a compleat education. The section on Mathematics begins, for example, with the simple definition: "Arithmetic is that branch of mathematics dealing with computation by numbers. . . . [Its] principal processes are addition, subtraction, multiplication and division." The chapter proceeds briskly but comprehensively through algebra, logarithms, vectors, plane and spherical geometry, and trigonometry to a stirring conclusion forty pages later deep in the bowels of differential calculus. While Bowditch as a navigational university is unexcelled, Bowditch as a literary experience is purely enjoyable. Consider the majestic and artful simplicity of this sentence: "The tidal phenomenon is the periodic motion of the waters of the sea due to differences in the attractive forces of various celestial bodies, principally the moon and sun, upon different parts of the rotating earth." At first I was intimidated by the sheer size and scope of the book (it weighs ten pounds), but later I came to love it, to consult it in moments of navigational perplexity, and to browse in it for pleasure. My copy cost seven dollars from the United States Naval Oceanographic Office, surely one of the publishing bargains of the century.

August 28

JEANNINE: Melissa's moody condition has worsened. We will have to face it as seriously as if she were physically sick, but there's no medicine in our chest to cure her ailment. Our psychic shakedown has really turned up a crisis.

She gets angry at the slightest provocation and swears like the saltiest sailor. I think she can't sort out her real feelings because they're masked by intense resentment at being forced into a choice she didn't really want to make. She feels trapped in this venture, boxed in a corner with no escape.

But it's hard to know what's going on in her head. She really brought all of us down last night by getting mad during a card game. I sent her to bed and told her that I wanted her in the morning to write down how she feels about the trip to see if she could express why she gets so angry. This is what she wrote:

> Yesterday I didn't feel too happy. Partly I think I was sort of seasick and partly because I thought people were making fun of me. I was in good spirits until we had the Hearts game. Then when Matthew dropped the Queen on me and everybody laughed I didn't like it.
>
> I think all of you didn't like what I did. I'm sorry I got mad but that's just me. I can't help it if I have a temper.
>
> When you ask me to do the dishes I put up a fit because I don't like being thrown around the galley like a bouncing ball. One time it knocked the wind out of me and it hurts. Besides the sink is too small. I'm not used to it and there's no place to stand. Either you have to stand up and bend way over or sit down and turn sideways and I can hardly reach the sink that way so I don't like to do dishes.
>
> I don't want to cook because of that stove. If we had a better stove I would be cooking two meals a day.
>
> I can't think of anything else to say 'cept I'm sorry.

Of course, her moodiness could be physiologically caused, rather than a psychological reaction. I know that

Melissa's moods are closely tied to her body-state. Even when she was a young child, strange angry outbursts without visible motivation would sometimes occur just before dinner. As soon as she ate she was cheerful again. I learned it was best to ignore the outburst and give her something to eat. She didn't even realize she was hungry. Maybe the moodiness we are seeing now is a physiological reaction to the motion of the boat—her own particular brand of seasickness.

Earlier this evening Melissa was really impossible. She raged around like a dark squall inundating everyone with her frustration and anger. After the dinner mess was cleaned up I went out to the cockpit to take a watch. She was there—tight-lipped and sullen. Where was my lovely cheerful daughter; what were we doing? This was not our glorious dream of family unity. I started to cry and talk at the same time.

"Melissa, we've got to do something. We can't continue our trip this way; your happiness is too important to us. If you hate the boat, and hate the trip, then you should have the right to decide what you want to do. There are two alternatives, really. We could try to arrange with your grandparents or your Aunt Joy—or Holley even—to keep you for several months while we go on. You could fly back from Bermuda and we could cut the Africa part of the trip shorter and come back in a few months. Or, if you really feel strongly about it, we could even turn around right now and go home. You are an equal member of the family. Your needs are as important as anyone else's."

"That's not true!" she blurted out. "There's three of you and you all want to go. That makes three to one."

"Listen, Melissa. The Quakers make their decisions by a process called consensus. One person, if he feels strongly enough, can turn a whole meeting around. Because they believe that each person must act according to his own conscience, they really have to listen and respect someone who stands all by himself against the group. No one would abuse that right of veto because they trust and love each other, but sometimes a thing just doesn't get done because there's no 'sense of the meeting.' Maybe the time wasn't right, or it wasn't the right thing to do in the first place. Anyway, I believe in the Quaker philosophy, and so does Matt. We think it's the only way a group, like a family, can really trust each other. I'm not saying this very well because it's hard for me to talk without crying, but I want you to know that we love you, and if you really want us to go home, we'll go home."

"Oh, Mom, . . . I don't know what I want!"

"Hey, it's all right. Don't cry. You think about it and tell us when you know what you want to do, okay?"

By then we were both sobbing, arms around each other. *Aquarius,* insensitive to our crisis, was making her own way toward Greenland's icy mountains. I swung her back on course and tucked Melissa into her cockpit cocoon. Within a few minutes she was asleep. What have I done, I wondered? Have I blown the whole trip? This voyage means so much to Matt. What if she decides she wants us all to go home?

August 29

JEANNINE: Damn calm. Day of the Bird. He was a swallow I think, and he came with a mate who soon disappeared; we never saw where. He circled the boat several times, not able to find a still place and finally lighted on the boom preventer line which snapped and jumped in the wandering eddies of the calm. Soon we discovered that we could move quite close to him, and cautiously offered some bread. He clung to the line desperately until Matthew reached out his finger, gave a little nudge under the bird's breast and encouraged him to change perches. From then on he was tame, as if this new state of mind had always been his nature. The children fed him wheat germ and water, and, due to a moment of scientific brilliance on Matthew's part, a little tuna fish. Melissa held him, petted him, fed him, and exclaimed delightedly over how much tamer he was than her

pet parakeet. But Bill predicted the bird would never leave
our boat alive. He told us stories of land birds lost and
exhausted over the ocean that had perished on board boats
he had sailed. He reminded us that we were now seven
hundred miles from land, with Bermuda almost two hundred
ahead. But near sundown, perhaps feeling a bit stronger from
the nourishment, our bird made a few exploratory forays,
then took off for good in the direction of Bermuda. We were
sorry to see him go and half expected him to return, but he
didn't. It was a lesson in adaptability to see a wild thing
completely lay by his instincts and adopt a new personality
in order to survive. May we be so flexible if the need arises!

August 30
   MATT: Still obnoxiously calm. Bill reckons as how the
lack of breeze is due to the "Bermuda High," which, it must
be noted, is a meteorological phenomenon, not a state of
mind.

August 30
   JEANNINE: I don't mind the calm at all, even though
we're not progressing on our way. It's giving my body a
chance to recoup its forces. Thank God the ocean *doesn't*
stay the same. But there's something eerie about being still
on the ocean. When the air is moving, the universe is alive
and breathing. When the wind stops, you feel suspended in
a vacuum; the universe is holding its breath.
   The sun was warm today, the water inviting. We went for
a swim. Swimming in the middle of the ocean is somehow not
as uninhibited as swimming at a beach or lake. There is a
definite element of vigilance. Bill declined to join us saying,
"I never go in unless I have to," the comment of a professional diver.
   It would be nice to paint a picture of floating in meditation on our backs in limitless space, experiencing the ulti-

mate expansion of consciousness. Actually, we never closed our eyes; we went in wearing diving masks for the best possible vision through the water, circling immediately to take in the full sweep of the surrounding area. I swam close to the boat looking continuously over my shoulder, peering down into the blue fathoms, expecting to see some dark shape cruising in the depths ready to shoot up and swallow me in one snap. My sensation was of intangibility and apprehension. I was not related to any definable space. I occupied a membrane of surface tension, an anonymous interface between sea and sky. My only definition was *Aquarius,* my refuge.

As we searched the infinite blueness we were frustrated by the impenetrability of apparently clear water. Our gaze didn't stop at anything like bottom; it just faded out. And beyond the scope of that gaze . . . unknowns!

When no one was swallowed up we began to feel a little more confidence. Matthew unsnapped the jib halyard from its bail on the bow pulpit and brought it outside the shrouds back to the cockpit. He climbed unsteadily up on the after-rail, launched himself out on the rope with a great swing, and dropped off. It was a very satisfying experiment. Before long he succeeded in swinging all the way forward to the bow before having to bail out.

It goes without saying that the next logical step was to swing all the way around the boat. There were a few harrowing trials where, not having sufficient momentum to round the bow, he dropped off at the last second (it seemed) before bashing himself against steel-blue steel. Eventually there came a trial where all circumstances were right: his takeoff thrust was out and forward at just the proper angle; the boat rolled fortuitously over a wave giving his arc just a little more impetus; he gave an extra kick and twist as he rounded the bow, pulling in his stomach as he passed by the point of the anchor. Whooping in triumph, he swept pendulously back to the stern, having described an exhilarating circle of equal altitudes around the mast.

We cheered. And spent the rest of the afternoon trying to equal his feat, never stopping until the first signs of wind sent us skipping back to business.

August 31

JEANNINE: In Biloxi we had decided our shakedown should include evaluating the supplies we brought along for our *emotional* well-being as well as the efficiency of our nautical gear, a process that was postponed until late in the shakedown when the novelty of the voyage had worn off. Now we are just days from the point of decision—Bermuda is the last logical place to say, "It was a mistake, let's go back," and so we must ask ourselves how our psychic equipment checks out: our boredom extinguishers, sanity preservers, and stress harnesses. These items are important because both children are highly allergic to boredom, a condition known in our family by the word "bumbly." The symptoms are generally a rash of emotional itches: a feeling of being at odds with the universe, a propensity to whine, a decided lack of coordination, and a perverse determination to bump and break things. Although their individual reaction is unpredictable, Matthew often becomes aggressive and demanding, searching for something to alleviate his discomfort, while Melissa submits to irrationality and tears.

Like all allergies this one comes and goes in mysterious ways. I have never been clear whether boredom is actually the *cause* or the *result* of the "bumbly" state. It could be a simple mechanical problem—a slipping clutch between a souped-up brain racing ahead of itself, and the hands and chassis. Whatever the cause, it is a malady to avoid at all costs on a small boat.

For the most part Matthew and Melissa have supplied their own boredom extinguishers. Strange constructions are likely to appear in odd places around the boat. A tent-like hideout made from a poncho monopolized the foredeck one day. The inhabitants could check on the enemy by peering through a disguised periscope (the hood of the poncho). Another time a fort was built in the forepeak and barricaded from the slings and arrows of the *Aquarius* world by four inches of mattress foam. Melissa regularly rigs a private sun shelter between the hand rail on the cabin top and the life lines. She lies for hours snuggled underneath it on the side deck, participating in the adventures of Nancy Drew and Trixie Belden.

Matthew manufactures weird things from paper—from origami birds and kites to "gigly twirls," a kind of construction, usually highly decorated, that moves in the wind. Some are variations on a paper windmill, others are totally original. There is one whirling merrily at the top of our fiberglass radio antenna right now.

When we asked him before the voyage what kind of boredom extinguishers he would like to bring, he mentioned a B-B gun, and we bought one. For a target he trails a plastic bottle on a long string off the stern; he and Matt compete for marksmanship on the bobbing afterdeck.

The bobbing *foredeck* is another matter. When we are headed into the wind, especially under power, the children use the foredeck like a trampoline. They store momentum by coiling their knees as the bow lurches upward; at the zenith of its pitch they leap into the air as high as they can, letting the deck fall away below them. It is a long ride down. They have rigged two "leashes" they can hang onto while making their flights so the boat doesn't move out from under them altogether.

I think we're correct in assuming our psychic equipment has passed inspection; we haven't begun to exhaust our supplies, at least so far.

August 31

MATT: The calm finally tranquilized itself to death, and just in time. Another day and it would have soothed us right out of our minds. The wind returned yesterday afternoon as a gentle breeze out of the southwest, and by nightfall was blowing fairly hard from dead astern. We slacked *Aquarius*'s sheets and she spread her arms to the wind, of which there was an armful, and began nearly to fly—surfing on the backs of the big rolling waves, carrying us onward at last toward Bermuda. Bill and I shot a round of stars at twilight, the most important sights of the passage. Unless all our calculations are off, Bermuda should be just beyond the horizon— Bermuda and the reefs that encircle it on all sides except the southeast, like the unforgiving spines of a sea urchin. Our final sight put us about seventy-five miles west southwest of the island, and gathering darkness revealed on the horizon dead ahead a soft luminous glow—the loom of the lights of Hamilton, it could be nothing else! We seemed to be coming in right on target. At our present speed of almost six knots we could expect to raise the ten-second flash of the Gibbs Hill lighthouse about four in the morning. But events did not follow such a smooth schedule.

I stood watch from one A.M. to three, and while I didn't expect to sight the beacon, I kept a sharp lookout. All of us were edgy about this first landfall. It would prove the success or failure of our navigation, and maybe of the voyage. Too many yachts have come to grief on Bermuda's reefs for us to take them lightly. Our strategy was to approach from the southwest on a heading which paralleled the southern verge of the islands, keeping us south of the reefs with plenty of searoom to make any necessary course corrections after we sighted the light. According to our chart the Gibbs Hill light should be visible about twenty-six miles out to sea. Our arrival couldn't have been more perfectly timed. We ought to raise the light just before dawn while it was still dark enough to be clearly visible, and by the time we were close in with the island we would have full daylight to help us.

About 2:30 I had a fleeting sensation of light scratching at the periphery of my vision somewhere off to the south. It was another fifteen minutes before I could be certain of it in the woolly darkness; a random flicker somewhat forward of the starboard beam—a ship probably, or a fishing boat—that would not be unusual this close to Bermuda. Certainly whatever it was lay too far south of our course to be the Gibbs Hill light. As if for reassurance the loom of the island continued to brighten steadily, directly ahead. It had been eight days since we'd seen any lights but our own, and I watched this flickering thing idly, waiting for it to steady down. If it was a fishing boat the flickering would surely grow constant as our distance narrowed and the intervening waves ceased to chop it into segments. But the flashing continued, and, as the light drew steadily abeam, I began to see a pattern in it.

A pattern? A cold finger touched me and I scuttled below for the stopwatch. As I timed the light my safe tight world of positional certitude, so reasonably constructed of star-sights, charts, and logical deductions, fell apart in one swift explosion of uncertainty. Only navigation lights flash in regular patterns, and this one was now emitting an unmistakable twelve-second pulse. It had to be a navigation light, but it *couldn't* be the ten-second Gibbs Hill light—or *could* it? Suppose it was an entirely different light; in that case where were we? I looked at the chart. It showed a single light on this end of the island. Was the chart out of date? The inscription in the lower left corner read "Revised March 2, 1970." Practically fresh from the printshop. The loom that should be Bermuda was still hanging steady on our bow, but it only confused me now. Cold tentacles of panic clutched at my stomach. I imagined sharp coral reefs reaching for us somewhere out in the darkness. Was I mariner enough to unravel it all, or should I call for help? I shouted for Billy.

The tone of Bill's voice got more and more serious as he considered the situation. "The light we see is certainly flashing every twelve seconds," he reasoned. "This *could* be a new light not shown on our chart, maybe a sea buoy set to mark an approach to the island, but it isn't normal procedure to place lights of so nearly similar timing so close to each other.

On the other hand, it's not a bit unusual for a light to be two seconds off its assigned rate. I don't know what we're seeing, but for safety's sake I think we have to assume that it *is* Gibbs Hill light, and it's way off to the south of us which means the reefs could be under us *right this minute!*"

In panic I switched on the depth sounder. The scanner showed no bottom, at least to the limit of its two-hundred-foot range.

"Come on," said Bill. "We can't afford to hold this course a minute longer. These reefs are steep-to and we could be on them before we know it." Our urgent voices had brought Jeannine from her bunk and together we wore *Aquarius* around 180 degrees until she was sailing directly away from the loom, retracing her course perhaps into safer waters.

"Okay," Bill said. "Let's figure out what to do. It seems reasonable that Bermuda should be where that loom is— that's where our last star fix told us it would be. Let's see what the radio direction finder has to say."

Somewhat skeptically I pulled out this new and still untried navigation aid. Bill showed me how to tune in the Gibbs Hill radio signal and swing the antenna until it gave us a bearing on the beacon. The results were unequivocal: our radio direction finder believed the beacon lay under the loom, not at the mystery light.

"I guess we're seeing a temporary light that's not on our chart," Bill said after some thought. "Maybe the Navy put it there to mark a submarine exercise area or something. Let's ignore it and head for the loom."

"Okay," I agreed, "but for heaven's sake don't turn off the depth sounder."

My watch was long done by now and I turned in for a few hours of uneasy sleep. Around five Jeannine roused me briefly. "We've got the Gibbs Hill light in view, dead ahead," she said. "It's flashing every ten seconds."

September 1

JEANNINE: Gentle swells rolled in from the east toward the rocky coast as we made our way along Bermuda's southeast shoreline toward the passage leading into St. George's harbor. Like so many crabs scuttling in and out of their holes, we popped our heads out of hatches to check the scenery, then popped below as we scrambled to make everything shipshape for the customs officials: their opinion of our seamanship would rest on the pristine appearance of our little craft more surely than a woman's opinion of her new daughter-in-law is formed by the shine on her floors.

We pulled the cleanest clothes we could find from our lockers, Matt bringing forth a pair of radiant white pants that he obviously had been saving for just this occasion, an extravagance of vanity at which even he had to smile.

The channel entrance moved up on us. Melissa and I stood on the foredeck checking out the channel markers. As we rounded the first buoy and started through the channel the scent of land struck us full in the face. What a sweetness! It smelled as if all the jacaranda and gardenias and honeysuckle and jasmine in the world were concentrated on this small island.

"Well, we really made it," Melissa smiled.

"Of course we made it; didn't you expect to?" I asked.

"I really wasn't sure. I guess if we can make it to a little island like Bermuda, we can make it all the way across to the Azores, huh?"

"Are you saying that you've decided to go with us?"

"Well," she smiled again, "I guess I'd rather stay with you, even if you *are* crazy."

I swallowed and busied myself coiling the docking line which we would soon be throwing ashore.

10

Bermuda

September 8

MATT: St. George was a stage set. Entering directly from the windy reaches of the Atlantic we found ourselves at first disoriented by these tourist vistas. Everything appeared smaller, older, more theatrical than our American eyes were prepared to accept; it was not entirely simple to separate the real from the replica. For example, the two-masted square rigger lying becalmed in concrete just opposite our mooring place clearly wasn't real—a pseudo-ship built to freight tourists. Nonetheless it was a jolt having her for a neighbor. The pillories, too, were an obvious hokum. They occupied a place of prominence on the King's Parade, the wide flagstone square where we first stepped ashore, and their function was obvious from the swarms of tourists with cameras buzzing around them. We watched the bustle with wonder and amusement. Bermuda, or at least St. George, was just a little too quaint to take seriously—a colonial Williamsburg in short pants.

But these simple generalities began to fail as we ventured further from the boat. The atmospheric old tavern by the edge of the Parade, for example, looked ancient enough to have hosted Bluebeard himself, and it *was,* but the beer tasted real, and among the schoolteachers from Boise and the secretaries from New York were patrons who looked and talked like genuine locals. Well then, what about that antique stone edifice occupying the middle of the Parade? It was called the State House, we learned, and its stones had been laid in a mortar of lime and turtle oil in 1619, seven years after the founding of St. George and one year before the *Mayflower* landed at Plymouth. Certainly the State House was real, town business was still carried on within its chambers, but it was also a tourist attraction, and this puzzled us at first. We weren't used to having our Disneylands mixed with real life.

Did it matter? No, we decided, warming to Bermuda with a rush. We rented bicycles and set off to explore the island, puffing along country lanes lined with camera-conscious pastel cottages, exploring old forts, stumbling unexpectedly onto wonderful jungles hidden behind crumbling walls where weeds, flowers, lizards and birds lived in profusion. The arrangement of everything we saw seemed casual but compact, and we were astonished to learn how crowded Bermuda is: more than twenty-five hundred people on the average inhabit each of its twenty-one square miles (compared with fifty-seven persons per square mile in the United States)—and when you multiply this multitude by six —the number of tourists that visit Bermuda anually—the demographic problems seem truly staggering. It is as if White Plains, New York, had decided to live on half of Nantucket Island and were visited each year by the entire population of Birmingham, Alabama! Yet Bermuda did not appear crowded. I think the inhabitants have achieved this miracle by keeping everything small—the houses, motor cars, highways, shops and municipal buildings seem about two-thirds normal size, and surprise! the scale seems to fit the shape of humans much better than our own. Maybe we have something to learn.

It was not long before we felt quite at home here—more residents than tourists. As a matter of fact, we *were* at home: we carried our home with us, sailing it from place to place, and for the first time I began to appreciate the unique advantages of this arrangement. For ten years I'd traveled widely on photographic assignments, living out of suitcases in characterless motel rooms that had been mass decorated according to some executive's idea of Mr. and Mrs. Average Citizen's taste. Nowhere could I find anything of myself, and I camped in those rooms reluctantly, pitching a tent of personal mementos about myself to remind me of the person I was. If the assignment was lengthy I began to suffer from a pecular malaise that must be familiar to most people who travel for a living. I would begin feeling disjointed, alienated from myself, depersonalized by the commercial anonymity of my temporary world, against which I sometimes reacted with fear or hostility. I think it must be the same for most tourists; I consider being a tourist very hard work. Yet I like to travel, and now *Aquarius* has provided an escape for all of us from many of the anxieties of travel.

In Bermuda it was our haven, the repository of our books, pictures and other personal possessions. The polished woodwork and cabin appointments reflected us as intimately as had our apartment in New Orleans, and whenever exploring St. George grew tiresome, we could retreat to this personal floating turf and feel refreshed and whole again.

There were other reasons we began to feel like residents of St. George. We had business to conduct here, the important business of final preparation for the Atlantic crossing, and it led us into personal relationships with the townspeople. Every day our separate tracks fanned out across the cobbles of the King's Parade. I became a familiar figure at the hardware store off the north corner of the square; the manager greeted me at least ten times daily as I completed final repairs on the boat. (I think *Aquarius ate* brass screws!) At the marine repair shop down King Street I was known to the man in the musty front office. His establishment made several mast fittings and a crank for Methuselah which I returned twice because I had got the dimensions wrong. He charged me $10 for all their work—a gift more than a business transaction. The Barclay's banker knew me well. I sat in his office on the east side of the Parade several afternoons as we tried to conjure forth a money order lost in the bowels of Western Union. For days all elements along the system denied its existence, but at last, encouraged by a physic of plaintive cables, the money burst forth with a loud jangle astonishing us all.

One morning I clattered across the Parade looking like a mechanized Mexican peasant. My donkey was an asthmatic motorbike borrowed from a yachtsman along the quay, and in place of the traditional woven baskets of produce, my steed carried a rattling bundle of five-gallon hydraulic fluid cans scavenged at the jetport on St. David's Island across the harbor. With our fifteen-gallon fuel tank, the cans gave us enough gasoline capacity in deck cargo for fifty-five hours of engine use, plenty for charging the battery daily, running in calms, and negotiating the harbor in the Azores. With a crank, a new battery, and a watertight seal for the deck gas cap, Methuselah seemed well primed for the crossing.

On another St. David foray I visited the United States Airforce Meteorological Station to petition the oracle for favorable winds and fair weather. A crew-cut sage scratched his head and rummaged his satellite photos and weather charts, then foretold this gloomy augury: "The Azores High has been holding pretty far north this summer, forced there by a succession of tropical disturbances moving westward out of the Cape Verde Islands. 'Pears to me, you'll have light winds all the way—and most of them out of the east."

A dismal prophecy. I made a note to sacrifice two chickens before we embarked.

Jeannine, too, left her tracks across the Parade, but her excursions to the supermarket on Duke of York Street just off the square were not always happy ones. The price of foodstuffs was dismaying; the quality of produce (all imported) was disappointing. She had planned to stock up on fresh foods before we set sail—large quantities of long-lasters like potatoes, carrots, cabbage, onions, oranges, grapefruit, and enough fresh vegetables and meat to last as long as our ice. But being a frugal boatwife she just couldn't bring herself to pay the incredible prices. A medium-sized watermelon was marked at four dollars; five pounds of potatoes cost another dollar; there were no cabbages. She would pace ambivalently up and down in front of the vegetable counter with Melissa:

"Green peppers would last a while. How much are they, Melissa?"

"Fifty cents each, but they don't look very fresh, and the tomatoes look like they've already crossed the Atlantic in a sailboat."

We put to sea somewhat understocked with perishable food and considerably underjoyed with the quality of Bermudian greengrocery.

Melissa became a well-known figure on the Parade, an equestrian figure at that. She met a carpenter named Brownie working near the dock one day, and during the course of a long conversation, Brownie learned of her unquenchable enthusiasm for horses. By coincidence he owned three such animals: one kicked, one bucked and the other, a gentle brown mare named Antigua, became Melissa's regular afternoon companion. No money was exchanged; Brownie just admired little girls who liked horses. Melissa and Antigua would begin their daily circuit at the stable in the hills above the harbor, wind down through the town, and clatter at least twice around the Parade before ambling up the hill again. She had no need for boredom extinguishers in Bermuda.

Matthew's big adventure was a lesson in scuba diving:

MATTHEW: We made friends with Mark, Wayne and their parents, Bill and Nancy, from a boat called *Fiddler*. One day they took us to Castle Harbor where we planned to go diving. We had three scuba outfits, plus masks, fins and snorkles for everyone. I was looking forward to scuba lessons. After lunch on *Fiddler* we put all the scuba gear in a dinghy and set out toward a shallow place with rock walls and caves that went in a few yards and stopped. It was time for some lessons.

In learning how to scuba dive I had to leave my equipment on the bottom and without mask, fins, or tank, I had to find the regulator, put it in my mouth and clear it while my eyes were burning. Then I had to clear the mask and get the tank and backpack on while I was upside down. The tanks were heavy and I felt clumsy. Last came the fins. It was hard to maneuver without them and I had to kick to stay down. It felt strange to be able to breath underwater and my mouth was soon dry, but it was fun and exciting. We never found any really good coral reefs so we all went back to St. George where we had dinner and went to bed.

September 10

MATT: Bermuda's ambiance snared even Bill Seemann. Ignoring commitments in New Orleans, he tarried days, making seaman's forays to the bars and bistros of Hamilton across the island and helping daytimes with the work on the boat.

On the eve of Bill's departure we sat late in the cockpit reminiscing over a bottle of red wine about the adventures and pratfalls of the voyage so far. Our talk turned to shake-downs and what we had learned from them. On sudden inspiration Jeannine got out pencil and paper to list the most heartfelt lessons for future reference: (1) *Never trust anyone else to be competent.* Whether it's a dock watcher tying your line or a *Seaducer* leading you aground, the ultimate responsibility for the boat is always with the person in charge and can never be fully delegated. (2) *Never leave anything unfixed.* A hundred lessons convinced us that the repairs we avoid today will come back to plague us tomorrow. (3) *Never go into a strange port at night unless you are sure of everything.* It's better to anchor off or heave to and wait for the morning. Biloxi taught us that, with an added corollary: (3a) *Grounding is not necessarily disastrous.* (4) *Never go anywhere without an engine crank.* It's foolish to trust batteries. (5) *When in doubt, turn back to safe waters.* After the Gibbs Hill light experience, we don't need reminding.

Remembering the multitude of possessions lost overboard, Jeannine added one final lesson: (6) *In the cockpit, never take your bottom off a pillow when the wind is blowing.*

Jeannine laid aside her paper. Bill's quiet laugh reminded me that he'd be gone tomorrow, and in a few days we'd be off ourselves. Tonight was our last chance to benefit from his wisdom.

"Bill, what do you think? You're our mentor in this enterprise as much as anybody, and you're about to leave your fledglings on the dock. Are we ready to go? Have we learned enough to make it safely?"

There was a long silence while Bill refilled his glass. "Yes, I think you're about as ready as you could be, considering the lateness of the season and the time you've had to prepare," he answered seriously. "You've done a good job with *Aquarius,* and after sailing to Bermuda with you, I'm not worried about your ability to take care of yourselves. If there's one thing that still bothers me, I guess it's this: I don't think you have enough respect for the sea, and that's something you can only learn from experience."

"Thanks, Bill," Jeannine said softly. "We'd never be this far if it weren't for you. I'll be thinking about your words all the way across."

Phil arrived the next morning. I looked up from adjusting a cockpit winch and saw him crossing the tiny bridge to our moorage on Ordinance Island. We all bearhugged on the quay. He looked exactly as I remembered him from New Orleans, apparently unchanged by prison except for shorter hair and a grin he couldn't contain. I cleaned out a cabin locker for him and as he unpacked his gear—mostly necessities I'd suggested in a letter: seaboots, oilskins, rescue light, even a so'wester hat—I realized how much he must trust us, putting his person and his life so completely in our hands, accepting our competence before there was any way of testing it, allowing this voyage to be his first important experience in the free world. A heavy responsibility, I thought, hoping we were up to it. Before there was chance for much talk, Phil was off with Bill Seemann for a sail on a nearby boat—a good chance to get his feet wet.

In the afternoon when they returned, I asked Bill about him—how did he take to sailing, how might he react at sea? He was green but enthusiastic, Bill thought, and very eager to learn. If attitude were any guide, it should be a good crossing for Phil. What more could we ask?

We said goodbye to Bill at the door of a taxi on the Parade. A firm handshake, a warm hug and a few tears from Jeannine, and he was off. With his departure we were on our own—for real now, no one to hold our hand or take in the jib on a blustery night. The urgency to be off doubled, and we worked for the next few days like demons with Phil lending a welcome hand. He and Matthew replaced all the screws in the mainsail track, he performed innumerable errands around the town, and his presence augmented our company in new and subtle ways. After eighteen months of isolation, Phil saw the world quite freshly, and through his eyes we became aware of things in ourselves and around us that we took for granted. His obvious enjoyment of simple pleasures and his quiet and ever-present wit relaxed us somewhat from our mad pace. We began to realize that the urgency of diminishing time and stress of inexperience was turning us into automatons: new adventures should be savored *while* they're happening, not afterward.

The contrast between our frantic hustle and the easy ways of more experienced sailors was nowhere more evident than in the crew of a large and glamorous ketch whose arrival from Grenada we witnessed one afternoon. She was well over sixty feet of polished mahogany and was being sailed to New York by a young crew from a yacht delivery service when diesel trouble developed that forced her in to

Bermuda for repairs. The yacht's company did not seem distraught by the delay. They rented motorbikes and set out on perilous voyages along the two-lane highway to Hamilton in search of diversion. One evening a mishap occurred (the details are not entirely clear), in which the first mate and his machine came to a parting of the ways. The bike halted quite suddenly at a highway post; the mate came to rest in a nearby ditch. Thereafter he wore his left arm, quite jauntily, in a large white cast, and his companions seemed more content to adopt the slower pulse of St. George. The skipper and his merry men often could be found by day on the sunny terrace of the tavern, by night in a small but exceptionally spirited black bar on a back street. Aboard the yacht a steady stream of friends came and went, among them two student nurses unearthed along the byways of Hamilton.

I watched them as I went about my duties. They fraternized easily, these children of grace. They lived with swagger and freedom in that young man's province where responsibilities are limited and the world seems ready to open all its oysters on command. They were weighted down by none of the grubby family concerns that crabbed my style and that of other yacht dwellers along the quay. And so I nursed a tiny coal of malice against the easy livers on the beautiful boat. They're playboys, I thought, sexual Tom Sawyers conning the whitewash off unsuspecting Becky Thatchers with their big yachts that belong to other men. Yet I recognized in my envy the times when I myself had moved with that same felicity—often when riding the tide of a good assignment, all my cameras clicking at the happy moment of inspiration and the fever running strong. Then women in hotel lobbies glanced at me and I felt a kind of power. It was different now. The Atlantic loomed ahead and I was much too busy being a diligent ant to leap with the grasshoppers.

It was Phil who cured me of my spite. He made friends with the yacht's crew and soon I found myself joining him in the expansive saloon below deck with its *gimbaled dining table*—a luxury I could never imagine! I met Jack, the young skipper who had delivered hundreds of boats of all sizes and seaworthiness up and down the coast of North America.

"You must have sailed some real clunkers in your time," I suggested.

He replied with ringing sincerity, "I never sailed a boat I didn't like." *Never?* It dawned on me that Jack must *really* like boats, and that maybe we had a few things in common. By the end of the evening we had exchanged a dozen sailing yarns and lies, and were firm friends.

The night before they left, Phil and I took our ease in the deckhouse of the big ketch while Jack poked around in the bilge, fretting out some problem with the boat's electrical system. I was surprised to see him a little uptight on the eve of departure. I had thought that emotion was reserved for neophytes like myself, but maybe that's what "skipper" means, carrying a knot in your gut because a part of you is always worrying about the boat.

"You'll like the Azores," Jack told me. "I've been there twice. The people are great. There's a guy who has a café in Horta—the Café Sport—he'll take care of anything you need, arrange supplies and repairs, introduce you to people. And he won't charge you for his help."

I was suspicious of foreigners who offered services without charge. "What's his name? How do I find him? And why is he so helpful to people he's never met?"

"He likes yachtsmen, that's all. And I don't know his last name. Everyone calls him Peter—just Peter. When you arrive in Horta ask anybody for the Café Sport, you'll find him there."

11

Crossing the Great Water

September 12

MATT: We finished the last step of preparation last night, too tired and too late for a comfortable departure. This morning bright and early Jeannine mobilized all hands for an epic scrub down. *Aquarius* had grown disgracefully dirty during our ten days in port. By noon we were ready to leave, but curiously reluctant to cast off ties with Bermuda. We dawdled. I took some pictures. Then Phil and I mounted the stairs to the St. George's Dinghy Club bar one last time to blow the foam off one last round before heading into the Atlantic where breweries are scarce.

I watched Phil sitting in the dark quiet of the bar, reflecting on how often I'd be looking at him in the weeks to come. I had few doubts. Phil was good company—quiet and steady, a fortunate addition to the Aquarius family. There was no one I'd rather have along on this voyage. Yet what did all our varied associations add up to—the student-teacher relationship, the prison correspondence, the new relationship in Bermuda? I'd seen enough proven friendships go awry at sea to know that the same forces which cement people together ashore may drive them to opposite ends of a small boat. There was a lot of water ahead of us—a lot of unanswered questions. Would Phil take to voyaging like a natural sailor, or prove to be a hopeless lubber? He was eager to learn, but how would he adjust to a month of constant rolling and pitching? Would he be incapacitated by seasickness? And how would all of us cope with living together for a month in the closest possible quarters? All of us were flexible, but were we flexible enough? Only the passing days could answer those questions. The sea hadn't tested us yet, but I knew it would and when that time came we would learn much about ourselves and about Phil.

We emptied our glasses and returned to the pier. A few friends gathered. Goodbyes were said. In the last moments I worked out an arrangement with a cruising family staying behind in Bermuda. "We'll send you a postcard from Horta. If you don't hear from us by October fifteenth call the Coast Guard." It seemed casual, almost dangerously so, but it was as much insurance as most voyagers take and I knew our friends would honor it; they'd sailed enough to understand the importance. It took only a moment to step aboard and cast off the lines, a simple action, but one I'd rehearsed in my mind a thousand times: our departure for the Azores with eighteen hundred nautical miles of ocean ahead. I glanced at my watch, it was one-thirty. I felt a surge of confidence, and some apprehension, too. We were as ready as we could ever be; no reason to delay further, we must put out at once and learn what the sea held for us.

I touched the starter. Methuselah responded immediately, as primed and ready as we were. The lines came aboard; water grew between the boat and the pier. When would *Aquarius* nudge against a friendly quay again? We churned smoothly out toward the harbor mouth. A "bon voyage" or two from the shore and we turned our faces and our minds away from land.

The cliffs of Town Cut passed on either side, St. David's Head towering away to starboard. Now the sea swell began to lift us as we negotiated the channel buoys. *Aquarius* responded unsteadily with the alcoholic roll of a yacht under power. I moved forward to the mast and the familiar ritual began, the pas-de-deux of making sail:

Sail stops off. Jeannine at the helm bringing the yacht into the wind. Quick heaves on the main halyard. Mainsail climbing the mast. Jeannine lifting the boom from its crutch at the critical moment, the tiller pressing against her thigh. *Aquarius* moving off the wind, sea pressure on the helm, a new will and consciousness in the wood, the boat's rolling no longer manic, responding to a new rhythm improvised by wind, sails and swell.

On the foredeck now. I'm doing my jib dance—the choreography rehearsed in countless sail changes. Jib halyard coming off its cleat, carried forward in my hand to meet its own other end shapshackled to a bail on the pulpit. Quick snap transfer from bail to jib head. Snap. The sail already hanked to the forestay. Now a backward two-step to hauling position, flat-barefooted in the middle of the foredeck. Both halyard ends taut and dancing in my hands. Quick heave. Heave. The jib running up. Sail-flapping noises, then a profound void of silence opening suddenly as Jeannine cuts the engine, its alien throbbing stifled in every rib and frame member. *Aquarius* coming alive in its natural world. Sea sounds entering the void, gulls crying, rigging creaking, the boil and slither of sea water pressed aside by the moving hull.

At the mast now, sweating the halyard taut around the winch. We're moving! I feel tourniquets loosed in my head, pores exploding in the expanding silence, tears rumbling in my throat. In the cockpit Jeannine snugs in the jibsheet. Heavy bronze clamoring from the winch. Both sails drawing nicely now in the fresh breeze. *Aquarius* settling over, pressing forward, liquids streaming out behind her. I return to the cockpit. We touch faces. No need for words. It has begun.

By 1430 we had cleared the sea buoy, heading northeast, pointing up toward latitude thirty-six north where I hoped the winds and currents would be more favorable. By 1800 as the light began to soften, the heights of Bermuda were only a cluster of humpy whales dim on the horizon.

September 12

MATTHEW: At two-fifteen we passed the last sea buoy. I was glad to be on the sea again without any fruitflies or churchbells to bother me. The seas were very small, about two feet. We had an easterly wind, which was not good because we wanted to go in that direction. I spent the rest of the day lying around in the cockpit waiting for the day to end. We had learned on the run to Bermuda that it usually took about four days of brisk weather to get used to the sea. During that period we are all very sleepy and seasick, except Dad. But, as I said, the waves were small and the boat didn't rock much.

I slept in the cockpit that night because I hated it down below. In the galley there was always something sliding back and forth or some block outside going click . . . click . . . click . . . every time the boat rolled. The galley was the worst place. The cups in the shelf would rock or the silverware would make a tinking sound. To me it was like a Chinese water torture with the water on my head going drip . . . drip . . . drip. . . . It could drive you crazy. I couldn't sleep below even if I wanted to. Besides, being out in the fresh air looking at the stars was better.

When I sleep in the cockpit it seems strange to me because I frequently wake up in the night and see one person on watch. Then I close my eyes, and without realizing that I have slept a couple of hours, I open my eyes one second later and see another person sitting in the exact same place. Then I shut them for another second and see another person. So the night goes on like that until the sun blazes in my eyes in the morning and I wake up.

Sunday, September 13

MATT: 0500, the morning watch, my favorite. I witnessed the sun's rise this morning, an appreciative audience of one while the rest of *Aquarius*'s crew slept. Silent applause for each pink cloud. Muted bravos when the sliced orange poked its blazing rim above the horizon. Pleasant anticipation of the morning changes brought by the sun. What kind of a day would it be?

One change the sun always brings is a wind shift. This morning the wind moved back toward the east, a course it held yesterday afternoon until nightfall drove it further south. I understand now why there is always so much boring detail about wind direction in most of the voyaging books I've read: the wind literally determines the course of your life. Will it be an easy day or a hard one? The wind will decide that for you and there's very little you can do about it; so describing the wind is a way of describing your condition of life at the moment.

The Arabs have a word, *'Nshallah,* that denotes an attitude toward life very akin to the psychology of going to sea in a small sailing boat. *'Nshallah* means "It is God's will." The devout Muslim appends this word to almost every thought to express his belief that all events are determined by God; that he is but a leaf floating helplessly on the sea of life and must accept philosophically whatever fate deals him. At sea, a small boat and its crew are so much at the mercy of wind and weather that it is pure waste of energy to rail against them; and part of the challenge of moving from land to water, I think, is learning to accept whatever is dished out without worrying too much about what may lie ahead. If the day is rough you're going to be uncomfortable and you might as well accept it. If the weather is beautiful that's a blessing to enjoy without concern for tomorrow.

Anyway, east winds are our fortune for the day—and an adverse fate at that. It means holding the boat hard on the wind, a course that is slower and rougher; but nothing can spoil my pleasure at this first sunrise at sea. The beginning of our longest ocean passage has been ideal so far, and I'm trying to follow my own advice and not worry about the rough weather that I'm sure lies ahead.

September 14

MATT: We're settling down, re-establishing old routines, getting our sea legs under us, beginning to look around. Everyone is still a bit queasy, Jeannine and Phil look especially peaked, but another day should see them feeling fit. I can afford to be philosophical, the motion hardly affects me at all.

This morning during my watch I was reading Christopher Columbus's journals and a passing reference to a sea bird evoked an electrifying connection for me between his voyage and ours.

Rabo de Juntos, "Red Tails" Columbus called them. His flagship attracted their curiosity about halfway between Gomera in the Canary Islands and his San Salvador landfall. They were a welcome sight to Columbus, these large black-and-white birds with their incongruously long, forked red tails. He took them for a sure sign land was near. (All the way across he made similar misinterpretations of seaweed, gulls and floating debris.) According to Alexander's *Birds of the Ocean,* the red-tailed tropic birds probably are found in the Pacific, but their white-tailed cousins have been wheeling and circling over us ever since we left Bermuda. Old salts call them "bosun birds" because they wear a marlin spike in their tails. I can understand why Columbus thought they were land birds; it is hard to believe such extravagant creatures could have any legitimate business to conduct this far out in the Atlantic. They appear more suited to boudoirs; a short flap to the corner taildresser would seem their speed. Yet here they are miles from the nearest cocktail lounge, swooping skillfully, quite the most flamboyant sight in our lonely ocean.

Bosun birds are not our only link to Columbus. The same

old seaweed is still going around and around, making its circuit up the Gulf Stream from San Salvador, being hustled across the North Atlantic in the coattails of the westerlies until it catches the Canary Current and is borne back along Columbus's southern route to the West Indies again. This morning we fished some up for closer inspection. In the water it looked dead as it floated in long windblown streaks along the surface, but at close hand it revealed crisp juicy leaves, succulent stalks with grape-like clusters of tiny green globules that kept it afloat. I'm sure the weed must provide food for myriad sea creatures but its most important function in our scheme of things has been to spoil the fishing. After a few minutes of action the silver spoon we drag behind us would invariably snag a curd of weed. And what fish would be attracted by a luncheon of undulating seaweed sandwich?

Aside from birds and weed, we haven't seen much so far. No ships at all, and surprisingly, no fish except for an occasional squadron of flying ones. The first morning we entered their territory I stepped confidently on deck with a frying pan expecting to collect a breakfast of unfortunates that had flown aboard during the night—just as I read in all those South Sea adventure stories. I did find a couple of flying fish, but they were delicate little things, about four inches long with fine silvery wings. We had oatmeal instead.

What else have we seen? Thor Heyerdahl spoke of encountering debris and oil pollution all the way across the Atlantic on his fabulous reed galleon, *Ra,* but in our corner of the ocean the only sign of man's dominion has been, oddly enough, fluorescent light tubes. "Look! What's that floating off the port bow?" (Something important, certainly. Maybe a message, or at least a crate of plums!) A scramble for the binoculars and the treasure is revealed: another fluorescent light tube.

September 15

MATT: 0300: This is the hour when the *Aquarius* family slumbers most heavily. The wind is steady and the seas relatively calm. In two hours it will be dawn and I can decide whether to work another star fix or not. I will probably be lazy. At dusk yesterday I got the most perfect star fix I've achieved so far. The three lines of position converged so beautifully on the plotting sheet that I felt quite certain of our position: some one hundred fifty miles east-northeast of Bermuda. It's very reassuring to be able to put a mark on a plotting sheet and say, "We are here," even though at this stage in our journey it doesn't make a hell of a lot of difference. Later, as we near Fayal, knowing our position will become much more important.

Navigation is usually spoken of as an art, not a science, and I'm beginning to learn why. While it's possible under favorable conditions to plot a position at sea to within several miles or less, the variables of wave action, wind drift, and current can never be worked out with complete accuracy. If land is near, especially dangerous land such as we encountered approaching Bermuda, it's safer to allow for all the variables in such a way that you assume a position closest to danger. Then set your course and make your calculations with that position in mind. Just how much error to allow for is a matter only experience and instinct can teach—that's where the art comes in. I don't find the techniques of navigation too difficult, but I can understand why the art could take a lifetime.

I tried to give Jeannine and Phil a navigation lesson yesterday. The experiment was not a complete success. I chose a noon sight because the paperwork is easy, explained the workings of the sextant, and delved briefly into the mysteries of the *Nautical Almanac*. After a few tries they began to get the hang of swinging the sextant and each produced reasonable enough altitudes of the sun, so I sent them below to do the figuring. When I next looked in, the papers were on the floor and two bodies were on the bunks gazing at the ceiling with glazed expressions. The teacher didn't have to ask, it was motion sickness, not mathematical complexity, that defeated navigation.

September 16

JEANNINE: "All ships! All ships! All ships! This is Bermuda Harbor Radio . . . Bermuda Harbor Radio . . . Bermuda Harbor Radio!"

These friendly words in triplicate greet us every morning; assure us that there are no hurricanes roaring into our vicinity beyond the ken of our barometer; inform us of the precise hour in Greenwich, England; and bring us the comfort (like a silver cord tying us to our astral body) of knowing that there *is* a familiar world peopled with humans and electronic instruments out there somewhere. But every day Bermuda Harbor Radio is a little harder to find, a little weaker, a little fuzzier with static and interference.

Today was a tough one. Matthew wrote a good description.

September 16

MATTHEW: The waves were eight or ten feet high. There was strong but steady wind. We were all feeling a little queasy. The boat was in a mess; it looked like a house that had only sick people in it and everybody was too sick to clean up but not too sick to make a mess.

The steering was hard. The adults took most of the watches and we were always taking seas over the deck. I cleaned up the forepeak and rested there all afternoon. It was like a rainy day with nothing to do. I finished *Andromeda Strain,* a very exciting book. Only one other thing happened. The ice box turned into a disaster area. The shelf had jostled loose and fallen into the melting ice. All the precious chocolate that we had been saving got soggy. The butter was okay —just wet. The apples and some eggs survived, too. We had three eggs left. The raisin bread got deep-sixed along with other unidentifiable floating debris. Dad cleaned everything out holding his nose. He cleaned it until it smelled like soap.

September 16

JEANNINE: Thank God, Matt doesn't get seasick. I couldn't have faced that mess. On rough days like this I retreat. My body is ignored. It is not important if my hair is combed, my face washed or my teeth brushed. The clothes I wear are for utility, not beauty. The tasks I perform are from necessity, not love. My energy is drawn inside, jealously contained. My body craves anonymity. I am not "woman," not even "person." My mind desires only that the hours and the miles should pass.

I have become an authority on seasick pills. This brand makes me very sleepy. Those don't actually put me to sleep, but I do feel shaky and dizzy if I try to sit up or do my work. These knock me out completely for about twenty-four hours. After careful evaluation I can make this objective and scientific summary: none of them keeps me from being seasick! I have just taken the third variety again to make sure that I haven't misrepresented the facts; after all, one shouldn't draw conclusions without . . . without repeating the experiment . . . several times and I . . . I really feel . . . zzzzzzzz.

September 16

MATT: *Is it hard living on a ship? Do you have a washing machine? Does your father drive at night? Do you fish from the boat? Do you ever get mad at your sister? Do you go to church? Do you have a TV or radio?*

Children's questions about the voyage. Matthew is a celebrity of sorts at P.S. 56 in Rochester, New York. He was adopted by the sixth grade after an article and pictures of our voyage appeared in the Rochester *Times Union.* The pupils have been flooding him with letters and questions ever since.

We are told there is a chart on the classroom wall to help them follow our progress, and that they are studying the countries and ports we visit. In Bermuda Matthew received a flock of interesting questions from these children who have almost no idea of what it is like to be at sea. They have helped us take a fresh look at our daily lives.

How does your boat run at night when everyone is asleep?

With Phil along, night watches have not been much of a problem. We adults stand two hour stints in rotation, beginning about ten in the evening. If the wind direction is such that we have to sit and hold the tiller, two hours is long enough. But now that I've learned to make the vane gear behave better, it has been relieving the helmsman about seventy percent of the time. That's equivalent to at least three additional hands and night watches usually amount to little more than sitting on the companionway steps or out in the cockpit (it's nice under the stars) checking the compass occasionally and casting a wary eye around the horizon for ships. Undoubtedly we could "run at night when everyone is asleep" (provided we could solve the problem of four bunks and five bodies), but so long as there is even a remote possibility of collision with a ship I feel we must maintain regular watches. From eye level the horizon is about three miles distant and a ship steaming blindly in our direction at twenty knots would run us down in nine minutes. In practice, we have been sighting a ship's masthead lights long before it's on the horizon, giving us considerably more leeway.

Before we left New Orleans we were treated to several horror stories of yachts run down at night; no one objects to keeping a lookout. It's one of the rare times when it is possible to feel truly alone on the boat, to re-establish dominion over one's inner territory, to relax the tensions of living in tight quarters. I do most of my writing at night—there's nothing to interrupt the flow of ideas. But if I'm feeling lazy, I'll spend my watch hours braced against the companionway steps dialing through the shortwave channels in search of intelligible signals from the outer world.

Do you get up before your father goes to work?

The change from a dark to a daylight regimen takes place slowly. The official end of night watches is 0600, although sometimes they drag on until 0800. The last person off watch rousts out a child (usually Matthew, who sits sleepily in the cockpit until the boat comes to life or until he can justify rousting Melissa). We adults are inclined to remain anonymous bundles in the bunks as long as possible, but Jeannine is usually up before nine and has breakfast going on the stove.

Who washes the dishes?

Cleanup follows with everybody taking a turn at the jobs (I get easy duty in the galley in return for most of the boat maintenance) and the day settles into its normal routine. In reality there are two daily routines, one for heavy weather and another when the sea is mild. If it's rough, Matthew and Melissa are apt to spend most of the day in their bunks either reading or combatting the gastro-reverberations of motion. Matthew becomes very quiet with seasickness. Melissa, his opposite in most things, protests loudly, but normally doesn't get as sick. Jeannine's reactions to motion are well documented, but I am becoming increasingly worried about Phil. He hasn't accommodated to living at sea as easily as I had expected. He came aboard in Bermuda with an armory of antibiotics to combat an infection, but so far it has been the infection, in unholy alliance with our well-known adversary, *mal de mer,* which has carried the day. Except for his watches, Phil spends much of his time burrowed into a bunk in mute and feverish misery. I watch the fever with some anxiousness, looking for signs of change or deterioration. If he doesn't begin to improve soon we will have to decide whether to put back to Bermuda or not. Putting back would be bad news for Phil and for us too. Given the lateness of the season, we'd probably have to cancel the voyage of *Aquarius.*

What kind of work do you do on the ship?

Watchkeeping certainly is the most work, but in favorable weather none of us stands formal daytime watches.

Whoever is in the cockpit keeps an eye on the boat while the vane gear does the actual steering. If the sun is hot, Matthew or Jeannine will soon begin petitioning for the erection of the sailing awning, a cockpit-sized vinyl bonnet that hangs in a web of guy ropes just above our heads. Everybody likes the awning except me. It does make the cockpit cool and comfortable, but the boat is much more complicated to handle when it is rigged. Everytime the mainsail is swung across the cockpit a guy rope must be dropped, and an unexpected jibe could easily carry the whole contraption away. Anyone charging heedlessly forward to untangle a jib sheet is apt to suffer abrupt strangulation from one of the ropes. Once the awning is rigged, it's not difficult to find a volunteer to tend the boat, and since it does have its advantages I am certain to lose all arguments so long as anyone has the energy to put it up.

Is it hard living on a ship?

We live on a boat, not a ship. A boat is any vessel small enough to be carried on a ship, and there are times when I wish we had one around to carry us. Even so, most of the time our life *is* easy. The days are balmy and we live outdoors, a cosy family group congregating under the cockpit awning. There is reading, dozing, sunning; the miles slip away almost unnoticed. A quality of uncluttered leisure reigns sovereign. We never seemed to enjoy such leisure ashore and I think it is at the root of the physical and emotional well-being all of us except perhaps Phil are beginning to feel.

Melissa often practices her flute, and the rest of us have tried various craft projects. Matthew is the most consistently crafty. He learned knotting from a book, graduated to macramé, and has now replaced all our tattered lampshades with artfully macraméd creations.

Aquarius provides me with more "craft" projects than I care to think about. Some piece of gear is always breaking or getting out of adjustment, and I have only begun to whittle away at my list of "essential" improvements. Since I have no way of foretelling what weather or emergencies may lie ahead, the only prudent course is to prepare for the worst by keeping everything at its best all the time—by definition an impossible goal. It's fortunate the captain-navigator-electrician-plumber-mechanic-carpenter-sailmaker-rigger likes his work.

Do you have a washing machine?

We have only enough fresh water for drinking and cooking now; it's been my major concern this morning. We left Bermuda with four tanks brimming: a twenty-five gallon fiberglass tank amidships under the galley sink, a thirty-five gallon galvanized tank in the forepeak, and two fifteen-gallon flexible plastic waterbags snugged into odd-shaped fragments of space beneath the forward bunks. All the tanks feed hoses interconnected to a hand pump located at the galley sink. Next to it stands a salt-water pump which supplies all our needs except drinking: dish-washing, people-washing, laundry, even cooking (one-third sea water and two-thirds fresh water in the vegetable pan yields properly salted food—sea-salted, at that). Besides the fresh water, we are carrying six or seven cases of tinned fruit juices, a good supplementary water ration.

But this morning, only five days at sea, the twenty-five gallon fiberglass tank ran dry. What a disaster! At that rate of consumption, almost double my calculations, we would run completely out of water on the eighteenth day. It didn't seem possible, there had to be some other explanation—we've been downright niggardly with water.

Finally I tore apart the engine compartment and slithered around on my back for half an hour looking at two-way valves, water hoses, and cockroaches. Once, as the boat righted herself momentarily on a wave, the remaining inch of water sloshed around in the ailing tank and I noticed a formation of droplets gather rapidly along the outside rim. Thirst Gremlin Unmasked! The shifting fluid had obviously cracked the tank, and our precious water had leaked into the bilge—a good argument for not putting all your aqua in one basket, especially a fiberglass basket. Only sixty-five gallons remain, but at least I know where the water has gone and why. We'll probably have enough to get us to Horta, but no water festivals for the crew of *Aquarius*—and no margin for error.

What other tasks for the day? Solving the water mystery was a major accomplishment; now if I could complete a few minor jobs I'd be happy. But first, a noon sight. The sun doesn't wait at the zenith of his daily arc, I must be ready when he is. This morning from the pages of my *Nautical Almanac* I worked out the approximate time of astral noon, about 1145. With the hour hard upon me I hurried below for the sextant, returned to the cabin top and began shooting sights of the sun about once a minute. Old Sol seemed unconcerned with my fusillade, but I must have slowed him some for he climbed more and more reluctantly toward his rendezvous at the daily divide. At the apex he seemed to balance ponderously for a few moments, an incandescent circus elephant poised on a pinnacle. I kept shooting until the sextant told me the sun was definitely descending. Then I descended too—to the cabin for some quick figuring. Noon sights are so easy to work they seem like cheating. In a few minutes I had our position fixed at 35° 18' North, 58° 12' West—about three hundred forty-five miles east-northeast of Bermuda. We were just short of the 36th parallel, where I hoped to find a wind change that would allow us to take a more easterly heading.

My next job for the day was mounting cheek blocks and cleats on the boom to secure reefing lines so that tying down the sail during reefing would not be such a monumental struggle. Like so many others listed in my repair book, this job has been deferred time and again. I began by disordering the cabin. The engine cover boards that were strewn about during the water-tank investigation had been replaced, and now I re-strewed the cabin with bunk cushions, tools, and the boards covering my tool locker. Everything took twice as long because of the motion of the boat; but finally holes were drilled, blocks and cleats bedded in sealing compound and screwed firmly to the boom. Meanwhile, Matthew began lunch, a casually catered affair of sandwiches fabricated on the bridge deck. Once I narrowly missed stepping in the cream cheese while driving home a final screw; another time the boat lurched suddenly and I saved myself from a plunge into the open icebox only by desperate gymnastics. There was no washing up. The sun had begun to do its work on us, and what few dishes there were, we tossed in the galley sink to await a later disposal.

Do you like taking lessons from your mother?

The afternoon torpor had set in. Jeannine and Phil dozed on bunks in the main cabin. Matthew was finishing his net. Melissa lounged in the cockpit reading a Nancy Drew mystery, hauling at the tiller with a negligent foot whenever a lull in the breeze threw the vane gear off course. There have been no ships since we left Bermuda, and she seldom looked up.

About three, Jeannine roused herself abruptly. "What's everybody doing?" she asked with unconvincing heartiness.

"Same thing you are."

"Well, we can't let the day slip by. What about practicing Morse?"

I sensed a schoolteacher's conscience troubling her as she rummaged through the "everything box" for the Morse Code bleeper. The rest of us had given our consciences the day off, but we settled sleepily in the cockpit for a lesson anyway. We had all memorized the code, but our rate of sending and receiving averaged two grunts and a groan per hour. Learning Morse is more than an academic exercise, it's the only way to receive complete and reliable weather reports now that Bermuda Harbor Radio is fading into the outer ether. We tapped out practice passages from Chapman's *Small Boat Handling* and Eric Sloan's *Weather Book.* As the lesson progressed the textbook sentences became more easy to predict and decode, and we resorted to our own inventions, producing wilder and wilder messages as our enthusiasm grew. Matthew broke up the lesson with this: "He lightly smashed the eyelash that bound him to the Coke machine."

"Time to charge batteries." A universal groan greeted these words of gloom. They meant an hour of living with Methuselah, the geriatric Greymarine. We tolerate Methuselah because we need him, but none of us loves him, although I admit to a grudging respect for his endurance. Somehow a combustion engine is never really at home on a sailing machine. Methuselah has lots of not-so-secret vices. He smokes a lot, and I suspect emphysema from the noxious blue fumes that seep into the cabin. I suspect, but I have no desire to investigate. What use is an exploratory operation that turns up a terminal illness? Perhaps because of his smoking, Methuselah coughs a lot, but mostly he carries on hour after complaining hour with a heavy teeth-jarring rumble. He also suffers from low blood pressure, another ominous sign. His oil gauge has dropped almost ten pounds of pressure since the voyage began. I tried ignoring it for a while, but finally in Bermuda I pulled the oil pressure relief valve and stuffed a few washers behind the valve spring. They helped, but I know only radical surgery will cure Methuselah's maladies. I only hope he prevails unto the end of the voyage, and if he does, we'll give him an honorable send-off to that Great Grease Pit in the Sky.

Since we pay dearly for the power Methuselah churns out —the electricity to light the cabin and *Aquarius*'s running lights, the power to drive the radio, depth sounder, bilge pump, and tape recorder—I am likely to be crochety when the children leave lights burning unnecessarily. "Turn that goddamn light off! Do you think batteries live on air?" They regard my bitching as a tedious nuisance, but it doesn't stop them from wasting electricity.

Before Methuselah had finished his grinding, supper preparations were underway. Tonight Melissa was cook-designate, an office she didn't entirely relish, and Jeannine agreed to help her. They sat in the cockpit together, my two long blondes, peeling potatoes, carrots and onions. Melissa may dislike cooking, but she loves to *peel*—and to scrub, scour and clean. As soon as the fumes of Methuselah had blown away, Jeannine began browning the last of our fresh chicken (it's corned beef hash henceforth from here to Horta) and teaching Melissa how to make gravy. Propitious smells emanated from the galley. Phil and I exchanged significant glances. It promised to be a good meal.

And a good evening. After supper we sat in the cockpit playing Password. Matthew and I practiced ESP and won easily. Venus appeared; the sky turned apricot, then claret, heliotrope, ultramarine. When the little passwords were no longer visible in the little plastic windows of the Official Card Holders, the game broke up and the various Aquarians filtered down to their bunks below.

Phil took the first watch. He sat on the companionway steps listening as I read from Jules Verne. Reading aloud is a new custom for us, and it's surprising how much we enjoy it. It seems a fitting way to end a day, as well as a painless means of imparting to my children some awareness of literary classics they might otherwise miss. We like stories that relate to our own experiences. Since New Orleans I've recited the remarkable Mississippi voyage of Huck Finn and Nigger Jim. I've read sections from Moby Dick, and lately I've been recounting the adventures of the mighty Captain Nemo. The children consider Jules Verne a bit "flowery" but they like the action that comes between descriptions of flora and fauna.

Bedtime stories take Jeannine back to the days of teddy bears and Little Red Riding Hood.

"Jeannine, are you awake?"

"Zzzzzzz—Sure I am."

"Okay. What did I last read?"

In a mechanical voice she manages to repeat the last sentence verbatim, but the children and I are on to her.

With Phil faithfully on watch and consciousness fading rapidly, we composed ourselves for sleep. That is, most of us did. Jeannine had gone long before us.

12
Mid-Passage

September 17

JEANNINE: "Hey! Hey! It's a rainy day in the middle of the Atlantic!"

I heard the kids conspiring up on deck. They had been trying for the last three days to convince me that every little squall we saw was a "rainy day mid-Atlantic" because they knew I had a few treats stowed away for that particular occasion.

I came into the cockpit prepared to be dubious, but it *was* raining and it looked like the sky was generally overcast.

"Let's try to catch some rainwater off the sail," I said, hoping to divert their attention. This was the most rain since departure—maybe we could catch enough at least to wash our hair. Matthew held a pan under the boom to gather the run-off. We tasted the first cupful.

"Aaghhhh! It's salty!" Melissa spat over the side.

"Not enough rain yet to wash the sails. We need a real downpour. Maybe later this afternoon we'll try again."

"Mom, it *is* drizzling—what about our surprises?"

"Yeah, Mom! You *promised!*"

I started to give in. "Well, how about a little schoolwork first, and then a treasure hunt for dessert." Whoops and cheers from the crew. Melissa retired to the forepeak with a

French workbook she is really enjoying. It is simple and well programmed with enough pictures that she needs very little help from me. She has picked up a lot of vocabulary and can put short sentences together, so we converse a lot; and her pronunciation is excellent.

Matthew decided to do a typing lesson. Both kids are about one third of the way through a self-teaching book which they started on the way to Florida. Their progress is remarkable considering how hard it is to type when the table is slanted. Matthew has managed to experiment with every possible place to type—forepeak, cabin, companionway, afterdeck. He adjusts the height of the typewriter with the same meticulousness and determination that he searches out persistent noises in the night. (And that is no mean determination! I am always astonished to open one eye in the dead of night and see him prowling around the galley, probing, testing, stuffing hotpads and dishtowels in strategic places between jiggling plates or rattling cups. I can't help but commiserate with his frustration, especially when I see him go to such extremes as to don foul-weather gear on a rough night to go out on deck to wrap up a clattering block.)

I settled myself down to turn out some rhymes for the treasure hunt. Hiding the clues was another matter. It's really hard to be secretive on a thirty-one-foot boat. First, I confined everybody in the forepeak while I tiptoed around the cabin; then I chased them into the cabin while I did my sneaky business in the forepeak.

The hunt iself took two hours. From a spice bottle to the fishing tackle box, from the depth finder to the coffee pot they tracked down note after note until, just at the edge of frenzy, they located a cache of comic books, life savers, plastic balloons, Yo-Yo's, and Silly Putty. They were more than delighted with their haul and remained engrossed in the forepeak for the rest of the afternoon. For a couple of dollars and a few inches of space it was sure worth it, *and* (chuckle, chuckle) I have enough for a few more rainy days still tucked away.

The sporadic drizzles were not enough to wash down the sails. My hair will have to stay stiff for a few more days.

We carried our rainy-day celebration to a logical conclusion. Brownies! I had bought a case of brownie mix at the railroad salvage yard. They were the most appreciated of all our goodies, especially since the demise of our beloved chocolate bars in the Great Ice Box Disaster. Matthew wired together the rickety rusty oven while Melissa mixed the brownies. (We have one more precious egg—that means only one more batch of brownies. Eggs were just too expensive in Bermuda. Next time I'll take ten dozen, no matter what the cost. They play a million roles, from sticking pancakes together to cheering up another dinner of corned-beef hash.) I wore my sexy blouse and long skirt. Matthew wore the same red-and-blue-striped shirt he has worn since we left Bermuda. (I think he is trying for some kind of record.) It was a lovely rainy day.

September 17

MELISSA: Toward the end of the day it started getting calm. The rain stopped and by evening the water was almost glassy, and we were all sitting in the cockpit with the sails down and the boat drifting. Suddenly Phil pointed to something in the water. We all ran to the back of the boat. It was a shark about twice my size and I am four feet eight inches! The first shark we've seen the whole trip.

September 17

MATT: He wasn't in any hurry and he was so big you felt more inclined to gauge the boat in sharks than to measure the shark in feet. At best *Aquarius* was less than four of this fellow in length. We stood at the life line and looked directly down at him swimming just below the surface only a couple of feet away. He was so clearly visible it seemed there was only air between us. Very impressive. I thought quite a bit about that tiny particle of space separating us. Standing on the deck of a boat, the distance was adequate; in the water it would be nothing. Ocean is the shark's element. He has lived there quite happily for hundreds of thousands, maybe millions, of years and probably will always be around. By temporary sufferance we also live in the shark's element, but only by constant vigilance can we maintain that precarious but urgently important separation. My thoughts strayed to the tightness of hull fittings, to that small but persistent leak in the rudder stuffing box, while the shark swam quietly away.

September 18

MATT: Almost a week gone and we've yet to sight a ship or any other evidence of living humans inhabiting this planet—only that twice-a-day, disembodied voice, polite and colonial, reciting from Bermuda the accumulated weather observations of ships all over the North Atlantic Ocean— only that to convince us we proceed in company. I'm so lonely this morning I can taste the emptiness. I need a ship —anything—to bounce my aloneness off, to prove by reflection my own existence. My thoughts ring like hollow drums, their impact magnified by the surrounding vacuity. I had the same eerie sensation sailing to Bermuda, but not until we had been lying several days in St. George's harbor did I understand why every action performed in port seemed so much *less significant* than at sea.

At sea the horizon is three miles away—an exact circle of blue all around. You live like a grain of rice in the precise center of an immense blue platter. For the most part nothing happens anywhere else on that platter. A squall, a jumping fish, a flight of sea birds is all that ever disturbs the vast emptiness, the vast *eventlessness* of the surrounding space. On the grain of rice, by comparison, the pressure of events may be very intense; sentient humans living too closely together, generating great densities of movement and emotion.

The motion of the boat itself is an unceasing and often highly charged activity. And it's all amplified by the surrounding space; the slightest finger twitch or whisper takes place under the magnifying glass of enveloping emptiness. A scientist working in the Bell Telephone Labs' "Silent Room" thinks the ringing we perceive in our ears when there are absolutely no other signals to interfere, is a result of the brain's neuro-amplifiers turning up the "gain" control to a higher sensitivity level in the search for something to hear. Maybe it's this "gain" effect that turns every intrusion into our magic blue arena—a ship, a jet trail, a floating bit of debris—into an event of major proportions.

I know I'm not alone in these lonely feelings. Matthew and Jeannine, at least, share them with me. I've uncovered their confessions in the log book:

> *Matthew:* When the sea is glassy calm you suddenly realize how big the ocean is and how lonely you are. It looks like you're in a big room and if anybody came in, they would immediately look at you, but nobody ever comes in the room.
>
> *Jeannine:* When I look out to sea I always expect to see something. Even after several days of seeing nothing, when I come from below I make a careful examination of the horizon. There will be a whale spout which I can point out and surprise everyone. Or a giant manta jumping. Or perhaps I will see the mysterious island of Antilia which early cartographers placed in varying positions across the Atlantic. Columbus looked for it too. The anticipation is keen. At night I'm sure there will be a friendly light on the horizon, or at least a flying saucer disturbing the quiet order in the sky. I always expect to catch a fish too, when I polish up the spoon, spit on it for luck and toss it over the side. Matt is usually happily enjoying the present while I'm busy anticipating the future.
>
> I have just come up for my watch and have completed my scanning. What? Nothing but water? Again?

Saturday, September 19

MATT: 2130 hours. As he turned over the duty to me this evening, Phil unstrapped his expensive Japanese wristwatch (by now the only working timepiece aboard except for the navigation watch) and handed it to me so I would know when my time was up.

"When your bloated and decomposed body is washed ashore," he said with a little smile, "this watch will be found on your wrist still keeping perfect time—*wound by the action of the waves.*"

That cheerful note ended one of the most eventful days of our voyage so far. It began almost twenty-four hours earlier, about midnight yesterday as our faltering breeze gave a final gasp and died. Phil and I sat in eerie silence, except for the occasional flop of a sail, on a perfectly glassy sea. The swells in the moonlight looked like gently rolling Ohio farmland, except that they really rolled and the boat rocked as they passed under us. We decided to turn in, took down the jib and lashed the main tight to act as a damper to our rolling. Although we had seen no ships for six days, I turned on the masthead light and we stretched out for the first uninterrupted night's sleep since leaving Bermuda.

Next morning something awakened me early. Maybe it was the first stirring of morning breeze subtly altering the way the boat rocked. I've developed a kind of kinesthetic third ear that awakens me like a nervous mother to any new motion of the boat.

I came on deck into the warm early light. *Aquarius* sat at the center of her blue desert, nothing in sight, as usual. Jeannine was spread out on the forward part of the cabin top, soaking in the morning stillness. She often gets up very early and goes out quietly without disturbing anyone to have the peaceful early time by herself. I have no idea what passes in her head at this hour, but I love her soulful habit of letting nature pour in—and I watched her quietly for a few minutes. Then we came together, touched, and watched the ripple patterns as patches of moving air on the water turned themselves into something worth sailing about.

"It's a good breeze," I said, hopefully. "We'll get two knots out of it easily."

"No," Jeannine maintained, "it won't give us a knot."

"What do you want to bet? One in the forepeak?" (Our usual bet: the winner has his way with the loser in the forepeak—a nice arrangement where nobody loses.)

I raised the genoa and *Aquarius* set off, but much more slowly than I had anticipated. About this time Matthew lifted his blond head out of the companionway, and we appointed him "fair witness" to cast the chip log, record the speed and decide the winner.

"What's the bet?" he asked.

"One in the forepeak."

Matthew smiled wisely and said nothing. I believe he regards lovemaking and everything that goes with it as some weird form of adult strangeness, but he's very tolerant of adult strangeness.

I stalled and whistled for more wind. The chip log was cast and recast amid inordinate delays to get the rope untangled. Still we proved to be making little better than half a knot. Bill Seemann says I'm an incurable optimist.

Around noon I came on deck to relieve Melissa of her watch. I found her curled comfortably in the cockpit absorbed in a book while the vane gear did most of the watching. I glanced around, and there, almost on top of us, was a ship! "Ship!" I cried. "Ship!" After seven days of empty horizons it was such a shock to receive this sudden visitation. Eagerly we scanned the new occupant of our world. It was a rather small undistinguished freighter, *Freubel Asia* by name, and as we watched, the red, gold, and black flag of West Germany was hoisted at her taffrail. She drew rapidly closer and then came to an almost complete stop. The crew lined her foredeck waving to us. We sat on the cabin top of our little boat and waved back, feeling very grand, very salty and adventurous.

Phil went below to get a camera. I switched on the radio. How does a sailboat address a freighter in the middle of the ocean? Ridiculous to wait on protocol. I forged ahead. "This is the sailing yacht *Aquarius,* WY 9864, calling *Freubel Asia.* Come in, please." Eventually a very polite German voice answered me in schoolbook English. Where were we from, and where bound, the voice wanted to know. "We're out of New Orleans, bound for the west coast of Africa."

"I don't understand you. I don't understand where."

"New Orleans to West Africa." It sounded grand, almost presumptuous from such a small boat, but I was presuming to feel grand. Was there anything they could do for us, anything we needed, the Voice of Freubel inquired. "Tell them we want to come aboard for steak and ice cream and hot showers, Dad." "Ask him to tow us across the Atlantic." No, I assured him, there was absolutely nothing we needed, nothing at all—well, perhaps if he insisted, a report on the weather. And a position check. The voice seemed delighted to be of help, and was back in a minute with a position (within a few miles of my own estimate) and the assurance that there would be no meteorological disasters during the next twenty-four hours.

"Would you like to talk to the Captain?" Herr Voice continued. Did the skipper of the intrepid ocean voyager *Aquarius* wish to speak with the master of *Freubel Asia*? Did he, indeed? Indeed he did . . . Captains conferring in mid-ocean. *Captain Herron wanted urgently on the bridge! . . . Captain Herron! . . . Cargo shifting dangerously, Captain . . . Up to you to save us, Captain . . . Yes . . . Yes, of course. I'll be along directly . . . Excuse me, my Dear . . . Duty before pleasure . . . .*

A new voice in gold braid appeared at mike-side wrenching me abruptly back from fantasyland. The voice addressed me in courtly, Old World language. "Good day to you, sir. . . . Is there anything we can do for you? . . . You have a very fine sailing yacht there."

"Thank you, Captain *(tongue-tied)* . . . Thank you." We

wished each other good weather, safe passage, and goodbye. Screw churning, *Freubel Asia* drew ahead leaving the crew of *Aquarius,* and especially her captain, glowing in its wake.

Within an hour the wind started backing to the west until it was almost astern of us, and began to intensify. We spread our sails and flew before it. The wind continued to increase and the seas piled up behind until it required a fine concentration, quick timing and a sure hand on the helm to prevent *Aquarius* from breaching to and backing either the main or the jib. Jeannine was steering, doing the job with some lack of attention, and inevitably the main backed. Our preventer line saved us from a disastrous jibe, but with the main filled from behind it became almost impossible to bring the boat back on course. When eventually we did manage to wear her around, the main swung back across the wind filling from the other side with an explosive report and slamming its leach into the upper shrouds where it caught behind them, breaking a batten and threatening to tear across.

Cursing like Long John Silver, I rushed to the foredeck and managed in the soaking spray and violent motion to get the pole off the genoa and the sail down so we could run up into the wind and lower the wildly racketing main before the wind tore its head off. As I struggled with the sail I got madder and madder. It seemed as though all the tensions and frustrations of the voyage suddenly converged on this one incident—all my fears and my anxiety at being out here in the midst of this lonely ocean in a frail boat with the people I loved most in the world, people who, incredibly enough, had trusted me to guide them on this mad adventure, trusted me in spite of the fact that I had never made a crossing, had never in fact made any long passage, was, in fact, when you stripped away basic seamanship and simple bravado, quite unqualified to undertake such an ambitious and possibly insane voyage. Normally my fears and feelings of responsibility tend to work themselves out in excessive concern for the boat—for having each piece of gear working properly, for executing every maneuver in seamanlike fashion, for keeping everything in its place, the boat clean and well ordered.

(I'm convinced these goals are worthwile. They certainly increase the safety and comfort of everyone aboard, but there's no need to pursue them as I do, like an anxious mother hen, clucking neurotically whenever anyone flubs his seamanship or treats the nest more like a barnyard than a boat.)

When the mainsail was restored, the crisis over, and the boat back on course, I stormed back to the cockpit and dropped the heaviest stone I could think of on Jeannine. "You're an *inattentive* helmsman. I've watched you time and again put the boat in trouble by not attending to the goddamn course. It's about time you learned to consider the boat when you're at the helm."

It was the Captain speaking, not Husband or Lover, and the "inattentive helmsman" set her jaw and stomped below. I could hear her banging around in the galley, a harsh word to Melissa, a resounding thump to an unfortunate pot, and then into the forepeak. Silence from the forepeak. The tightness in my stomach gradually subsided. (Why is it in a quarrel one person cures the tension in his gut by transfering it to another?) Eons passed. I relinquished the helm and went to Jeannine lying tight and angry in the forepeak. Tears, then words. "This goddamn boat works against everything I do. It makes me so sick I don't feel like myself—don't act like myself and I know you don't want me. When we're sailing we're like strangers. We don't talk to each other. We don't touch each other. We never make love."

What can I say? Maybe a few things. I say them. We close the door to the forepeak. Gently. Clothes on the floor. There's never enough room on this damn boat to get your pants off gracefully. Bodies together. Skin. Touching. The afternoon is warm. The wind is fair. We defeat the sea.

September 20

MATT: What a night and a morning the funky old ocean has given us! Before dark last evening the wind was up beyond where a prudent sailor would be tucking a tidy reef in his mainsail. To be honest, I'm not always prudent and I don't like reefing at all. I'm a little afraid of it even—it's a large sweat and a small danger because we haven't rehearsed the mechanics of reefing down to a smooth drill, as we have making sail. In our fumbling there's always the danger of breaking gear or tearing the sail. Consequently, I tend to put reefing off as long as possible, hoping the wind will moderate, the seas will be stilled, or the Hand of God will appear in a golden shaft of sunlight, commanding the elements to spare us. Usually I am left, as last night, pacing the cockpit, gazing anxiously into the advancing weather and hoping for a lull that never comes, until the decision is finally forced and I take my station at the mast to reef under wind pressures already too advanced for comfort or safety.

Fortunately no serious accidents attended our reefing drill last night, although it was a monumental struggle to stretch the sail tight at the leech cringle and lash it fast to the boom. But once I'd exchanged the genoa for the working jib (with the foredeck alternating between moon rocket and precipice), *Aquarius* settled down to behaving like a lady— a half-tight lady in a barroom of drunken waves. Melissa and I were the only passengers up on the observation deck last night admiring her performance. Phil still has not recovered from the tailspin engendered by infection and seasickness, although he shows slow improvement. He and the other passengers groaned below in traditional attitudes of discomfort. Supper, that elegant repast at the captain's table, was canceled.

The night passed with plenty of discomfort but little actual difficulty. The wind backed further and we were able to set the vane gear, which had proved useless when running dead before the wind. By morning we were making very good time—between five and six knots—in eight- to ten-foot waves that marched down upon us in ordered ranks from some unseen marshaling point beyond the horizon, their plumes blowing in the breeze. *Breeze* is the correct word, the *officially* correct word. Although *Aquarius* was rough-riding the waves at a steeply canted angle and occasionally taking a dollop of salt water into her cockpit to season the constant spray, the wind measured only *force six* (22 to 27 knots) on the Beaufort scale, by official designation a "strong breeze." Force-six wind is not unusual at this time of year. We had three or four days of force six on the passage to Bermuda, but we've never gone beyond that intensity. I know we can handle the present weather without difficulty, it's what's ahead that causes me to scan the horizon with trepidation.

Let me pause and pay tribute to that admirable admiral, Sir Francis Beaufort, hydrographer to His Majesty's Most Britannic Navy between 1829 and 1855, the originator of all these "forces." Beaufort, a contemporary of the redoubtable Horatio Hornblower (historians agree they never met), was wounded as a lad of twenty-one near Málaga while covering Cornwallis's retreat down the Iberian Peninsula before Bonaparte. Eight years later, in 1803, he devised a practical scale for measuring wind velocity, dividing it into eighteen steps, or "forces," from dead calm to bloody unbelievable. Beaufort's scale is based on observable changes in sea conditions (you don't need an anemometer to estimate the wind velocity) and has proved so workable it is still in general use. Of the three best-known seafaring Sir Francises, Chichester and Drake gained the greatest fame, but Beaufort bequeathed us the most useful tool.

September 20
   JEANNINE: How long will it be before I feel at home in this environment? Take me to the mountains with a tent and a few supplies and I am happy; my childhood summers were

spent in the woods. But I still don't know what to expect from the sea. What is it like when the waves are twenty feet high? I can't imagine it.

The boat is another being, not a friend—an acquaintance so far. I know the parts of her well. I have scrubbed and sanded and painted everywhere. But at sea, with the wind in her sails I am still ill at ease with her. There is an awkwardness between us, as if our eyes have never really met. When the wind shifts and *Aquarius* slows and struggles through the water, I try to reset the sails but I am never sure of myself. The steering gear is a mystery. My mind is always reluctant to apply itself to understanding how something mechanical works. Just tell me how to drive it; that's all I want to know. (There's that damn specter of the "feminine mystique"! How often it still haunts me.) It's so much easier to let Matt set the steering vane than to deal with it myself, although I know if I really wanted to I could figure it out. It certainly doesn't require strength. On land I do battle with this inertia, this deep-seated copout that says, "I am only a woman." But when the sea robs me of my sense of well-being and my stomach quivers, I take the ancient path of least resistance. There is no extra energy for learning something new, for taxing my brain or my body beyond stasis. I disappoint myself.

September 20

MATT: The wind is down, and about 2200 this evening I sighted a light—the second ship in two days. We must be in the shipping lanes now. I watched her fearfully, mindful as always of stories about small boats cut down in the middle of nowhere by merchant ships; but she crossed our course about a mile astern and then lay to with her engines idling —a muffled black enigma in a dark night. I tried to raise her on the radio but the air waves were as silent as the darkness. Finally I turned on our spreader lights and lit *Aquarius*'s sails so the freighter could identify us as a yacht—not a life raft or some other motionless blip on her radar screen. After a few moments she moved off into the darkness, as anonymously as she came.

September 21

MATT: Phil was poking around on deck this afternoon with a camera—a hopeful sign that he is recovering from whatever has laid him so low. I watched him searching for pictures, an inscrutable process in which nothing seemed to happen until abruptly he would point the lens at some arrangement of objects that to my eye was totally devoid of picture possibilities. I photograph in a very different manner, usually with a definite objective in mind, and I will try dozens of variations until I find one that suits me. Recently, though, it's been very hard to pick up a camera. I've been giving myself so thoroughly to seamanship that I've not had the mind for photography; and I discovered long ago that I can't photograph with half a mind—it's unsatisfying and the results are terrible.

I know Phil's intuitive picture hunting works because I've seen the results. While he was in prison I put together an exhibition of his photographs for a gallery I once started in the French Quarter of New Orleans. His images were remarkable and they separated quite distinctly into two groups: a harsh, arid series of dehumanized urban scenes from his years in New York—bleak housing projects and construction sites, a blankly menacing transit bus, a chain-fenced schoolyard suggesting a concentration camp. The resemblance to the prison world he later inhabited was striking. The other group couldn't have been more different: pictures of his friends and lovers in the country, in commune settings—all smiles and foliage and flowing robes. I called the show: *Phil Stiles 22614: Images of Freedom and Confinement,* and used for the announcement his mug shot with number beneath, which he smuggled out of prison. The photographs were captioned with excerpts from his prison letters. It was a good show, the best the Listening Eye Gallery ever hung—and its last. I think I know Phil better from those photographs than I do from living so closely with him.

September 21

JEANNINE: Bodies accommodate. It is their salvation. Our bodies have been accommodating to the new environment in different ways: for one thing, we have lost weight. It doesn't seem to matter how much we eat, although I think we do eat less, and of course we are a bit limited in supplies of ice cream (a former staple) and butter (my secret passion). Matt has lost three inches off his waist and has become really lean and hardy. His pants are no longer fashionably tight—in fact they're decidedly saggy. He says it's from the constant muscle accommodation to the roll of the boat, but it's more. There is a tension that accompanies this new role of "captain." It's like the "executive monkey experiment" where two monkeys receive an electric shock simultaneously but only one is given access to the switch to turn it off; it is always his responsibility to jump for the lever to stop the shock. One guy gets shocked for no reason and can't do anything about it. The other guy turns it off for both of them. Guess who gets the ulcer? The captain, right? Well, of course Matt is not about to get an ulcer, but I think the responsibility does make it hard for him really to relax when he has a chance.

While I have lost some weight, what bothers me most is a general loss of tone in my muscles (except for my abdominal muscles which are well exercised). I crave exercise. When the kids start feeling confined they race around the deck playing tag, or put up the hammock and swing. I have tried yoga. It works on the foredeck when the seas are calm, but most yoga exercises already require excessive feats of balance without adding the boat's motion to the task. Also, a wash of cold sea water while concentrating on the *plow* is very disconcerting. I have developed my own unique multidimensional yoga. Since I have no horizontal floor space I have adapted some of the exercises to vertical space. Standing on a companionway step, I can brace a foot up against a corner of the hatch and do leg stretches by bending my head down to touch my knee. It must be similar to the regular stretch because it hurts the same way. Helpful though it is, vertical yoga doesn't substitute for the pounding heart and heavy breathing of fast bicycling, a tennis game, or a run around the park at home.

September 21

MATT: We've been traversing this ocean for nine days now—time I tried to summarize where we've gone and what we've gone through. Most of this time we have basked our way through typical Caribbean summer weather—hot sunny mornings, brilliant blue skies with cumulus clouds piling up into towering thunderheads toward late afternoon. If one of these squall centers happened to pass over us we underwent a half hour of violent wind with just enough rain in hard-driven sheets to wash the salt from the sails. We usually found it prudent to shorten sail, since summer squalls have been known to unleash winds of near hurricane strength. A half hour of stifling calm usually followed the wind and *Aquarius* would roll sickeningly while her sails popped and flapped in epileptic fits. Then the balmy southeast breeze would return, someone would reset the vane gear, and we'd be off again on a starboard tack along the north-northeast track that we followed until September eighteenth, when at last we gained the Thirty-sixth Parallel. There we turned and began running almost due east toward the Azores. A day later our fine weather deserted us, and we plowed through almost two days of moderately heavy winds and seas.

Noon today found us six-hundred and sixty miles east-northeast of Bermuda at latitude 36° N, longitude 52° W. We've covered about a third of the 1,788 nautical miles to Horta. Our average daily run has been about seventy-three miles, our average speed about three knots. Experience has demonstrated that a hundred miles in twenty-four hours is a very good daily run for *Aquarius.* Ninety miles pleases me very well, and yesterday's run of one hundred fifteen miles caused the captain to dance gleefully on the foredeck.

All in all, we're about on schedule for the passage of twenty-five to thirty days I predicted in Bermuda. But that prediction I thought was conservative; secretly, I'd hoped we would be much further along by now.

September 22

MATTHEW: Yesterday I talked to Mom about my birthday. It was supposed to be the twenty-fifth but I was afraid that we would have rough weather that day so I made a deal with her to have it on the next calm day. Yesterday wasn't calm so I had to wait until today to see what kind of weather we had.

I got up this morning and was glad the sea was like a mirror with small swells. Two black birds were flying around looking for fish; Dad said they were petrels. I didn't think you saw birds in the middle of the ocean. Everyone was up by then. We tried a little fishing with the casting rod and caught a good-sized dolphin fish. It was blue with yellow fins. We ate it for breakfast and it was very good. All of us wasted the morning just drifting along with no wind to sail by.

Around two o'clock Mom decided to give me a treasure hunt. She said she would give me one present today and one on my real birthday, and save the rest for surprises along the way. For two or three hours she worked on the treasure hunt. It was a long hunt with crossword puzzles and Morse messages to decode. The hardest part was the crossword puzzle. I finally got the last message which said: "Your present is at the top of the mast. There is a rope tied to it but as you can see, it is too short to let your gift down so you must splice another rope to the short one, and then you can get it down." By this time I was very anxious to get my present so I took the other rope and just tied the two together. Dad didn't like that at all because he wanted to get those ropes spliced together. What I got was a digital computer in kit form. It teaches you how a computer works and at the same time does your homework for you. I put it together and played with it for the rest of the day.

September 22

MATT: Last evening *Aquarius* was locked so deep in calm it seemed there never had been nor could be any wind to disturb her peace. The barometer was high, and we decided to join it, we were so delighted at this unexpected vacation. For the first time our tape recorder came out, and with it a small but choice stash of goodies.

Jeannine, Phil and I sat around the cockpit. The children played on the afterdeck. The tape machine emitted sounds of Bach via the Moog Synthesizer, and flute duets by Bach's progeny, Wilhelm Friedemann and Karl Philip Emanuel. Judy Collins sang and the stars appeared—unbelievably brilliant in the smogless air; we examined them through binoculars. Sirius, the Dog Star, blazed above us, a caldron of brilliant reds, blues, greens and crystal white—each color transmuting swiftly and mysteriously into another.

Then came different music: Brazilian Supernova taped at a private recording session by a friend of ours in New York, the rhythms more complex than anything I'd ever heard except perhaps Indian Raga. I found myself astride the bridge deck, letting the roll of the boat move me, balancing lightly, using the boat's motion to fashion new body rhythms in concert with the music. It was a completely new experience, a different kind of dancing with the dance floor moving, the feet never losing contact with the floor. My body began to understand in a new way how to move on a boat—lightly, easily, letting the boat's motion project the body movements, never fighting the pitch and roll. It was the difference between confidence and fear, between stoned and straight, and gradually a new relationship opened up between myself and the boat. I had never really trusted my body to the boat before. In heavy weather I used to scuttle forward, tense and crab-like, clawing at every handhold while my stiff and fearful form was thrown violently by every sudden motion of the boat. This evening I began to understand that a relaxed body will protect itself from harm with only minimal attention from the conscious mind. It was frightening at first to drop my guard, and I half expected to fall, even in the easy motion of the calm, but nothing happened. My stoned body was totally relaxed, rocking, enjoying it. The others became aware of what was happening to me, and soon four of us were moving: Matthew on the afterdeck, Phil in the cockpit, myself straddling the bridge deck, and Jeannine grounded to the cabin floor below—all swaying and oscillating ecstatically to the rhythms of *Aquarius* Rock.

September 23

MATT: This windless morning marked our eleventh day at sea. We are more at home now, and the experiments of the early days are beginning to solidify into routines and rituals—some general, like cooking, watchkeeping, navigating; others, personal and particular.

One such ritual I call the Opening of the Cans. Whenever our diet begins to seem too dreary Jeannine digs down into a secret recess and brings forth something lovely. It may be a can of peaches, a fruit cocktail, a tinned pudding, or simply pineapple juice, but her offering is always received with passionate acclaim. Food has become very important to us. Our fresh fruits and vegetables are long gone. In their place, a lusterless procession of canned succotash, green beans, instant mashed potatoes, and corned-beef hash makes daily forced marches through our galley; and the fine art of food fantasy has been raised to new heights.

The effect on impoverished palates of a covey of perfect peach halves, lying unblemished and golden in a sauce of their own sweet juices, is simply indescribable. We hover

around the magic can with unfeigned greed. Muttering im-
precations, Jeannine grasps the can opener, but something in
her manner suggests defeat before she has begun. This is our
new, expensive, stainless steel can opener, purchased in Bermuda to replace our old, cheap, rusty can opener that never
worked. After a few weeks in a salt environment this one has
became rusty too, and performs no better than its miserable
forebear. Jeannine has been patient with can openers much
too often. Her crescendo of curses fails to hasten the little
wheel on its ineffectual journey around the can top. After
several futile circuits, the apparatus is handed to me and I
manage somehow to hack the cover off. The container is now
open for our reverent inspection. There is a moment of profound silence and then the can is handed to Matthew and
Melissa for apportionment. No congressional district was
ever divided with more vigilant regard for the rights of its
constituents.

"Matthew, how many peach halves have you had?"
Melissa inquired.

"I've had three halves of peach halves; Mom and Phil
have each had two and a half halves of peach halves; and Dad
has had one complete peach half."

"Okay. I've had three halves of peach halves. That
makes thirteen half halves altogether, and there are nine
more halves of peach halves left in the can. So you and I get
one and a half halves each, Mom and Phil each get another
whole peach half and Dad gets two and a half peach halves.
Oh damn! That leaves us half a peach half short. Matthew!
What are we going to do?"

The crisis is averted, as always, by Jeannine giving up
enough of her portion to square the account. Something in
mothers gets satisfaction from sacrificing to the family weal.
I wish I could say the same. By any accounting Melissa and
I are the greediest ones—Melissa quite openly and without
shame, while I am a secret glutton. I have discovered that
while feigning indifference to the whole process, I nevertheless know at each moment exactly what the score is, and I al-

ways manage without appearing pushy to get my just desserts. Privately I cherish this absurd ritual of gastro-democracy.

Not so Phil. After a year and a half of jailhouse food served in lock-step portions, his soul cries for the free indulgence of every personal appetite. Although he has never once complained about food, I know that the restriction of our diet is one of the most difficult privations for him to bear; and not having had a part in stocking the boat, he can't appreciate that every cubic centimeter of *Aquarius* has been crammed with all the provisions she can carry. (In a post-crossing post-mortem, he voiced one of the memorable complaints of the voyage: "If canned peaches is where it's at, I don't see why you didn't strap a couple of extra cases on the cabin top.")

September 24

MATT: Doldrums! Damnable, dolorous doldrums! We've been deadlocked in doldrums for almost three days—suffocated, suspended in a wind vacuum that won't quit. At first it seemed almost miraculous in a whole ocean of rushing air to find ourselves parked in a pocket of dormancy. Jeannine reveled in her release from the motion; she became bouyant again. Phil used the respite to finish recovering from whatever it was that held him down so long. I shouldn't complain; the calm has had its blessings.

It spread its blanket over us late Monday afternoon. The wind grew light, then flukey, and I looked for a change of wind direction which usually follows this set procedure: a general quieting down to little huffs and puffs; then silence broken by sighs from every point of the compass; a few halfhearted deathbed revivals of the dying wind; more sighs and silences; an intermission of a half hour or so, followed by tentative and intermittent rustlings from a new direction; more silences, then a light but definite breeze that soon settles down into something sail-filling. But Monday the wind resigned for good, and all of us relaxed into a solid night's sleep.

Tuesday was a wonderful day. Tuesday was a lie-in-bed Sunday after ten weeks of Mondays. We logged (drifted?) exactly eight miles. I remember doing only one thing remarkable. I dropped an empty yellow gas can overboard and watched with awe as it drifted down, down, down, through the immense water sphere beneath us, growing tinier and tinier but no less distinct until finally I lost its track a thousand sea miles under. All day our watership, *Aquarius,* floated quietly on top of this chimerical crystal sphere. We also fished.

Wednesday the calm drifted into doldrums. I don't know if that's the correct meteorological term but it describes the change in the climate of our emotions. Tuesday we enjoyed the peacefulness and tranquility of our delightful calm. Wednesday we were driven batty just sitting, sitting in the solid heat. There was a growing enthusiasm for motoring, but with more than half the distance still ahead, I was reluctant to use up much of our fuel reserve.

We tried fishing once again and discovered that *Aquarius,* having become a more or less permanent fixture of the ocean around 36° N, 52° W, had collected a congregation of neighborhood fish under her bottom. Mostly they were dolphin fish, hungry but wise. Jeannine threw out a plug on our light casting rod and a dolphin struck it within seconds. But we lost the fish trying to boat him—the tackle was too light—and for the rest of the morning the wily fish ignored our every lure and snare.

By afternoon popular pressure for motoring was intense. I gave in, aroused Methuselah, and let him plug us along for about three hours. We logged thirty miles Wednesday and by nightfall were throughly fed-up, pissed-off, dragged-out, and brought-down by our predicament. All we needed was a doleful albatross perched on our pulpit to convince us we'd blundered into some supernatural void and would sit there forever. Calms are fine; doldrums are too much of a good nothing.

But at three-thirty Thursday morning Jeannine and I were roused from our bunks by a new sound and a new motion. The wind had returned! The empty mainsail we had left up to steady the rolling of the boat was filling with a steadily freshening breeze and *Aquarius* was swinging her head back and forth across the wind, sniffing it like a skittish mare. Mother-naked and laughing, we tumbled into the cockpit to raise the genny and set the boat on her way.

September 25

MATTHEW: It was a hot day, my real birthday, and we were all sweaty so we decided to stop the boat and go for a swim. Everyone jumped in except me. I waited to see if anyone got eaten. No one did, so I clipped one end of the jib halyard to the bowsprit and held the other while I stood on the pulpit, swung out over the water, and did a belly buster. I had swung like this before, but not in such rolling waves. It was much more fun to swing with the roll of the boat because I went out a lot farther. I tried it again from the stern and managed to swing all the way forward, right around the bow, and all the way back to the stern again before I dropped off. Our anchor sticks out a little at the bow of the boat and when I came within one foot of it I had to do a little twist to keep clear. This was the first time I managed to get all the way around.

I tried it again, got past the anchor and just as I let go of the rope I saw a five-foot shark. I scrambled out of the water, ignoring what my father had told me about moving slowly if there were sharks, and yelled "SHAAARK! SHARK!" As soon as Mom, who was the only one in the water, heard me she scrambled out too! Everyone told me I was seeing things until Dad said he thought he'd seen it too. Then they all shut up.

Later on, Dad wanted to take some pictures of the boat

from under water. That meant I had to go up the mast in a bosun's chair and keep a shark watch. They left me up there for an hour. I didn't see any sharks but I did see Dad under water. He looked like a waving mass of color.

Finally we raised sail and moved on. I got a cribbage board and some books for my real birthday, but the computer was the best.

September 26

JEANNINE: I enjoy baking bread; it is a calm deliberate creation. The rhythm works its way into your metabolism. You can't hurry it. Bread has its own life and its own growing to do and it makes you wait. Since it is not to be dominated, it is a companion, a free spirit. Fresh bread is the most welcomed food to come out of the galley. But making it at sea is an art that still needs refining.

I have a folding oven which sits over the burners of the stove. It does all right for brownies, but I've found that bread is easier and better baked in a pressure cooker—a circle of asbestos underneath so it doesn't burn, twenty minutes of high heat until steam starts to escape, followed by one hour of low heat. The jiggling cap is not used, so the effect is much like that of the old cast-iron Dutch oven my father used to bake cakes in over an open campfire.

My first attempts utilized honey, whole wheat flour, and wheat germ—a successful combination at home. But at sea the dough seemed heavy, never rising sufficiently. Perhaps it was the age of the flour or the fact that the rising never took place at a steady temperature like over my pilot light at home. I tried keeping the rising pot in a bath of warm water. This took constant nursing and did not seem to make any appreciable difference to the apathetic dough. I felt the need for lighter flour but I had no white flour at all. Finally in one desperate experiment I tossed in a box of corn muffin mix. The bread was delicious! A high golden New England Anadama with a wonderful flavor. We ate it with a memorable tin of Danish Camembert.

Bread making today ended less successfully: I started late in the day so by the time the dough was ready for baking everyone had settled down for the night and I found myself with the first watch. I clamped on the lid of the pressure cooker, adjusted the flame and settled down on a berth to relax. The boat was sailing herself and I needed only to pop my head out of the companionway every ten minutes to check our course and to scan the horizon for lights. I read for a while. I was just lapsing into a pleasant reverie when I heard a tremendous crash and sat up to see the entire stove, pressure cooker, and a pot of prunes (which had been enjoying a gimbaled throne on the second burner) in a jumbled heap on the floor. The skin of our last lemon which had served several purposes (the last of which was to add some faint remaining essence to the prunes) crowned the pile.

I examined the supports of the stove which allowed it to swing freely back and forth with the motion of the boat, keeping vital fluids safely undisturbed in their containers (would that I were supplied with such a mechanism) and found that the supporting pins had been neatly sliced off by the sawing action of the stove. I figured there wasn't much hope for the bread, but I put the stove back together, wedged it into a place on the counter where it wouldn't slide around, engaged the pressure cooker, and lit the fire. From the heel of the boat and the position of the pot, I estimated that if the bread had any life left to it at all, it would probably end up looking like an upside-down Frisbee with a forty-five-degree set. An hour later I opened the pot and my worst suspicions were confirmed. I understand now why sailors have such a reputation for cursing.

September 27. Four descriptions of a rough night:
MELISSA: It has been really rough since last night so we have stayed in our bunks and read and slept. I feel good when

its rough but I don't like to steer when we're sailing before the wind.

MATTHEW: We have had many squalls and we have been really thrown around. Everything is falling apart and no one wants to put it back together again. The dishes have started piling up and the foul-weather gear is thrown down on the floor because there's no good place to put wet stuff. Little odds and ends have started accumulating in corners and there are ragged rolls of toilet paper and paper towels hanging above our heads. Another Disaster Area turned out to be the storage area under our bunks in the forepeak. We found all our paper things soaked. We tried to squeeze the rolls and dry them in the sun, but a blast of spray would get them wet again. They're ugly hanging inside and it's depressing to use wet toilet paper! But that's all we have.

In rough weather like this everyone usually sleeps except the person on watch.

JEANNINE: If this is to be an honest account, then it must include all excursions of experience and mood—the highs and the lows as well as the in-betweens. Today is definitely a low; last night was nasty:

There is nothing more exciting than being called out of a cosy warm berth (where you maintain precarious homeostasis by curling up your knees and jamming yourself between the wall of the cabin and a piece of canvas stretched from bunk to ceiling, keeping a blanket over your head to dampen the knocking, banging, rattling, and roaring from without) to take a two-hour watch. Two hours! You sit up, scratch here and there a skin that feels like it belongs to someone else, and immediately your stomach starts jumping around. You pull on a stiff pair of pants, a stiff pair of socks, a slightly soggy sweater, oilskins and boots, and lumber out to the cockpit to see what good ol' Mother Nature has for you tonight.

Oh great! Three squalls in sight and the boat is running before the wind, surfing along at about six knots. (*Aquarius* takes to following seas like a neophyte hotshot skier takes to the slope—ass-end wigwagging all over the map.) It's all you can do to hang onto the tiller so you're too busy to mind the rain in your face. The boat is flying along a phosphorescent highway but you can't stop to look because your eyes are glued to the compass needle, which is playing some kind of sadistic game with you. No sooner are you able to halt its flight toward 120 degrees than it makes a wild leap backward toward 60 degrees. Your feet are braced against the opposite side of the cockpit. A cup or two of water has found its way into one of your boots. You are hunched over the tiller using all the strength of both arms to thrust and hold and pull. Two hours! Despite the annoyance, you feel a strange rebellion— a wild desire to shout taunts and insolences into the night for treating you so unfeelingly.

As the minutes drag into the second hour your stomach gets increasingly more anxious. (Eric Slone described seasickness as a "nervous breakdown of the stomach muscles.") You start to sweat. Suddenly you feel that familiar rush of saliva into the mouth and you know there's no hope. There you are again sprawled over the lifelines puking up the depths of your duodenum—like some lame boxer always on the ropes. And then back to the tiller.

You've really got to love the ocean when it's beautiful, you hate it so much when it's mean.

MATT: *Aquarius* surfed before the wind all night, making a sensational six, six-and-a-half knots. No moon—it was pitch-black except for the phosphorescence of our bow waves. We banked and turned down sea after sea, sending soft sheets of luminescent foam out on both sides, sliding down a slalom of neon meringue.

We each stood a two-hour watch, paying our dues in earnest. The helmsman would sit crouched over the compass, ready to respond when the boat veered off as she did continually, leaning his back into the tiller as she rounded off the crest of a wave in a great half-circle of foam. It was tiring but exhilarating, worth the price to be moving well again after so many days of half-calms, or so many headwinds, with the boat pounding along hard on the wind, and everything uncomfortable. I said to Phil tonight, "I've been hard on the wind so long, I can't get it up any longer."

This morning the wind shifted back to the northeast and *Aquarius* started her rocking-horse rhythm once again. Like every morning after a hard evening there was nothing happening aboard. One person on deck, everyone else in the sack. About nine Phil called down and informed me in his casual way that a ship was bearing directly down on us. I rushed on deck, and sure enough, a medium-sized freighter was making almost straight for us. Through glasses, which jumped around in my hands, her name looked like *Baalbek* (could she be Lebanese?) but suddenly I realized the characters were Russian and simultaneously Phil spotted the hammer and sickle on her stack. There was no question about her nationality or her destination. She was Russian and on this course she had to be headed for Cuba. The cold war, international geopolitik, all those complexities I'd almost forgotten about came back to send a chill down my spine.

We waved to her in a friendly fashion but there were no answering waves though she passed within a few hundred feet of us with most of the crew on deck. We tried calling her on the radio but still no answer, and in a very short time she was hull down on the horizon as we stood watching—feeling very strange to be passed that closely without a word of greeting.

September 28

MATT: Every twenty-four hours I transfer our daily
position from my plotting sheet to a sailing chart so I can
watch the little X's march purposefully from St. George to
Horta. Lately their stride has lengthened. After dawdling
disgracefully in the doldrums, we began moving on the 24th
—really moving through the wild night of the 26th—then
turned to a more northerly track as the wind backed to
east-southeast. I decided to follow the path dictated by the
wind. On the 26th we were still one hundred forty-five miles
south of latitude 38° 32′ North, the parallel of Horta, and
could well afford a northerly diversion from our route. By
yesterday the wind had developed a nasty edge and we were
pounding east-northeast at almost five knots, and paying
greatly in personal comfort for our good speed through the
water. We made one hundred fifteen miles and earned every
inch of it.

Today the wind was even stronger. I eased off the sheets
this morning to take full advantage of it and give *Aquarius*
a more comfortable course. All day we boiled along, our
speed varying between five and six knots. By late afternoon
as we prepared for evening star sights, I began to feel a stir
of excitement—today might be a record run, and we badly
needed some kind of record as an antidote to mid-voyage
depression. Our slow progress over the preceding weeks had
begun to wear on us. I could sense it in the complaints about
food, in Phil's silence, in the way Melissa resisted taking
watches, in the piles of salt-soggy clothing collecting on the
cabin floor. The captain needed a victory, however modest,
to keep the hands from growing restless, and so he proposed
a small wager: extra rations of pudding to the person who
came closest to guessing the number of miles to Horta. If this
were a windjammer the prize certainly would be duff pudding with currants, but in tune with our modern steel auxiliary, we settled for Campbell's Bounty Pudding—from a can.
Charts were consulted, the wagers sealed, and we turned to
the stars for an answer.

Star sights are the only celestial observations of the day that by themselves yield a definite position. Consequently, I usually compute our daily runs from star sight to star sight, and no subject, even food, is attended with greater interest. For purposes of navigation, twilight is a very brief period. It extends from the moment when the brightest star makes its first faint appearance in the sky until that less tangible instant when gathering darkness obscures the line of the horizon. Since accurate sextant work requires both star and horizon to be visible at once, the limits of twilight are inflexible—a period of slightly less than half an hour. I've learned to prepare carefully for it.

About four this afternoon I thumbed through the *Nautical Almanac* to the tables for September 28. Under "Rising and Setting Phenomena," I found the period of useful twilight and worked out the "local hour angle" of the star Aries for approximately mid-twilight. The local hour angle of Aries is a reference position for locating all the other stars; it is also the key that unlocks a crafty little volume called *Sight Reduction Tables for Air Navigation*. These tables tell me more surely than could my friendly neighborhood astrologer the seven stars most propitious for celestial naviagtion on any given evening. I copied the compass bearing and elevation of each star into my navigation workbook; preliminaries were complete.

The focus of preparation now shifted to Matthew, cook for the evening; he had to have the meal finished and cleared away before twilight. Nothing goads the navigator to foam and cuss more profusely than putting his foot in a plate of half-eaten spaghetti while stumbling around the cockpit in search of an elusive star. Supper was prepared and devoured: canned peas and corned-beef hash with brown rice from yesterday's lunch. By the time we had ravaged a commendable salad of artichoke hearts, the sun had departed and the sky in our wake was a fading cerise. Dishes were cleared and stacked in the galley. No time for dessert; we would enjoy that later. The hour was upon us.

I took my sextant from its box and checked the light that illuminates the arc and micrometer drum. Jeannine lit the kerosene cabin lamp and propped herself beneath it, the paraphernalia for recording sights—logbook and pencil, chronometer and stopwatch—gathered in her lap. Our preparations proceeded with the smoothness of long-established ritual, but it has not always been so. In the beginning I tried doing it all myself: locating the stars, shooting the sights, recording the time and elevation. What a mess! The cockpit was strewn with starfinders, flashlights, logbooks, stopwatches, and navigation tables. I could never find what I wanted and the pressure of trying to finish within the rapidly dwindling minutes of twilight generated a kind of astro-hysteria, which had a disastrous affect on accuracy. After an hour of futile calculations I would usually emerge with the gloomy announcement of conflicting results.

Tonight we are organized. I snap on the compass light and climb into the cockpit. The wind has dropped a little with sundown but *Aquarius* is still moving well and rolling enough to make holding a star in the sextant's mirrors a bit difficult. The stars of the celestial extravaganza tonight will be six Arabs and a Greek: Alpheratz, Enif, Altair, Rasalhague, Alkaid, Kochab, and the lovely Arcturus. Who are they? *Where* are they?

The sky is a bland bright blue with only a single twinkle low on the horizon just off our stern. I'm not fooled by my old planetary friend, Venus; she's been upstaging stars from that position for most of the crossing. Arcturus is the bright one. "Where's Arcturus?" I shout to Jeannine. She consults the figures I've jotted down in the logbook. "Elevation twenty-five degrees, twenty-two minutes. Bearing about three hundred degrees." I set my sextant to the elevation and pan the instrument across the horizon where the compass tells me Arcturus should be. A point of light I could never see unaided appears mirrored in the eyepiece, apparently floating in the sea near the horizon.

"Arcturus, baby! There you are." A quick adjustment of

the micrometer and the star rises to the horizon. "Found it, Jeannine. Are you ready? *Mark!*" At the call, she tags the stopwatch and I pause in the cockpit to read off the elevation registered at that instant on the arc of the sextant. I do this carefully, methodically; and I do it twice. Experience has shown there's vast scope for error here. "Twenty-seven degrees, twenty-three point five minutes—" Jeannine writes down the elevation, 27° 23.5′. She has already worked out the exact Greenwich time of the observation from the chronometer and stopwatch. Now she sets the watch going for the next observation. I can see her through the companionway, blonde head framed in the soft glow of the oil lamp as she notes the new time in the logbook. I am glowing, too. It's a kind of love duet we carry on, singing star azimuths and elevations to each other (not exactly "O soave fanciulla" from *La Bohème* but certainly more passionate than computer language). I enjoy the technical cohesion of our star sight teamworkmanship. It makes the other cohesions better, too. If work and love are the most rewarding expressions of human energy, as Wilhelm Reich suggests, then the greatest reward is to find them both in the same person! Happiness is fondling your favorite navigator.

Meanwhile, four or five new stars have become visible. Since the Air Navigation Tables make use of the brightest stars, there is a good chance anything I can see must be among the elected seven. I pick the brightest, high in the sky almost on the starboard beam and sight over the cockpit compass for an approximate bearing. "What do you have that's high and bearing about one hundred ninety-five degrees?" I ask Jeannine.

"What about Altair—one hundred eighty-three degrees bearing with an elevation of fifty-nine degrees three minutes?" I set the sextant to this altitude and swing it in the direction of the star. Almost immediately it pops into the scope, riding just above the horizon—Altair for sure. But I lose it—boat jumping around too much—and try as I will I can't bring it back again. *Altair, my Flying Eagle, fly back to me. Can't waste time with this goddamn star. Twilight flying, too. Try another method.* I set the index arm of the sextant to zero and point the scope upward directly at Altair. When I have it—a double image of the star, the two points almost superimposed, one in the scope, the other caught in the mirror—I drop the instrument smoothly toward the horizon swinging the index arm forward at the same time so the mirrored image of the star remains in the eyepiece. After a couple of tries I am able to force a marriage of star and horizon. "Got you, you mother! Mark!"

The other stars go reasonably well, although I have some trouble with Kochab way out on the rim of the Little Dipper —too many similar stars too close together for positive identification. As I tick off the sights I think how much I like the names these Arabs bear, names tugging me back into an earlier age when magic and science lived amicably together. I found their names translated in Bowditch. Alkaid: leader of the daughters of the bier. And Rasalhague (how I murdered his name until I looked it up!). In Arabic, *ras* means "head." RAHS-al-HAIG-wee: head of the serpent charmer. By now it's nearly dark. I never do find Alpheratz, the horse's navel. I have to struggle so long to find a horizon for Enif, the nose of the horse, that I feel like the other end of Pegasus's anatomy. But I do have positive sights for six out of the seven stars. Not a bad twilight's work.

Plotting the sights was almost an anticlimax. I settled myself under the cabin lamp with the paraphernalia of navigation spread on the cushion beside me. Unfortunately, *Aquarius* is much too small for the luxury of a chart table, but I have learned to work sights on the surface of a stiff notebook propped in my lap. In such a confined space, a protractor is better than parallel rules and just as easy to use.

The pencil work was easy. The Air Navigation Tables reduce calculations to a couple of minutes' work per sight. The actual positions were worked out on the plotting sheet, a large blank chart laid out with compass rose and distance scale. Plotting sheets are the scratch paper of modern navigation.

This evening I was very pleased. My lines of position intersected as if by prearrangement. Only intransigent Kochab stood off about eight miles from the common hub formed by the other intersecting lines. I banished him with my eraser. Probably what I sighted wasn't Kochab at all. After the uncertain navigation of the last two days this precise fix brought a sense of relief—the smugness of a thrifty housewife with all her linen in order. (It's comforting to know where in the ocean you are.) Best of all I could compute the results of the Stupendous Aquarian Mid-Atlantic-Bermuda-to-Horta Sweepstakes. My dividers giant-stepped across the plotting sheet to the mark at last night's probable position: one hundred twenty-one miles for the previous twenty-six hours' run, and one hundred twenty-five miles covered in the twenty-four hours before that—two hundred forty-six miles in two days! *Aquarius* had never done better. Jeannine exclaimed. Melissa smiled. Phil looked happier. We examined the bets. My optimistic estimate had been six hundred miles to Horta. Jeannine had guessed six hundred eighty and Phil, seven hundred forty-three. Matthew and Melissa had chosen six hundred forty and six hundred fifty respectively. Another chart was withdrawn from under the cushions of the starboard bunk, the Great Circle Sailing Chart of the North Atlantic Ocean. On this chart, the continental land masses are weirdly pushed out of shape, but a straight line drawn anywhere represents a Great Circle sailing route, the shortest distance between two points. I measured and computed: six hundred ninety miles to Horta. Jeannine, the winner, was just ten miles off the mark. The pudding was hers, and the navigator retired, brooding, to his bunk. Where did he go wrong? Ninety miles error in his estimate—a full day's sailing. Let's see, ninety miles divided by the distance already run (1,100 miles) gives an overestimate of about eight percent. Well, Columbus overestimated his daily runs by a consistent nine percent, and he didn't do so badly. Statistics are rarely so comforting!

September 30

MATT: I wish I could understand what's happened to Phil. This afternoon I tried to show him how to balance the boat—a matter of drawing in or letting out on the sails, or changing their size so the boat will sail herself easily at a given angle to the wind without undue pressure on the helm. It's a subject of some importance, since the vane gear won't function smoothly without help from the boat. I got about three sentences into it when it became clear that Phil just wasn't interested. He's reacted the same to all my attempts to teach seamanship, whether it's navigating, tying knots, or changing the jib. I think he's given up on the boat, and I can't seem to get through to him. It's not the sickness that is holding him down now—he appears fully recovered—but the depression that accompanied it never went away, and his interest in sailing never revived. Consequently Phil has remained so unskilled that I don't dare call on him in a real emergency. He stands his watches willingly enough, and helps out whenever he's asked, but that's about as far as it goes.

This evening, Jeannine's feelings boiled over. She had worked hard over supper, trying to produce something different out of our limited repertoire of cans, and had done reasonably well. She scooped the results onto a plate and handed it to Phil, who retired to a corner of the cabin with an acknowledging grunt. Jeannine was hurt:

"Phil! Can't you *say* anything? What's the matter? Are you angry with us? Are you disappointed with the voyage? I can't even make *contact* with you anymore. When we left Bermuda I hoped we would all grow to be a real family—lots of talk—lots of give-and-take. But none of that's happened. I can't even get a *word* out of you!"

Very quietly Phil replied that the only other times he

could remember having felt so sick, he'd always been in the hospital. Jeannine withdrew. No one knew better how thoroughly sickness could drain personal energy.

Phil has not complained and we have been relatively unaware of the extent of his discomfort lately. If he were not so reserved maybe we could understand each other better. As it is, the communication seems difficult. I hope we can re-establish his good spirits; it would be better for the morale of the whole crew.

13

Pico's Pike
or Bust

October 1

JEANNINE: The barometer has been incredibly high, lifting our spirits and producing an intoxicating optimism. Yesterday we stretched in the sun, hung our clothes out to dry, and congratulated ourselves for a turn of good luck. Captain and First Mate laughed and played and banished everyone from the foredeck for some privacy under the bright sky.

But we celebrated too soon. In the afternoon the wind began to build and the waves got decidedly higher, although the sky remained clear and blue. We told ourselves it was just a windy day, tomorrow would be fine again, but night brought steady intensification.

By morning the barometer had dropped from 30.6 to 30.0 inches and we estimated the wind at force six. We had progressed only seventy miles in the last twenty-four hours. *Aquarius* was struggling now under single-reefed main and working jib, but we were reluctant to reef further because the Azores seemed so close we wanted to make as many miles as we could. The cloudless sky belied our notion of storm. Almost imperceptibly the wind hefted itself on to force seven, and the barometer, as depressed as we were, dropped to a new low at 29.7. We had never seen it that low. What was it telling us?

Around lunchtime we realized we were fooling ourselves; the weather wasn't going to go away. In spite of the beguiling sky, we were already into something very bad indeed. Lunch was a hurried, worried sandwich affair. Feeling decidedly green, Phil and I took to our bunks, but within minutes Matt was calling me out to help.

I struggled into foul-weather gear and weaved out to the cockpit, where my stomach promptly rejected its sandwich. I have learned that it is more efficient to lose a meal gracefully than to fight it down, willfully attempting to control a belligerant autonomic nervous system with the under-developed powers of my cortex. (Someday yoga and I will conquer the sea, but this was not the day.)

I looked around, amazed. The elements were engaged in some power trip, an anarchic display. In the tight dry cabin under a warm blanket I had successfully insulated myself from the physical and psychological assaults of the tempest. Out here noise and spray quarreled around me; the waves had grown to an aggressive maturity. I had left my shelter; I was exposed. Oh, Lord what waves! No longer boyish, live-and let-live spirits, they now communicated immediate, unmistakable authority.

"We've got to go to a full storm reef," Matt shouted as he turned over the tiller to me. "I've really waited too long, but I'm not sure it's a good idea to head her into the wind for reefing against these waves. We've never had waves like this! What do you think?"

"Well, we reefed while powering downwind once and it worked pretty well," I answered. "We won't have as much wind velocity if we're moving with it rather than against it."

"I don't know. Do you think you can keep the boat in better control if we're not fighting the waves?"

We surged upward as a big one rolled under us. "Yeah! I do! It's going to be tricky enough for you to keep your balance up there on the cabin top while you're tying the knots!"

"Okay. Let's try it!"

Anxiety and inexperience helped us make that decision. They were not reliable counselors. With the mainsail tightened down amidships there wasn't much pressure on it and our run downwind felt right, but as soon as Matt loosened the main halyard to reef, the wind caught the slack leech and tried to wrap the sail around the mast. Before we could blink, the head of the sail had whipped into the upper shrouds and was torn almost completely off at a point about two feet from the top.

"Son-of-a-bitch!" Matt clawed the flapping sail down to the boom. I eased the boat off the wind, then began to run downwind, fumbling with the engine controls as I considered our mishap. It was serious but not a calamity. Methuselah responded and the tiller became enervated once again. No question what to do next. The mainsail was our stability and our salvation, it must be repaired. We needed all our options in this weather.

"Hand up my ditty-bag!" Matt shouted into the crack between the hatch cover and the closed companionway door.

For three hours he sat on the cabin top braced against the boom, his safety harness snapped to a life line, and stitched, racing the increasing winds and oncoming darkness while I ran the boat westward under power, toward home and the setting sun, eating up the wrong-way miles—the hard-won, wrong-way, turn-around miles. Moving mountains heaved under us as I tried to keep her steady so Matt would not be thrown off. In the valleys we could see nothing but snow-capped walls around us rising to twenty feet or more. When we gained the heights we looked down across the ranges where the snow boiled off into spindrift and melted into the air. It was awesome! We bobbed, a blue seagull, over the rollers. As long as I could keep from catching a wave sideways, *Aquarius* simply lifted up one side and skied down the other.

In the midst of all this turmoil a strange agitation near the boat caught my eye. It was an immense sea turtle thrashing awkwardly at the surface as if he had suddenly forgotten how to swim.

"Hey! Matthew! Melissa! Come see a turtle!" The hatch slid back and two yellow-crested slickerheads cautiously emerged from the safety of their nest below.

"Wow! He's huge! What's he doing way out here?" Matthew shouted above the wind.

"Why is he struggling so hard at the surface when he could be down below where it's peaceful?" Melissa asked. "JESUS CHRIST! Look at the WAVES!"

"Watch out!" I shouted. "Here comes a big one!" The children ducked inside and slid the hatch closed just as a wave slammed across the bulwarks and doused us with spray. Matt stopped sewing and wrapped himself tighter around the boom while *Aquarius* lurched sickeningly up on the verge of the wave, leaping like a jet toward the distant sun. For a split second she hung suspended as the wave moved out from under her, then she dived heavily downward, crashing with seven-ton impetus toward the bottom of a valley which kept dropping out below us. The impact rattled our teeth and sent up a fabulous spray, but we weren't dislodged. *Aquarius* calmly righted herself as if to apologize for trying to fly. The turtle had disappeared.

Matt threw me a look of concern and thanks. Our eyes met with a jolt of recognition. Here we were at the "decisive moment." This was what it was like to be in a gale at sea! It was a moment which, in our virginity, we had approached with considerable apprehension. But now that it had arrived, it was not fear we felt but an intense concentration of emotions—joy, awe, exhilaration, humility—a justification of all moments. We knew the ocean now, more intimately. We had unclothed and touched secret aspects. What the future held for this relationship was not important; we had lost our innocence and we were not afraid. That was enough.

How I loved this crazy man in front of me, quietly repairing his sail as if he were in his front living room instead of in the middle of an absurd ocean. And how complex a love —changing continuously from admiration and friendship to gratitude, from sentiment to sensuality and ecstasy. For all its variations, there is a simplicity, an essence. We are caught up together in a primitive engagement with life—a struggle to be alive. And more, to FEEL alive! We meet the waves together. We are mates.

We finished the sewing and tied the last points of the storm reef just before dark. Out came the new storm jib, never before used. We were going to try heaving-to—a maneuver we had only read about in books. The jib had to be backed on the port side but there was no block in a good position to receive the sheet. No time to rearrange things now; Matt threaded the sheet through an eyelet on deck and ran it back to the cockpit. Warily I switched off the engine and lashed the tiller to starboard. *Aquarius* lay just off the wind, controlled and steady at last.

As we clambered below, Matthew greeted us with hot mushroom soup. What a gift! When I am ninety I will still remember the taste and the creaminess and heat of it.

"Well," I said with a wry smile as I sipped the welcome soup, "Billy was worried that we didn't have enough respect for the sea! I guess I understand now what he meant."

Phil grinned, "Okay, so now we have respect for the sea —maybe even fear of God!"

We were aware of the new motion. The boat was rocking quietly, without strain despite the force-eight commotion outside. So this was what "heaving-to" was all about! *Aquarius* had relaxed and so could we. From our separate bunks Matt and I reached out and squeezed hands, wearily, satisfyingly, and then we slept.

October 2

MATT: I have new regard for the sea-keeping qualities of sailing vessels after last night. By the time we finished repairing the main, tying in a storm reef, and fighting the jib to a decision on the foredeck, the world around us had begun to look like a Winslow Homer version of *Walpurgisnacht*. I'd never been at sea in weather like this and from what I knew of her past history, I was sure *Aquarius* had never ridden out a full gale either. But I was conscious as I went about preparing the boat for heaving-to that I was working from the pages of many half-remembered books; I was working from instinct, too. If I didn't know gales, I at least knew this boat and her ways. I could sense when she was riding easily, or when laboring under too much pressure, and I felt confident she would tell me of any false moves.

When we brought *Aquarius* off the wind under her new rig and she steadied down immediately, heeling moderately, lying in the folds of the waves like a duck, I knew the wind would have to rise to whole new dimensions of fury before we began to suffer any real damage. It was a victory, a successful initiation, a world of doubt and apprehension lifted from my shoulders. But when I thought about it, it didn't seem strange that *Aquarius* and ourselves, all neophytes to this weather, should have managed so well. We were all recipients of a tradition of seamanship and naval architecture based on hundreds of years of experience. *Aquarius* came by her sea-kindly ways naturally—they were built into her hull and rig. We picked up our skills from books, from the word of friends, and by doing, but the techniques have been tested and refined through long usage—on the decks of Portuguese caravels, square-rigged clipper ships, and modern racing yachts. Properly applied, they work even for neophytes. But we're freshmen no longer. We've taken our midterm exam and passed it well. I know there will be other tests along the route, but after last night I retain a certain confidence; nevertheless, I hope we never have to face a Final.

We took shelter below. Closing the hatch cover was almost like switching off the storm. It was so quiet and snug in the cabin, the motion so easy compared to the tumult above, that I stuck my head outside again to be sure there hadn't been a sudden lull in the storm. I went out once more to tie down the self-steering gear, which was trying to bang its head off against the after-pulpit, and then we turned in— Jeannine to fall immediately into the sleep of the righteous dead. I stretched out in my oilskins, sea boots, and safety harness, prepared to go on deck in a moment if an emergency developed. I intended to make hourly inspections of the rig and sails through the night; but somehow my wristwatch raced during those brief moments when my eyes were closed, and I averaged no better than a look around every two hours or so. We'd seen a ship at dusk, a big freighter taking heavy seas at her bow, and we discussed maintaining a watch all night, but we were bone-weary. For once we trusted to luck and the brightness of our running lights.

In the morning shortly before dawn I sensed a slight easing of the wind. By the time there was light enough to turn off the compass light, the gale was blowing itself out. At 0930 I tried for a sun fix. I was prepared to find that we'd given up fifty miles or more to the gale, but the morning sun line showed us anywhere from eighty-five to one hundred twenty miles west and south of our noon position yesterday. It didn't seem possible to lose so much, but I checked the sight for errors and we spent a gloomy morning wondering how long it would take to make up the lost miles.

The gale dissipated rapidly. By late afternoon a balmy southern breeze had replaced the ill wind from the east, and we were heading toward Horta again, broadreaching and making good speed in spite of the heavy swell. A survey of the boat turned up no damage from the gale save the split seam in the main. I resolved to have the whole sail restitched when we arrived in the Azores.

October 3

JEANNINE: This morning I got up for my watch (0600) and found that Phil had left the boat sailing by the vane on a course of 90 degrees instead of 120. This meant that the wind had probably shifted and I would have to readjust the direction of the vane, the lines on the tiller and the position of the sails. Ordinarily I would have been a little uptight about this operation, reluctant to test again my inept seamanship, but reflecting my attempts against Phil's apathy I was able to muster a certain confidence. Besides, the morning was full of energy and potential. Anything was possible.

I sat for a moment in the companionway quietly exercising the synapses between my senses and a sleepy brain, appreciating the steady breeze and moderate waves. The motion of the boat was pleasant and my body relaxed. The "absence of sickness" may seem like a less glorious condition than "state of well-being" but to cease being seasick is, in relative terms, to enter a state of rapture and peace. "Wellbeing" is hardly adequate. The sun was pressing for recognition on the horizon. Blocked by low banks of dark clouds, it insistently probed, seeking any promise of access to the sea.

I steered back on course and started with the sails. We had fallen off the wind so I tightened in on the jib and the main. *Aquarius* responded immediately. She seemed pleased to hasten her pace. I sat back to wait for signs of luffing in the main, glancing again at the horizon. Where the clouds were poorly organized, the sun had concentrated its forces, breaking through here and there with great golden shafts. Above my head wisps of herringbone pink floated, turned to gold, and dissolved. The sun flaunted its splendor even behind its prison, threatening a display of superior power and ultimate victory. Its influence was irrepressible.

The main needed tightening just a hair. Then the jib correspondingly. It was just right. The compass steadied, the tiller grew easy in my hand. I moved, she moved. Hello, *Aquarius!* Reciprocity is such an important element of friendship. I fastened the steering lines to the tiller and turned to the problem of adjusting the direction of the wind vane.

The leading edge of the vane must be set into the apparent wind but sometimes it takes several tries to make it work perfectly. I estimated well the first time and did not have to return to the vane at all. I fiddled with the tiller lines until the boat was sailing herself, deviating only 10 degrees from course. I paused for a while to see whether she would come up or fall off any more. The dark cloud banks ahead had steadfastly maintained their position but their growing impotence was revealed by a brilliant white fluting which outlined the soft curves of their upper limits.

One more tiny adjustment to the windward line—just a centimeter. Some change caused me to look up. The sun had arrived. Blazing over the defeated clouds it proclaimed dominion over its sky kingdom in an ancient and undisputed territorial imperative, without a sound. My eyes were attracted by the light in my hair falling loose down the side of my face. A sudden feeling of warmth and affection came over me. I touched my hair. It was beautiful. I was beautiful.

The compass needle hovered decisively over 120 degrees. *Aquarius* was sailing perfectly and I was wonderfully pleased. I went below to make myself some coffee.

October 4

MATT: Where have the stars been all my life? Where have they been all the days I've lived in cities? Masked by street lights, neon signs, plaster ceilings and indifference. Well, what good were the stars? I never needed them and I guess they didn't need me; I hardly knew they were there. I found my way through the urban grids by maps and street signs. If I got lost I could always ask a policeman. Sometime early in life, my mother pointed out the North Star and the Big Dipper. She showed me how the two stars on the lip of the Dipper always point to the Pole. I was proud that I could always find North; it might come in handy. Sometime later, I guess probably in Boy Scouts, I learned to recognize Orion, Cassiopeia and, temporarily, a few others. I remember wondering why they all had unpronounceable Greek names, but I never wondered much beyond that. There were too many things to do.

Now there is not so much to do. The city is gone and I sit night after night in an open cockpit under a blazing canopy I hardly knew existed. I never saw these burning demons above the street lights. Edison has stolen the stars from all our cities. But now under the stars I have time to dream, time for aloneness with sleeping children around me, time for aloneness that is precious where five of us are together too much. This evening, dreaming, I talked to the sky:

Hello, Sister Moon and Sister Venus! You are my friends. We have traveled together and every evening I have watched for you to appear at your appointed places in the sky.

Sister Venus, you come early and faithfully to the skies and your light is radiant. You remind me that darkness follows closely, and that I must prepare my boat for the night. You direct my sextant to those Arabian cousins of yours who travel the same pathways each evening, who tell me where in all this measured expanse of ocean I happen to be. Hello, trustworthy Arabians! Syed Dubki, sheik of the northern sky, pointing always to Polaris. Aldebaran, the faithful follower, eye of the bull they call Taurus, guardian of the seven sisters of the Pleiades. Hello, Alkaid, Menkar, Altair, Hamal, Kochab, Mirfak, Betelgeuse, Fomalhout, Nunki—I found you first in the pages of my *Nautical Almanac,* puzzled at your strange names and wondered how in the universe I would ever be able to find you.

But gradually you became my familiar friends. I drew your altitudes on charts and watched your lines cross at unknown intersections of waves. I came to trust you, even to believe you would occupy the same places in the sky night after night. And I have come to rely on you to guide my little boat into a safe harbor. I understand the feeling men have had for you since they first became sailors—Phoenicians, Polynesians, Norsemen and Norman fishermen—those men who sat in open boats night after night and gazed at your ordered canopy, thinking of rocky coastlines ahead or small atolls lost in the Pacific.

Sister Moon and Sister Venus swimming in silver above me, I understand now why men worshiped your luminosity, named you with the names of gods, traced the outlines of favorite deities among your clustered beacons. Those ancient men were neither more credulous nor more ignorant than us, they simply had more space in them for awe and wonder, more minutes in their lives for looking, more time to marvel at the sky.

Times changed and we masked the sky with electricity; bound our minds with hurry. But you never changed. All our radiotelescopic probing of quasars and black holes and red giants could never dim you. Forgive my ignorance, Silver Sisters. I never saw you before.

October 5

JEANNINE: We are close to the Azores now, tantalizingly close, and the weather has been difficult and erratic. The wind fights our progress and we are resentful. Matt has pushed himself hard and when he finally sleeps it is with commitment.

Last night during my watch the wind shifted to the east, making it impossible to maintain our course; we were going due south instead of east. I felt it would be better to come about, but decided to check with Matt. I shook him gently and stated the problem.

"What do you want me to do?" I asked.

He mumbled sleepily, "Haul in on the stopwatch."

"The stopwatch?"

"Oh hell, you know what I mean. The *yellow* stopwatch!"

I repeated the problem. "We're going due south!"

"Don't worry," he muttered, "it's due to bottom error."

"Bottom error! What's bottom error?"

He pulled the covers over his head. "Oh, it's too complicated to explain now." In the dark Melissa giggled. I went back to my watch and changed tack.

This morning he vigorously denies saying any such thing, but Melissa is my witness.

October 6

MATT: The elements are conspiring to keep us from ever reaching the Azores. I expected kindness after the October 1st gale and the preceding days of wearing headwinds. And for two golden days we did enjoy glorious southerly winds. We were able to haul our wet everythings out on deck and sun them down to an acceptable Aquarius Dry. The steady breeze blew warm and *Aquarius* seemed to lope along, broadreaching easily, eating up the miles to the Azores—one hundred ten each day. These were the easiest sailing days of the voyage and I lulled myself into believing they must be our reward for enduring the rigors of the gale and the frustrations of contrary winds. I even speculated that the southerlies might hold all the way to Horta's harbor entrance. I should have known better.

Yesterday morning about five, our friendly southern zephyrs backed to the east and intensified with a cold bite whose message was abundantly clear: *Beware, little butterflies, the breezes of summer are gone and bad-assed autumn is here to hassle your mind and shrivel your golden wings.* Under zinc skies we battened down and beat wearily into the wind—port tack until ten, then haul around and starboard for the rest of the goddamn day. From 0515, the hour of my morning star fix, until 1830 when evening stars gave me another fixed position, we covered forty miles—forty leaden miles in thirteen grueling hours! I thought of the English explorer Humphrey Gilbert, in his journal of a voyage to Nova Scotia in 1583, who complained of "Winde so scant that our traverse was great." It didn't help to know that headwinds are nothing new.

Today it was worse. By eight P.M., almost twenty-six hours since the last position fix, we had advanced a mere forty-seven miles! The Azores are reputably close, no more than one hundred twenty miles by my reckoning, but so long as the east wind prevails they may as well be in the Indian Ocean. I can't even think about those elusive islands. My life has narrowed down to two realities: the outside world—gray sky, choppy sea, unforgiving wind and empty horizon (empty so long now it seems there is no terra anywhere ahead of us); and the more theoretical world of navigation represented by my grubby plotting sheets. On these I record the paltry victories of our eastward struggle: 0600 dead-reckoning position; about face and slog northeastward to a 1300 rendezvous with the sun; establish a position, come about and tack wearily southeast again. There is a heavy red line drawn horizontally across the plotting sheet at latitude 38° 35' North. It represents our theoretical course to a landfall on the westernmost point of the island of Fayal, a course which lies directly in the teeth of the wind. (Our actual track meanders north and south of this line like the spoor of a drunken ant.) Forty-seven miles to the north of the red line I've drawn a vague lumpy circle. According to Bowditch, which gives maritime positions for all the principal landfalls of the world, this lump should represent the beacon at Ponta Lagens, the southernmost tip of the island of Flores, itself the westernmost island of the Azores group—but I no longer believe even Bowditch. The evidence of my eyes scouring empty seas for twenty-four days is too overwhelming to credit a dubious circle drawn in a blank corner of my plotting sheet. Flores is said by believers to lie one hundred twenty-five miles west-northwest of the main islands of the Azores Archipelago. What nonesense! Even those first Portuguese colonists of Henry the Navigator doubted its existence so strongly it was not reported until 1452, some twenty years after the other islands had been solidly inhabited.

Nevertheless, *something* did appear out there across the gray water at about eight this evening. It was already quite

MATT

MELISSA

JEANNINE

MATTHEW

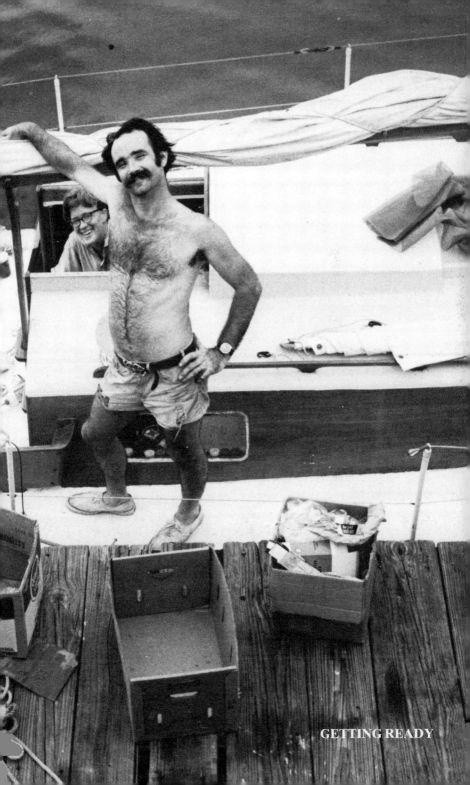

GETTING READY

DEPARTURE

BREAD

FISH

MID-OCEAN

LANDFALL

dark when I sensed a flicker off to the north, jabbing at the neurons in the periphery of my vision. For about half an hour my mind scoffed at the intermittent signals—it was a star, a passing ship—it was nothing. But the spectral suggestion of illumination strengthened persistently until I could sense the regular loom of a light arcing across the horizon. Electrifying arc! Could this faint bloom in the middle of cold nowhere be Flores? It was spooky and unsettling, this breath of solidity coming so dimly out of the cocoon-like darkness—a call from another planet, a cold hand lying on my heart. We were sailing almost toward it on starboard tack, and I wanted urgently to turn away. Although the light was still well below the horizon, perhaps thirty or forty miles off, I felt an irrational fear of closing with it. Familiar nothing seemed safer than a cold *something* on a dark night.

Anyway, Flores was not our destination and it would do no good to tack farther north of our course line. I put the boat about and turned resolutely away. Before midnight the arcing loom had faded below the horizon.

October 7

JEANNINE: Tonight we have been reading about the Azores in a marvelous fat blue book entitled *Sailing Directions for the West Coasts of Spain, Portugal, and Northwest Africa and Off-Lying Islands.* We tease ourselves with the descriptions of temperate climate, pleasant landscape, good harbor; the cultivation of fresh fruits, vegetables and flowers. We are sailing to Elysium!

> The climate of the Azores is particularly temperate and equable, the extremities of sensible heat and cold being, however, increased by the humidity of the atmosphere. . . . Viewed from a distance the islands do not present an attractive appearance, but on a close approach are found to be covered with vineyards, fields of grain, and groves of fruit trees. . . . The soil in such parts of the islands as are susceptible of cultivation is

very fertile, and fruits and plants of all kinds and from all countries can be successfully cultivated.

A Portugese janitor at the St. George Dinghy Club in Bermuda had told us it was grape-harvest time in the Azores. Grapes! I've almost forgotten what they taste like.

The volcano of Pico (pronounced PEE-ko), the island adjacent to Fayal, is over seven thousand feet high. We fantasize about sighting it on the horizon but we can't really imagine what it will look like—a small bump gradually growing higher and higher until it is seven thousand feet high? Who will be the first to see it? We adopt a new motto: "Pico's Pike or Bust!"

The tempo of Matt's navigation has picked up considerably. Where he once was content with three sights a day, he now seems to pop out of the cabin with his sextant almost every hour. This first landfall across the Atlantic is very important to him and he wants it to be perfect. Star sights at evening twilight have become more frequent in the last week but now he fixes the stars at dawn as well and this evening I even noticed him shooting the moon. Is it lunar madness or sick of seaness?

From the depths of our blankets and sleeping gear we dig out a bottle of champagne given us at our departure by friends who admonished that it was not to be opened until we sighted the Azores. We are ready.

October 8

JEANNINE: The transformation from dark to dawn took place during my watch. I sat in my favorite place in the companionway impatiently waiting for the sun. By my calculations we were within thirty miles of Fayal. According to the Sailing Directions, Pico should be visible on clear days for about seventy miles. The stars gave no sign of fading.

I remembered back to another night I had tried to hurry. I had just given birth to Matthew. I was as high on pure joy as I had ever been. Stoned by a remarkable physical experince and the sight of my own squalling fat baby at last. But after a few short moments with him and a brief hug from Matt I was whisked down the hall on my expressbed and Matthew was taken firmly and efficiently from my arms. "Poor 'mother' must be exhausted. Get a good sleep now, dear." Strange room. Whispering and movement in the hall, little bells ringing, pain between my legs. What did he look like? His hair was dark auburn. What color were his eyes? Did he look like Matt? Why did they take him away? I wanted to see all of him, examine each toe, smell him, nurse him, kiss him. I had waited nine months and two weeks for him. It was absurd to expect me to sleep. The night seemed endless.

My thoughts wandered and I leaned against the cabin and dozed a bit. When I opened my eyes again it was with disappointment. The sky was lighter now but the horizon was fairly well hidden on all sides by clouds and squalls; those directly ahead were dropping rain in intermittent gray patches. There were no sunny islands to greet me.

Occasionally the rain would clear. I noticed a long thin gray line stretching diagonally from the clouds down to my right toward the sea. It was a strange angle for rain to fall. The other gray sheets were more or less perpendicular to the horizon. I watched with interest. The line faded, reappeared, then faded again. I went below to get the binoculars and when I poked my head up again there was another faint gray line emerging from the clouds near the place where the first had been, this time descending diagonally to my left! The binoculars defined the line a little more distinctly. But it couldn't be land. It was too *enormous!* The point where the two gray lines would meet was well above the lower limits of the clouds. On the other hand, what else could it be?

I woke Matt up. "Come take a look."

We stood in the companionway with the binoculars, straining for confirmation. The lines became clearer as the squalls diminished. It had to be the volcano! We couldn't believe it could be so high. Then the tears were streaming out of my silly happy eyes and we were hugging each other. We did it! It took twenty-six days, but we did it.

"Wake up! Wake up! It's Pico's Pike!" There was a general clamoring and exclaiming from the kids as they emerged warm and sleepy from their beds. Phil was characteristically noncommittal. He quietly took note of the gray lines in the sky, grinned, and went back to his bunk. It was seven A.M.

By eight o'clock we could see the entire mountain and it was time for hot chocolate and champagne.

October 8

MATT: Warm champagne in the cockpit at eight in the morning. The bottle was beautiful—a gift from Bill and Ginny Osterholt in New Orleans. They wrapped it in brown paper with a lashing of tarred rope around the neck—nautical and very appropriate for a ceremonial drink in the shadow of our first landfall. There was no fine crystal for our warm bubbly, in fact no glassware of any kind had survived the crossing. We drank straight from the bottle. It seemed more appropriate, somehow, than plastic thermal cups.

(I have a sharply etched image of Jeannine standing in the sunlit cockpit tilting the bottle back with crazy abandon. There's release to be read in the reckless way she throws back her head. Until this moment I hadn't allowed myself understanding of how arduous parts of the voyage have been for her, or how hungry she is to stand on a surface that doesn't sway and tilt. So many times I've watched helplessly while Jeannine lay retching into the passing sea and nothing I could do would relieve her misery. The small attentions that she accepted so gratefully—a sympathetic hug, a glass of water to rinse her mouth, a washcloth for her face—only made me feel more inadequate. In many ways this voyage has been mine, although Jeannine and the children have been willing partners; and I've often felt an initiator's guilt when life was not smooth for them. Mostly I escape from the guilt by pretending the discomfort is not so great, or that it hasn't affected Jeannine's enjoyment of sailing. We both play this game. It makes it easier to get on with the business of crossing an ocean. But the self-deception is evident and when the sea is being particularly beastly, or on occasions like this when respite is imminent, I allow myself to know how much Jeannine has endured. Today is a real victory. But much water lies beyond the Azores. I wonder how it will go.)

The scene before us continued to change. The huge cone which first appeared as a slightly grayer eminence in the gray dawn, resolved itself into two gray cones, the smaller framed by a larger one leaning over its shoulder—no detail, but the awesome outlines becoming more distinct, more separate by the minute. Now the ambassadors came out to greet us—a dozen gray porpoises racing to sport in our bow wave. We've seen no porpoises since Bermuda, and we greeted them like returned friends. The kids ran forward to watch them play. Above us squadrons of gulls circled and screamed, diving occasionally to snare a fish. The sea that had seemed empty and almost lifeless for so long was teeming now with living forms and abundant energy. The presence of land, the bountiful food supply of the banks and rocky reefs around the islands, gave sustenance to thousands of living creatures. We could feel the pressure of life around us and we watched it hungrily. Jeannine got out a trolling line, tied on a big silver spoon and cast it hopefully astern. How long since anyone has taken a real interest in fishing? I kept a hopeful eye peeled for spouts and lumpy forms among the waves. The Azores have been a favorite haunt of the sperm whale for hundreds of years, and I promised myself we would sight huge and fabled creatures from the deck of our boat before the voyage was over.

The island was closer now, pressing me to decisions I'd been putting off. I rummaged among the charts and came up with *HO 1736: Fayal, Graciosa, Terceira, Pico and São Jorge* —the central Azores group. I had to deal now with the real and imagined dangers of rocky shores, hidden reefs, shoaling bottoms and tricky harbor entrances. After twenty-six days of sailing freely over the ocean, no coastline in sight, the only solid ground thousands of fathoms below, the chart seemed filled with menace. Those formations of X's lying along the coastline stood for rocks lurking just below the surface. A course south of the island would be a more direct route to Horta, but it lay almost in the teeth of a fresh southeasterly breeze, and I was leery of sailing with that rocky and unforgiving coastline in our lee. There was no legitimate reason to fear being driven ashore; to be truthful, it was fear of land itself that caused me to choose the longer course along the northern shore. It was the prospect of human society I feared most—the complex web of interrelationships we would step into the moment we stepped ashore. What sort of people would these Azorians prove to be? Scoundrels and pickpockets as Mark Twain reported in a book Phil had been reading to us? Would the port officials be suspicious and officious? And what of the legendary Peter, reputed friend to yachtsmen, whom I had heard so much about in Bermuda? Would he really turn out to be friendly or was this just another waterfront con? And how in all this swarming population would I ever find him? A thousand questions, a thousand unexpected fears assaulted me. To stay at sea seemed simple and curiously inviting. I was a salty bumpkin fresh from the rural stretches of the North Atlantic, terrified of the unknown hazards of the wicked port.

By noon the shoreline was close and the binoculars passed restlessly from eye to eye. Fayal is volcanic and the coast here steep-to with small villages nestled into neatly terraced slopes that sometimes reach to the water, but more often terminate in precipitous cliffs dropping hundreds of feet to a rocky and forbidding beach. The sea was easy in the lee of the island, but where the swell collided with the shore it was tossed by the rocks in plumes of spray twenty or thirty feet high.

At intervals along the cliff edge we could see ancient churches and light towers of black-and-white stone standing out starkly against the mountainside. Fields rose green and terraced behind them almost to the heights of Pico Gordo, Fayal's principal volcano. Each hedgerow and farm lane was lined with brilliant blue hydrangeas. The effect was of green and yellow quilting stitched with blue thread. Everywhere we saw beauty, order, thrifty husbandry and great antiquity.

We all got to work scrubbing decks, stowing gear and transforming the comfortable clutter below into a semblance of order. I was aware that we would soon be docking in a strange harbor under strange eyes, and I wanted to enter in style, "All shipshape and Bristol fashion," with the Portuguese flag flying from our spreaders and below it the yellow "Q" flag to let Customs know we requested pratique—clearance and permission to go ashore. I sorted out the flags and handed them to Phil to run up the flag halyard. He made a production of it, donning sea boots, foul-weather pants and slicker—even the yellow oilskin hat. I had witnessed this performance before when there was a little spray flying, and it made me impatient. It was as if Phil wanted to avoid any contaminating contact between his body and the sea. He lumbered forward with the flag, his boots and his body heavy with protest. But a flag snap had worked loose from the halyard and it was necessary to lash the bottom flag to the hoist. Phil seemed unequal to the task; in my eyes he seemed almost to be *enjoying* incompetence. I felt the irritation of weeks flash to the surface. Beyond watches, which he always stood without complaint, this was the only task I had asked of him in days. It would have been easy to lash on the flags myself, but something made me resist. I was tired of treating Phil with the deference due an invalid. With the end in sight I saw him now only as a recalcitrant crew—nothing more.

"Goddamnit, Phil. Find a decent piece of line and use a rolling hitch!"

"What's a rolling hitch?"

After four weeks on the boat it seemed impossible he couldn't tie one of the most basic knots. What's happened to Phil? What's happened to us all? Where's that ebullient friend who came bouncing aboard in Bermuda, full of good humor, fellowship and enthusiasm for the voyage? That person departed almost as soon as the headlands of St. George dropped below the horizon. Plagued by seasickness and infection, Phil has been little more than a lump on a bunk for weeks, saying little, going through the motions of shipboard life like a zombie, meeting my efforts to impart nautical skills with almost cataleptic resistance. He's performed his duties well, even heroically when the sea was bad and his fever raging. But he's shown little interest in the boat, no spark, no enthusiasm for weeks. As the illness waned we watched for the Phil we knew to return, but the damage had been done. The boat had become little more than a prison to him, a place of monotonous meals, overcrowding and restraint. He had served his time as he had at Danbury, quietly, passively, waiting for the end.

It was so clear to me now—the trap we had all fallen into, blinded by our romantic illusions of voyaging. What Phil had needed most after prison was freedom and release—bright lights, foxy chicks, good dope, lots of action. Instead he had unwittingly settled for seasickness, confinement and the unremitting companionship of a closely knit family. Small wonder so much irritation had built up during the hard-fought miles of the last weeks. Now, with Horta almost in sight, it was all threatening to erupt. I had almost invited a confrontation; but Phil kept the peace, ignored my jibes, finished his task. With the end so near perhaps he knew things would be easier ashore.

About four we rounded the point at the northeast extremity of Fayal and thrashed southward into the strait that separated the islands of Fayal and Pico. The wind was dead ahead and very strong, kicking up a nasty chop in the three-mile-wide channel. Many times during the crossing I had fantasized a heroic ending, bombing into the harbor under full sail, all colors flying. But a few calculations suggested it would take three or more hours in all the chop to beat down the channel, whereas Methuselah might bring us home in little more than an hour. I put the question to the crew and all hands voted without hesitation for the shortest, quickest, easiest passage to dockside. Unwilling to risk mutiny so late in the voyage, I fired up Methuselah and we plowed down the channel with the main still up to steady us. It was a sparkling afternoon, though cold, and the slanting sun turned the spray to diamonds as it came aboard by the bucketful. We were all on deck now in yellow slickers, and we must have made a brave sight after all, because a red fishing boat veered by us just off the harbor entrance and the crew cheered us: ten or a dozen weatherbeaten Azorian fishermen standing out in the chill wind in their T-shirts yelling and waving with both hands and laughing and cheering. We couldn't have wished for a warmer welcome.

My watch showed five-thirty as we reached in past the breakwater light, rounded up, dropped the main, and eased alongside the quay. A crowd of fifteen or twenty citizens had gathered along the quay above us, looking down on our docking procedures with great interest and animated discussion. I clambered up the rough volcanic masonry to drop lines over some bollards. A man stepped out of the crowd smiling broadly, and handed me his card. "Welcome to Horta," he said. "I'm Peter."

14
Fayal

October 9

MATT: Horta! I could hardly believe the solid rock that swayed so strangely under my feet. A thousand landborne sounds and sights and smells overwhelmed my rusty senses, and suddenly it was all too much—I wasn't ready to embrace this new place yet; I wanted to retire quietly to the familiar cabin until change had had a chance to settle in me. But events have their own pace, not mine, and soon a trim figure in a jaunty white uniform appeared at dockside. I glanced up at the spreaders. Our yellow quarantine flag was indeed flying, this must be the Customs official.

"Hello, I'm John," said the uniform. "Welcome to Fayal." (*Got to treat these Customs folks with respect.* I remembered the slightly pompous official in Bermuda shorts and attaché case who boarded us in St. George.) "Pleased to meet you, sir. Won't you come below? May I offer you a drink?"

"A drink? Certainly. I'm always happy to have a drink."

I thought his manner somewhat informal for the portentous business of warping us in, officially speaking, to the Republic of Portugal, but I found a place for him on the starboard settee and coaxed a drink from the meager stores that had survived the crossing: New Orleans vodka and a

squirt of artificial lemon juice. I tasted it on the sly and it was
terrible, but John seemed not to mind. He questioned us
about the voyage and cast a professional eye around the
yacht. Official business seemed far from his mind, so I asked
if he was a doctor, thinking of our medical clearance.

"Doctor?" A twinkle in his eye. "Is anyone sick? You all
look healthy. I'm chief pilot but I can summon the doctor
at once if you need him."

I explained that we were concerned about the formalities
of entering the country. "But you have already entered, and
we *accept* you. Yes, we *welcome* you! As for the formalities,
don't concern yourself. They can be attended to at any time.
Come, my car is near. Let us all go to the Café Sport and
celebrate your arrival."

And so we arrived at the famous Café Sport, known to
a select fraternity of yachtsmen the world around. In reality
it was a good deal smaller than I had expected: five or six
wooden tables in a modest room, a bar at one end, whaling
artifacts and whale-tooth carvings in cases along the walls,
everything very neat and snug. Peter Azevedo, the first to
welcome us to Horta, stood behind the bar, beaming from ear
to ear. Two gnarled fishermen drank their wine and watched
us quietly from one of the tables. A white-haired gentleman
with a dapper gray mustache, who reminded me dimly of the
pediatrician that cared for me as a child, sat at a corner table
stacked with books.

"Welcome to Café Sport," said Peter. "And please meet
my father, Henrique." The old man rose with a courtly
gesture and shook my hand. "You are the fifty-ninth yacht
to arrive in Horta this season," Peter continued, "and we are
happy to see you. The drinks are on us."

We sat quietly at a table, struck dumb by the miracle of
cold Portuguese beer, icy orange sodas, and salted fava beans
from a glass jar on the counter. Phil wore the broadest grin
I had seen since we left St. George. "It's over," he said.

The remaining hours flew by in a haze. We secured
Aquarius strongly against the wind which was now blowing

with determination from the southeast and sending salvos of spray over the seawall. John conducted us ceremoniously to the Capitolio, one of Horta's two restaurants. We ordered a table spread with an actual white tablecloth, a staid and landbound table too dignified for deep-sea rock-and-roll. John sat by while we devoured garlic steak topped by fried eggs and Azorian volcanoes of French-fried potatoes. The children were abnormally silent, a state they attain only in the ultimate stages of sleep—or rapture.

Sleep? Wild seahorses could not have induced us to bed down on *Aquarius* tonight. Besides, in a moment of marital weakness I had promised Jeannine a double bed all gussied up with genuine clean linen and isolated from the rest of the world by a certifiable door that closed with a lock. I mentioned these improbabilities to John, who took it as his last kindness of the evening to guide us into the safe anchorage of a nearby pension. Then the pilot of Fayal hauled wind and cast off for his own snug haven, having discharged his duties more handsomely than anyone could expect.

Rooms for all were procured from a sleepy porter. Jeannine and I hurried to ours for we had lofty ambitions for the remainder of the evening: (1) get loaded, (2) get twenty-six days of salt washed off our bodies in the hottest shower human flesh could tolerate, (3) get into the bed and each other in a style and splendor suitable to the occasion. The first ambition we accomplished easily, the second didn't come so smoothly. The beginnings of an October gale were shaking trees outside and making whistles around cornerstones. Inside a deep chill had settled into the bones of the hotel. We could not, as we so wished, blithely shed our woollies and leap into a steaming shower. We had first to coax some comfort from the subzero bathroom, a glacial white-tile affair resplendent with unfamiliar knobs and appurtenances. By intuition I located the valves which intercommunicated between the shower and a hidden reservoir of hot water somewhere in the bowels of the hotel. Regulating the temperature was another matter. The faucet was of two minds only, it provided water from either the Antarctic or Sahara under hairtrigger tension, but by employing the patient deftness I had learned at so much expense from my vane gear, I was able eventually to approximate Savannah, Georgia, on a steamy summer afternoon. We eased our bodies into the ambrosial stream, and just as the soap was running in Jeannine's hair and the outer layers of salt were beginning to soften and fuse with those closest to the skin— *zap!* Antarctica returned with icy vengeance. I cursed and fiddled with the tap while Jeannine shivered in a damp corner of our tile sarcophagus, but no invocation, no pleading, no hydrostatic cunning could entice another drop of warming fluid from that stern fixture. And so, with all our sensibilities heightened, we crept between the icy sheets to lie huddled together, stoned, salty, and shivering, until Morpheus drew his merciful shade across our misery.

October 15
  MATT: Fortunately all wounds heal, and the trauma of our bridal night in Horta was quickly soothed by the love affair that grew between ourselves and the people of this extraordinary town. We remained a few more days at the pension, solved the mysteries of its plumbing, and healed our salt-irritated cuts in its soothing waters. (A puzzle here. Why do salt sores take so long to heal at sea? Have we missed a vitamin or two?)

  We began to heal the other frictions too. It was as if the sea had been an irritant between Phil and ourselves, and by removing it we reverted to our former easy ways. We took breakfasts together at streetside cafés, we explored the town and the island, we slept long and late, we met afternoons at Peter's for a drink, we smoked together in the evenings, and before a week was out we had found the ease for a long talk about the difficulties of the crossing.

  It was not hard to understand in the relaxed atmosphere of Horta how our tightly knit family with its long-established habits and rituals had been as difficult for Phil as his self-isolation had sometimes been for us. There's no doubt we had been more anxious and uptight than we needed to be. We were concerned about the boat; nervous about our ability to deal with the weather ahead, and needlessly parsimonious with food and water. (As it happened, we arrived with plenty of water in our tanks. What a luxury it would have been to expend a few quarts of fresh water washing the salt from our bodies every few days!) Our worries seemed understandable by hindsight. We were doing it all for the first time. We had no experience to guide us save the secondhand experience of friends. We had never been at sea, never made a crossing, never weathered a gale, and we could not foresee how long our supplies would last. If this was understandable to us, to Phil it was nearly intolerable, coming as he had directly from an institution that was certainly the granddaddy of them all for uptightness, rigidity and inflexible regulations. When you add the unfortunate accident of his illness and his unforseeable addiction to seasickness, it's a wonder he survived as well as he did.

What happened to Phil—and to us—was very difficult to foresee. He began the voyage with enthusiasm and commitment. He had been a successful member of our household once before, and he was a close friend. Everything augured for happy relationships and a successful crossing for him—and almost everything went wrong. The wrongness was not expressed in open conflict, in anger or even very much in simple irritation. What we felt most acutely were the absences—the absence of joy and closeness, the absence of a family feeling we hoped would grow naturally from the experience itself. In New Orleans we prided ourselves on the kind of community feeling we had with our friends, and I guess we expected the same to develop during the course of the voyage with Phil. Were our expectations too romantic? Perhaps, but I prefer to view what happened as a kind of natural disaster of the sea, rather than to search for causes or flaws in our individual personalities. I think we were the unwitting victims of psychological pressures, physical disorientation, and a chance illness that we had no way of predicting; and I think it is significant that our relationship with Phil mellowed as soon as we were all back on shore. If there is a moral to the tale it must be this: Don't go to sea with *anybody*— your dearest friend, your lover, even your wife and children —until you have tested the association with at least a week, and preferably much longer, of serious cruising together. There are pressures that grow aboard a small yacht which may stress a relationship as it is seldom stressed ashore, and there is no way to predict how you will bear up until you have tried it.

Looking back on the Atlantic crossing, I think a lot of pressure was generated by too many of us being forced to live in too small a space. Scientists have made innumerable studies of the effects of overcrowding on rats, mice and others of our less cerebral brothers. The studies seem to agree that every animal requires for his well-being a certain minimum of space, and if he is overcrowded beyond his threshold of tolerance he begins to act in bizarre ways. Rats attack each other, some strains simply waste away and die for no apparent physical reason. Deformed litters are born, mothers eat their young.

Well, none of us showed any very clear tendencies toward cannibalism, but I think we did feel the stress of overcrowding and reacted to it in certain ways to protect our territory. A lot of our solutions came intuitively. We didn't hold any house meetings. The children staked off the forepeak as their territory—everything due east of the head and hanging locker. But far from huddling behind their walls, they usually slept in the cockpit or on the afterdeck (in good weather), or made forays against the bunks in the main cabin. The adults were not so fortunate in territorial acquisition, there being only two bunks for three of us, but we did establish certain preferences. Jeannine and I felt more comfortable in the port bunk, Phil seemed to reside mostly on the starboard, and of course each of us had his own locker for personal belongings. On the whole, I think the boat was too small for much staking out of personal territory, and Jeannine agrees. She believes we protected the rights of our *emotional* space instead. If emotional stress became too great or a personal relationship too abrasive, it was common for one or both parties to withdraw, to retreat into their private emotional space until the wounds healed. Sleep was one way of accomplishing this; night watches were another. If anyone wanted to be really alone, those nighttime hours were the ideal time for solitude, with the rest of the ship's company fast asleep, and the space above and around so immense, the stars so incredibly brilliant, that it was impossible to feel very cramped. We all looked forward to night watches.

Sometimes I retreated to the head for solitude. It has a door to isolate it from the main cabin, although not, unfortunately, from the forepeak. If the children were inhabiting their lair when I came to use the head they usually scuttled forth complaining loudly. The forepeak provided the only real privacy. When Jeannine and I wanted to be alone we simply crawled into the forepeak and closed the door.

I had only one real fight with Jeannine during the twenty-six days at sea. Considering how much we were together I think that was a lower than normal rate of quarreling. We both noticed that the emotional highs and lows of our relationship were less pronounced at sea; perhaps we inhibited our feelings because it was too risky to express them fully in such a confined space. There was no safety valve, no way the aggrieved party could go storming off to the neighborhood bar. Certainly there was less lovemaking than usual. It's possible we were responding to the stress of overcrowding, like the experimental mice, by limiting our procreational activities. Or maybe it was simply the discomfort of our situation and the fact that there were a lot of other demands on our time and energy. The state of your stomach and how tired you are has a lot to do with how sexy you feel. The voyage certainly hasn't affected us ashore.

I noticed early in the voyage that I got irritable and

sometimes irrationally angry at clutter and confusion around the boat, and I finally decided this was a reaction to "population pressure." Also, it became apparent early on that we were going to have to live and deal with each other's hang-ups in a way that had never been necessary before. In a normal family situation there is usually enough space between individuals so each can live a fairly separate life if he wants to. I have noticed this particularly with the children. In New Orleans they had their own friends, their own rooms, their own lives. It was possible for me to become very absorbed in my own work and have only a casual relationship with my children for days at a time. That can't happen on a small boat at sea. We had to deal with each other's emotional states almost on an hourly basis. I'm sure the wrong combination of personalities could tear a boat apart, but by the time we sighted Fayal our family had grown closer than ever before. The feeling has persisted ashore and I am sure it will grow as the voyage continues. In that sense, the trip has already been all that I hoped it would be. I wish it could have happened with Phil.

At the end of a week Phil decided to embark on his own voyage of discovery. We saw him off on an inter-island boat for Santa Maria, where the airfield is. (He flew to London, bought a motorcycle, we learned later, and continued northward to Sweden, where he met a girl. They toured Europe together on the bike, altogether a more satisfactory adventure for him than further voyages of *Aquarius.*) In Horta we quickly settled into a new life and a new and very satisfying daily routine.

October 21

JEANNINE: We took a room in the home of a *senhora* who spoke English. She and her husband lived alone and had one room to let—a pleasant room, quite inexpensive, with lace curtains at the two windows which opened out onto tiny balconies, a double bed, a couch for one child (they took turns on an air mattress every other night), a desk, and the best feature of all, a hot bath down the hall!

We balanced our living between the room and the boat. For the first time noisy messy work (on the boat) could coexist with quiet reflective work (in the room) without conflict. When the newness of being in a strange place had passed we settled down to an easy daily rhythm.

Foodgathering was a process I grew to enjoy, even though it meant getting up around five-thirty in the morning. At that hour I could already hear the wake-up sounds of Horta through the shuttered windows—the comings and goings of carts and cars on the cobblestones, and across the street at the butcher shop the pounding of a heavy cleaver and the whine of the electric saw as the butcher rasped through the bony cuts. Electricity was used sparingly in Horta; the saw was a necessity but refrigeration was a luxury, so only one cow was butchered each day. If I went early, at five-thirty or six, there was a wide choice of cuts; if I waited until a more American hour, eight or nine, only a few stringy-looking pieces were left. The shop usually closed for the day at nine-thirty A.M.

Standing in a long queue of townspeople, sometimes fifteen or twenty stretching out into the dark street, feeling conspicuous and strange, I would wait silently, smiling from time to time at the curious faces. While most of the merchants spoke a few words of English, the average citizen did not. I was limited to a few polite Portuguese greetings.

How do you describe to a butcher the cut of meat you want him to carve from an anonymous hunk of flesh hanging from a meathook? The first day I went there, the only word the butcher and I could get together on was *biftek*. He sliced off a small T-bone for my inspection. I was so relieved to see something I recognized that I put up four fingers. The four steaks weighed just over a kilo. Thinking that my foolishness would surely empty my wallet, but too embarrassed to tell him it was too much after he had already cut it, I let him wrap it in the plastic bag I had brought before I inquired the price. It cost $1.00 for some of the finest steaks I have ever eaten.

From the butcher's I would go across the street to the produce market for fruits and vegetables. In the early morning light it was a color trip—poetic, subdued, magical: yellow lemons in brown wicker; garlands of garlic like strands of baroque pearls; pumpkins halved, exposing an orange glow around a pithy nest of perfect seeds; not many tomatoes; no more of summer's fabled grapes; the last small black figs, sweet with the lateness of the season; green, green lettuce still sparkling with drops of ground mist; great dirt-colored tubers (phonetically pronounced *ignomish*); round white cakes of Pico cheese; sober, ruddy, friendly faces.

The market was formal (as that which follows a form, like sonatas or sonnets), laid out with shade trees in deliberate rows encircled at the base with whitewashed stones. At the back, raised by only a few steps, was a separate space delineated by a low-columned balustrade. Here long stone tables, fine and smooth like marble, were the last resting place for little blue mackerel, silvery fish, and pink octopi. I loved it. Everywhere the growing light filtered down through the peaceful canopy of leaves and branches.

Men were shopping as well as women. I paused to take that in—yes, quite a few men, some in uniform even, moving from table to table examining the produce, carrying net bags with a fish tail sticking out alongside a bunch of kale and a long loaf of bread.

By the time I returned to the room with my purchases it would be light. "Wake up! It's time to go to the *pasteleria!*" The pilgrimage to the bakery was a family affair, a ceremony undertaken with considerable reverence and pleasure. The objects of worship resided on shelves in a glass case—a reliquary of lovely yummy buttery pasteries wrapped around almond paste, cherry tarts, apricot cups, croissants. Our rituals of dividing the peaches on the boat were forgotten; caught up in a new religion we eagerly repeated the litany, "One of those, one of those, one of those."

Our breakfast choices cost only a few cents. For lunch, half a dozen submarine-type rolls would do; the *pasteleria* would make them with wheat flour if we ordered one day in advance. Next door we bought fresh milk for about eight cents a liter, sweet creamery butter and tasty cheese.

Mornings then, after pastry, were devoted to "school" for the children and to writing for us. "Aquarius School" got a little more serious about mathematics. Our original plan was to deal with math in Real Life Situations, for example, "If one-half pint of Resorcinal glue covers ten square feet, then how much do you need to glue a locker cover three feet square?" Or, "If one *escudo* is worth two and a half cents, then how much (in dollars and cents) do you have in your pocket right now?" Putting math in context is a great idea (in theory), but sometimes the context gets in the way of down-to-earth arithmetic. For instance, on the boat it went like this: "Since ten this morning we have been proceeding due east at approximately our present speed. How far have we traveled?" The solution might easily take an hour and anyone knows that an hour's worth of math is enough for one day.

An hour? How is it possible?

"Okay," says Matthew, "I'll throw the chip log and find out how fast we're going." Melissa rummages around for the stopwatch, pausing for a moment or two to visit the head and take in a few pages of an exciting book she's reading. Several more minutes are dawdled away while Matthew throws a practice run or two to get the kinks out of the line. Then a real throw is goofed because Melissa forgets to say, "Mark!" The line goes out again but this time gets tangled around Matthew's foot. Finally they decide we are going three and a half knots, put the equipment away and get back to their notebooks.

"We have to know how long we've been going at that speed, right? What time is it, Matthew?"

"It's twelve-thirty-five."

"So late? No wonder I'm hungry! Let's make a sandwich!"

So much for the arithmetic lesson. They got so they were pretty good at dead reckoning, but when I asked them, "What's seven times seven?" they couldn't answer. Alarmed, I drilled through the times tables: "Six eights!"

No reply. "Four sixes!"

"Twenty-four!"

"Five nines!"

Mumble, mumble. "Forty-eight? . . . Fifty four?"

Here was something I had assumed was socked solidly into their brains in third and fourth grade! I could locate the times tables in my cortex right next to the endless repetitions of "A noun is the name of a person, place, animal or thing," and "Thirty days hath September," and " 'i' before 'e' except after 'c,' " "Our Father," and "I pledge allegiance."

"Good heavens!" I exploded. "What's happened to your times tables?"

"Mom, kids forget things like that over a summer. Teachers always spend a couple of months reviewing basic stuff like that in the fall."

The incident alarmed me enough that I made it a point to drill in multiplication every so often until I was satisfied that they weren't going to be permanently crippled in the field of mathematics as a result of my neglect. (I even ventured to inquire about the nature of adjectives and pronouns from time to time, acknowledging albeit reluctantly that good old rote learning did have its place in education, after all.) I had ordered some interesting-looking math texts, the Cambridge Math Series, while browsing through various educational journals in the States, and they arrived in Horta shortly after we did. They were excellent—well thought out so that concepts were "arrived at" rather than "taught." The lessons practically explained themselves. If Matthew got stuck and I was busy, I generally referred him to the *Teacher's Manual.* Melissa required a little more assistance, but usually just a boost and she was off on her own too.

After a certain amount of "hard core" work like math and writing in their logs, they varied their choices among activities like typing, French, flute and art. They had some memorable drawing excursions in Horta which were described in Matthew's log.

MATTHEW: On the morning of the 20th, Melissa and I were doing school work. It was a beautiful day. When I had finished writing in the log and Melissa had done a typing lesson, Mom suggested that for the last part of school we should try to draw something. We decided to draw the park right next to where we were living.

It was beautiful. There was a pond in the middle of it and there were two swans both white with black beaks. There was an island in the middle of the pond with a small fountain on it. Behind that were palm trees and a very big pine tree. I started to draw the island when the spectators started to come. They didn't come all at once, but they came. First the adults. They would stand to one side and try to talk English. The most we ever understood was "Allo." Then the kids. They crowded in close so we couldn't move without hitting a few. They stood in front of us, in back of us and over us, breathing down our necks. There were always some little whispers and giggles. The park custodian came over and fixed us up with stools made of stone and burlap. This went on for about three hours. The people just kept coming and coming until all we could see were faces staring at us. A man with a pet bird came over to look at us. Melissa got sick of it so we went home, with the crowd following us like ducklings, "Quack, Quack, Quack!"

October 21

JEANNINE: Afternoons were generally reserved for visiting other places on the island or for the "noisy messy" ever-present boat repairs. We replaced a cracked spreader, painted the mast, repaired a broken cockpit seat and found a local sailmaker to restitch our mainsail (by hand). As a surprise for me, Matt built a folding bed into the passage of the main cabin so we would be able to sleep together on the boat, at least in port.

Occasionally we were able to involve Matthew and Melissa in these various constructions, but most of the time, just as they were settling down to some serious scraping or sanding, we would hear a chorus of shouts from the quay, "Futbol! Futbol! Mateo!" Neither of them wasted any time getting their soccer ball and piling into the dinghy to make for shore, to play strenuous and satisfying "futbol" for the rest of the afternoon. Matthew was so sore from the unaccustomed exercise that he asked for liniment one night. Most amazing was the amount of Portuguese they picked up as a result of the games. Numbers came naturally as they learned to keep score, but slang was important too. *Épa!* meant anything from "Hey!" to "Watch out!" to "Throw it here!" This was the kind of play we had tried to encourage in New Orleans for so long with so little luck—the equivalent of sandlot baseball that Matt used to love so much when he was a kid and that now seems to have passed from all but the black American scene.

Not to appear too pious, it must be admitted that we had our distractions from work as well. Sometimes we would hear a honk from the shore and Mario and his fiancée, Alda, friends we had met at the Café Sport, would beckon us from their car to come for a ride.

Mario knew the most beautiful places on the island and he shared them with pride. Close to the sea there were quiet bays, black sand beaches, and overhung cliffs where far below the waves carved violently at black stone sculptures. Climbing away from the shore, we looked across extraordinary vistas—tall grass like pampas bordering green rolling fields to delineate property lines and protect the crops from the wind; here and there the worn rounded cones of ancient volcanoes; beyond them the sun sparkling on the Atlantic and, across the sparkling water, mighty Pico, turning red and purple in the setting sun.

Descending, the road flowed gently ahead of us through banks of blue hydrangeas. We passed great wicker carts loaded high with corn, drawn by compliant-eyed oxen. The carts were on their way to the bluffs where giant figures in bright costumes stood sessile at the skyline. Their skirts, patterned of irregular black rock stitched together with whitewashed mortar, were planted firmly in the ground. Above the waist their bright red blouses with four stiff arms thrust out askew, could be rotated to face the wind by several men walking a great wooden lever in the desired direction. Inside, two massive round stones chafed at each other with only the corn to come between them. Windmills: planted in Portuguese soil by the early Flemish settlers.

Invariably we returned to Peter's; late afternoon was Café Sport time, as surely as it is also teatime, or cocktail hour in other places—time for good conversation with the regulars and a glass of Lacrima Christi. The children drank orange sodas, ate potato chips and fava beans, and watched Othon making scrimshaw. Othon was an affable, talented and very modest young friend of Peter's. He sat at one of the tables near the door. With a diamond-tipped pen he scratched incredibly fine drawings of whales and intricate three-masted square riggers into thin slices of whale's tooth, or whale's-tooth rings. Over the drawings he spread black ink, then wiped and polished the black away, leaving it only in the scratches. He showed Matthew and Melissa how to do it (once when we visited his home he gave them the first scrimshaw tool he ever used), and they made some drawings in ivory: Matthew, a sailing ship; and Melissa, a horse.

Behind Peter's counter, which housed carved whale's-tooth schooners, fine Portuguese sherry, various-sized ivory rings, and handmade black lace, he kept his scrapbooks of mementos, photographs, drawings and musings of the various yacht captains who had called in at Horta over the past ten years. The books were extraordinary historical documents of the crissing and crossing of small-boat traffic in the Atlantic Ocean—a chronicle of unique (and sometimes bizarre) human anecdotes. One man and his wife had crossed the ocean in a "duck," a military amphibious automobile. There was another yacht with two men aboard who ran off with a local girl. Mysteriously, there was only one man aboard when they touched in at the next port.

We poured over these journals with real fascination, peering into the faces in the photographs, examining the fittings and furnishings of each boat. It was like perusing a visitor's book at the top of a difficult mountain. What kind of people came to this far-away place before me? Are they like me? How do they express themselves? What sort of ships did they choose and how did they fare on their journey? What were the women like—tough? masculine? subordinate?

As twilight fell, Peter's clientele thinned and we made off for *Aquarius* and our steaks. Several times we invited friends to eat with us on the boat and they always very politely refused. We never knew whether it was social etiquette or the thought of our dinghy that kept them away, but we were at a loss to find some way to return the many kindnesses showered on us.

We enjoyed our dinners on the boat. It was home base; we puttered, played games, made music, and watched the lights in the town and the red and green running lights of the pilot boat going out to meet a late arrival.

Tucking *Aquarius* in, and walking back through town in the evening was a pleasant ending for the day. Sometimes the air was clear and crisp with a chilly scent, and Melissa would say, "Mom! I smell ice!" Another evening it would be San-Francisco-damp with just a light drizzle wetting the cobblestones. Quiet and familiar, dark except for the cafés and the movie house, the town itself was a harbor—not only was our boat in safe water, but our persons were in friendly hands. As we walked along dark streets, we felt uniquely protected from the stormy dangers that beset dark streets in other, more worldly cities. Never have we lived in a town where we felt so surrounded by honorable, generous people. It was a far cry from the picture of beggars and con-men painted by

Mark Twain in *Innocents Abroad*. Not once did anyone try to take advantage of us in Horta.

On the contrary: one afternoon I was in a little shop buying some socks for Melissa. As I reached in my purse, it fell off the counter scattering a number of coins on the floor. The shopkeeper came out from behind the counter to help me pick them up as I mumbled apologies. I didn't think again of the incident until, walking by the shop the next evening, I heard someone calling. The same shopkeeper came running breathlessly up to me and pressed three coins (about 15 cents) into my hand. "Here!" she said, "we found these on the floor when we were sweeping up last night."

The honesty of the people of Fayal was matched by their generosity. Everywhere we went shopkeepers plied Matthew and Melissa with treats. Unexpected mountains of French fries were heaped on their plates by the family who ran the Capitolio Restaurant. One afternoon Melissa went off by herself and didn't return. After a couple of hours I decided I'd better go look for her. When I stepped into the Capitolio to ask if anyone had seen her, the owner laughed, "She is going to be part of our family now!" He opened the door of the kitchen and there she was, peeling potatoes!

"Aw, Mom! Don't make me come home. This is fun!"

After that they always referred to her as their "extra daughter."

As we walked together toward our room at the *senhora*'s, Melissa's "family" was just closing the restaurant. "*Bona noche! Bona noche!* Until tomorrow!"

Such warmth! We passed on, recapitulating the events of the day with a sense of real satisfaction, loving this charming town and her people, seduced completely by the embrace of gracious Horta. Though the season was getting later every day and we could "smell the ice" in the air, we felt no urge to leave the safety of her arms for the sea just yet. Pastries and fresh milk were waiting in the morning.

October 25,

MATT: Harbors have fascinated me from the day I first began to dream of boats. On assignment in a strange city, my recreation was always messing around the waterfront, talking to fishermen, ogling yachts, supervising the unloading of freighters, watching the city conduct its aquatic affairs. I'm not surprised, at thirty-nine, to find myself wandering around a foreign harbor that includes among its many points of interest my own boat. The only surprise is how many years it has taken to get here.

Horta is a fascinating harbor for wandering. The people of the Azores have been obliged to "conduct their business in great waters" for many centuries, and have developed a special facility for managing boats—one that borders on the instinctive. As a photo-voyeur I love eavesdropping on the marvelous varieties of work and loafing that take place within camera shot of *Aquarius,* but I was surprised to find that bonafide citizens of Horta find their harbor every bit as interesting as I do. It's common on Sundays to see middle-class families arrayed in their sabbath best, strolling among the ropes and bollards, visiting boats, discussing everything, including the little blue American yacht with the peace emblem and waves of Aquarius flapping at its crosstree. Often I'd put my head out the companionway to find fifteen or twenty people ranged along the wharf above me. They were particularly curious about the baggy wrinkle which Matthew and Melissa had woven from old hemp rope collected among the docks of Panama City. It bloomed like cattails along our upper and lower shrouds, and I would try to explain its purpose to the docksiders though I could never find a way to say "chafing gear" in Portuguese. Often we invited these visitors aboard for a look at the rest of the boat, a tour that began (when the tide was low) with a pants-splitting slide down our starboard shrouds to deck level, some four to six feet below the quay. The difficulty of entrance tended to stem the flow of visitors somewhat, but we always enjoyed those brave enough to hazard the trip; it was a way of reciprocating the friendliness we encountered ashore. In the absence of language we communicated with smiles and gestures, and I was always surprised how fascinating they found our cramped quarters.

The fishermen visited us too, and their friendly curiousity was mixed with a professional concern for the safety of our boat. At first when they came with suggestions on how to arrange our docking lines or rig a fender I was a bit irked. After all, we had just completed an ocean crossing. What did they take us for, greenhorns? How wrong we were! Managing *Aquarius* on the open sea was one thing, keeping her safe in an island harbor was quite another—as we soon learned.

I had moved *Aquarius* to a new location in a corner of the harbor more convenient to the town. Peter loaned me several old automobile tires for fenders but objected strongly when I positioned the boat facing into a corner of the quay. I thought he was unduly fussy; I could always back out of the berth if necessary, and it was easier docking in that position. Jeannine wrote of what happened.

JEANNINE: It came up quite suddenly during a night we were sleeping in the boat, a fierce gale sweeping into the harbor from the north, the one direction unprotected by breakwaters. Matt sensed the change and came up on deck to find the waves beginning to slam us into the quay and the fishing boats around us casting off their lines to make for the other side of the harbor where it was a little more protected. Our position made it very risky to motor out. The wind and waves were bearing across the whole sweep of the harbor, blowing directly into our corner. Methuselah lacked the horsepower to back against them, and there was no room in front to pick up the speed necessary for a hard turn to port before we slammed into the corner wall. Fortunately some of the fishermen understood our predicament and offered to give us a tow.

All communication (and non-communication) took place in sign language, unintelligible attempts at Portuguese on our part and equally unintelligible English on theirs, a situation confounded by the darkness, the increasing winds and the rough water which by now was pounding us quite heavily against the wall. While we were untying our lines to get ready for the tow, the fishing boat suddenly took off. We were baffled. Were they leaving us? Had we misunderstood? Then we realized they were circling in order to throw us a line. Matt caught the line and quickly bent to make it fast on our foredeck before their boat took up the slack, but immediately they began shouting "PUSH! PUSH!" at the same time making *pulling* motions with their hands. Again bewilderment and precious moments lost, until we guessed that the rope in our hands was a light-weight throwing line, and that we should PULL to gain the towing cable. By now their boat was moving off again to keep from blowing into us and the wall. It was all we could do to pull in that heavy hemp, make it fast to a cleat, and then leap to fend off from the wall ourselves as they pulled us away. We landed relatively easily on the opposite side of the harbor, snuggled against the breakwater. In front of us the fishermen made fast their lines, then came back to squat on the wall above and observe our docking, holding a line for us here, moving a fender there, beautifully calm and efficient in the face of our anxious fumbling.

The wind picked up during the remainder of the night and by morning it looked like a serious storm. Angry clouds hovered over Horta and the hills beyond. The rising sun behind us penetrated the gloom only long enough to illuminate a perfect rainbow over the town, then it disappeared for two days. The fishermen came again and jabbered at us, pointing to the side of the harbor we had left the night before. Surely they can't mean that we should go back! But they were casting off their lines again. By now we had immense respect for their ability and judgment.

"Look, I trust these guys," Matt decided. "I think they mean to anchor to one of those buoys out in the harbor and they want to help us do the same." He nodded to the two who were waiting above us. They jumped down to our deck and helped fend off as their tuna boat again pulled us away. They led us to a buoy, then moved nearby to establish their own anchorage. It took both fishermen and Matt to haul up the heavy mooring chain while I handled the engine and the tiller. Finally we were fast, with two extra lines from the chain to the afterdeck for extra security. I cut off the engine and went below to make coffee for our wet friends while they waited for a rowboat to come and get them. They refused the coffee, as everyone here has refused our attempts to return their kindnesses. The waves were breaking over their dinghy and showering them with spray as they returned to the tuna boat.

October 25,

MATT: The storm continued for three days. It was strange being cooped upon the boat again, but I was reluctant to leave *Aquarius* untended with a full gale blowing. There was plenty of evidence from the tuna boats moored all around of how seriously the fishermen took the weather. Each boat was manned by a full crew and secured by double or triple cables to the mooring buoy. All day and all night the boats kept a helmsman on duty and their diesels turning over just enough to ease the strain on the cables. If a buoy should let go there was no chance of the boat going too. I fired up Methuselah every few hours to be sure he was ready for any such emergency. *Perola,* the tuna boat that had saved us from a brutal battering against the jetty wall, was moored just ahead and we had lots of time to watch the activity on board. Before long we could recognize individual fishermen and we shouted encouragement to each other across the angry water. It was remarkably like being at sea.

Two days passed. Our water tanks ran dry and we had begun to drink fruit juice before the gale slackened enough to permit very wet, adventurous trips to shore. At the first opportunity, the men of *Perola* invited us aboard for a meal. It was amazing what gestures alone could communicate, and fortunately boat people are mostly interested in the same things. Our visit began with a tour of the boat, a vessel totally unlike the slovenly Gulf fishing boats I was used to. True enough, *Perola* was a rough work boat, but she was maintained in a fashion that would do credit to any yacht. She was about forty-five or fifty feet overall, high in the bows with a decided flair and a generous sheer to shed seas. Aft, she dropped to a broad afterdeck, fully half her length with fish hold under. The engine room was in the bilges amidships and the crew slept forward of this in a tiny forecastle. The boat showed the effects of a season's fishing (they painted her a few weeks later) but every inch of her was spanking clean. She didn't even smell of fish!

I was most impressed with the engine room. A joy to any housewife—fresh paint everywhere and not a sign of grease, the big diesel gleaming red, all the pipes painted different colors and along the starboard side an immaculate workbench with a complete set of tools *inlaid* into a panel above the bench! How that space delighted my admiring mechanic's eye! I would have liked to remain there, perhaps with my own bed and light-housekeeping privileges, but a call from above summoned us to a tiny table where a large succulent pot of none other than tuna stew awaited us. Fresh tuna is a rich, strongly flavored meat and the stew was liberally seasoned with cinnamon or nutmeg. It was delicious but decidedly powerful for North American stomachs. I had the impression that tuna in different disguises is the unvarying diet on this boat. The fishermen poured us Pico wine, a rich, blood-red, slightly rough vintage, and they cautioned us against drinking too much. "I can handle my wine as well as the next man," I thought to myself, but I sipped cautiously, remembering my stew-stressed stomach.

As we prepared to leave, José, *Perola*'s engineer, a short fellow with humor and kindliness written in every wrinkle of his handsome face, presented us with a (graduation?) picture of himself. I remembered seeing him before, tooling around the harbor on a vintage Royal Enfield motorcycle that was as well maintained as the engine room. We thanked him, promising to reciprocate, swung down into the rowboat and were soon back aboard *Aquarius,* happy with the day, doubtful about the effects of the stew, and feeling that we were beginning to make real contact with Horta and her harbor.

October 29

MATT: There were a million things I loved to watch in that harbor, but probably the freight boats from Pico were the best. My favorite was *Picaroto,* a venerable wooden lugger of about forty-five feet, double-ended like a lifeboat but larger, beamy and high in the sides with thwarts braced along her length to take the strain of the gargantuan loads so casually boarded by her crew in their daily traffic between Fayal and Pico. *Picaroto* would willingly carry almost any cargo one could imagine: rustling beds of cornstalks, brown bags of grain, stacks of Pico cheeses, cases of Pico wine, firewood, squealing hogs. I saw her come in once loaded to the gunwales with ears of corn, and atop this great golden mound a little black automobile, and inside the little black automobile, a little black-cloaked priest. Priest and conveyance were hoisted together to the quay and they drove off to the noisy benediction of the cargo handlers.

It was fun watching *Picaroto* unload cattle. She could carry about twenty head standing haunch to haunch on the bottom boards in a most unsavory bed of straw, so tightly packed the men could not get down beside them and instead walked on their backs to adjust the cargo slings. The cattle bore large red crosses on their backs, the certifying mark of a veterinarian, I suppose, and with the men walking across them the scene reminded me of animated tic-tac-toe. Once a sling was secured under a steer's belly, two willing hands would begin cranking the manually operated derrick crane on the wharf. The sling would tighten and the chosen animal, wild-eyed and head rolling, would be raised above his brothers. As soon as his feet lost the touch of gravity the beast would become strangely docile, as if mesmerized by weightlessness, and would hang passive in the sling until swung in over the wharf and lowered to the pavement. A touch of his hooves broke the spell and the animal would come violently alive, snorting and stumbling, kicking against the wieght and hooking wildly at some imaginary adversary. Several knowing farmers would manhandle a rope on him and the feel of the familiar hemp seemed to remind him of domesticity again, for he would plod off as placidly as if he'd never been to sea. The sequence would be repeated with variations until *Picaroto* was riding high in the water. The lowing and laughing and cursing were beyond describing.

Without a pause for breath *Picaroto* would be refreighted for the return voyage (always with the *same* cargo, it seemed to me) and on top of the bags and bales and bundles would perch all the miscellaneous Azorians with business in Pico: peasant women with huge wicker baskets of produce, schoolboys, farmers, fishermen, businessmen. A man would duck into the cheesebox enginehouse set dead aft and a moment later I would hear the regular *thunk, thunk, thunk,* of the old one-lung diesel. Then amid great shouting and waving *Picaroto* would gather her ponderous skirts and lumber away from the quay. In a moment she'd be headed for the harbor mouth with a bone in her teeth, and before she was halfway out there'd be a flurry of activity forward and the dingy lugsail would clamber up the mast. With sail sheeted in and drawing smartly and all hands taking their ease now among

the piles and bales, *Picaroto* would slip from view behind the
breakwater light looking surprisingly trim and unconsciona-
bly picturesque. A few hours later she'd be back again.

What else delights me about this harbor? A million images, a hundred encounters flood my memory. It is impossible to catch them all:

Two men in a tiny dory. One is rowing, the other, on his
knees, is leaning far out over the stern, looking down intently
at the harbor bottom through a glass-bottomed bucket he
draws behind the boat. One hand holds a long bamboo spear.
Slowly the men row their way about the harbor, oblivious of
the activity around them. Suddenly the hand plunges down,
the spear is drawn up with a coil of writhing snakes pinioned
at its tip. It is an octopus. The man smiles, pulls the octopus
off the spear, drops it in the bottom of the dory, and returns
to his scrutiny of the harbor.

A boy about eight or nine pushes a homemade wagon
with his bare feet across the rough cobbles. The wagon is a
crude box mounted on the chassis of a ruined baby carriage.
One wheel is white, another black. Two wooden sticks jut
strangely from one end of the box like handles on a wheelbarrow. The boy is all alone on a wharf of busy dockworkers,
playing in some private world. I pass and he looks out at me
with strange, haunted eyes. "Hey! One 'scu!" The voice is
threatening. I smile at him but pass on, I know him well. The
command is his single refrain, spoken for form's sake more
than for need of the escudo, and we have come to call him
"One 'Scu." He is the only person in Horta who has ever
asked us for anything.

I pass along the wharf at midnight. The corners are full
of boxy shadows and all is silent. A freight boat rides quietly
at its mooring lines in the placid water. Perhaps it was caught
here by darkness, or the promise of an early morning cargo,

and its crew, all Pico men, have not been able to return to their island across the channel. A rustle draws my attention to a huge mound of corn stalks piled on the wharf. It is full of sleeping men.

Another winter storm is in progress but some mission, not my own, requires a visit to *Aquarius*. She is moored to a freight lighter anchored several hundred yards off the wharf. The new mooring is easier on *Aquarius* but harder on us. I launch Zodiac, our inflatable rubber dinghy, into the froth of waves. I am in a bad mood; this will be a rough trip and a wet one. I am wearing a heavy wool fisherman's sweater, wool iceman's pants, so'wester pants and parka, sea boots, watch cap and mittens. Maybe I can stay dry. I make it halfway to the lighter, fighting the blasts of wind and the vicious chop. A burst from over the sea wall lifts Zodiac and me out of the water, inverting us neatly and depositing us upside down in the icy brine. More angry than surprised, I right Zodiac, drag my sodden self aboard, collect the floating oars and continue furiously to *Aquarius*.

A tuna boat has returned from three days of fishing with a bountiful catch and the men are exuberant with success. The quay above them is crowded with workers and spectators and a big truck waits behind to haul the fish to the cold-storage plant. One man works in the slippery fish hold below, tuna stacked about him like cordwood, snagging the fish with his hook and slinging them back under the hatchway. The tuna are huge—some bulk the size of a man. Two fishermen lean into the hatchway with their gaffs and set the hooks through a jaw or a gill. A mighty heave and the fish comes slipping and sliding up onto the deck to bump among their rubber boots. The deck is awash with blood and the saucer eyes of the tuna stare blankly. Remarks from spectators at the size of the fish; a shout from the winch operator, who lowers his hook. The hook is set and the fish flies upward. Two men on the wharf snag it and sling it into the truck. Below another tuna starts its journey. The air is filled with shouting and laughter and the smell of blood.

I sense the history of this harbor everywhere. One day Peter showed us an amazing photograph of Horta in the mid-1800s. The harbor was crammed with great square-rigged whalers from New Bedford and Nantucket. The whole basin was forested with masts, laced with rigging. They came to chase the sperm whale, these early American big-game hunters, and they soon hooked the Azorians on the profit and danger of it. The local men first shipped aboard as able seamen, but soon learned the trade themselves. The rest of the world moved to exploding harpoons, helicopter spotters, and fleets of mechanized whaling vessels—and the whales moved closer to extinction; but the men of the Azores still hunt the sperm whale from open boats according to the time-honored and deadly rules of hand-to-hand combat they learned a hundred years ago.

Peter's photograph set me thinking about the constant interaction between the harbor and the town, about how thoroughly the harbor seems to have shaped the history and mentality of the island. It surely began in the early 1500s with the first Portuguese and Flemish settlers. But the whaling ships probably gave the Azores their first taste of foreigners in any number, and those ties still endure. It's not by chance that the largest Portuguese colony in the United States is located in New Bedford—every person in Fayal has at least one relative living there. It's not by chance that the only direct air connection with the United States lands first in Boston. Horta's greatest period of growth undoubtedly came with the development of trans-Atlantic steamer traffic. The harbor was a natural refueling station for coal-burning ships. Those must have been bustling and prosperous times for the town. The marks of it are everywhere: in the substantial stone buildings that line the principal streets; the faded signs in English above buildings that once housed thriving ship chandleries; the palatial Bank of Portugal, grand beyond any current fiscal necessity; the imposing Victorian mansions, relics of an era when every major maritime nation maintained a consulate here, and reduced now to modest service as private dwellings. The old coal warehouses still stand by the harbor's edge, unused and empty; the busy days are gone, probably forever.

I don't find it sad. The prosperity of that era turned Horta into one of the most attractive towns in the western world. The solid stone buildings and elaborate mosaic sidewalks evoke an age of skillful handwork quite consonant with the standards of medieval guilds. But the freshly painted façades, the immaculate streets and beautifully maintained interiors suggest that some miraculous influence stopped the process of aging the day the final stone was laid. A further blessing. Relative poverty and high import duties have spared Horta the worst artifacts of commercialism. The town is a delight and a benediction to the eye.

There I go again, praising poverty. It's not as simple as all that. Wealth and poverty depend to a certain extent on one's values, and to me the people of the Azores are in many respects wealthy. Material poverty is here, no doubt of that, but not the quality of impoverishment one finds in parts of Latin America and Asia, or the United States, for that matter. No real hunger, the agriculture is too skillful for that; no lack of clothing and shelter; and no vast extremes of wealth and indigence, at least not on the island of Fayal. But what the Azorians have in great richness is a *quality* of life that cherishes human values above all others. It is difficult to write about this and make any sense although it is easy enough to see if one has been here any time. The signs are in the faces that *look* at you, the clear eyes, the humor, the sense of beauty and order in the environment, the handiwork, the way people cherish and preserve old things, their attachment to children, their extraordinary regard for each other. I like to think these values were once American, too, that they could be found, for example, in the small upstate

New York town where my grandfather lived. But I don't know that for sure—maybe I am romanticizing—all I know is that those values cannot be found in any coherent sense in the mainstream of America today.

It is impossible to express to our friends here how much we admire their culture. The words come out sounding like the most superficial brand of flattery. I don't think the people I know in Horta are much aware of what their life looks like to outsiders; they wear it comfortably, unselfconsciously, like a well-used suit of clothes.

It is even more impossible to express to them our weariness with all the technological kitsch we have tried to escape by sailing away, or our horror at how aimlessly our nation seems to be drifting. The chasm between their view of America and ours is so vast that most of them can't even begin to evaluate what we say, and so they politely dismiss it without comment. To most Azorians, America is a *magic* place, as it must have seemed to the immigrants of the 1880s. It is a land of plenty and we can never explain to our friend Othon how little happiness America's great material prosperity has brought to most of us. Othon worked a summer in New Bedford recently, etching whaling scenes on pieces of ivory in a scrimshaw sweatshop maintained by a fellow Portuguese. The hours were long and the pay modest, but he came home with a small fortune by Azorian standards, and he wants to go back. Who can blame him?

We can never explain to Peter why we prefer sitting in his handmade café to wolfing a hamburger in polystyrene McDonald's. The technology of the Azores could never hope to produce the seamless plastic efficiency of McDonald's, and so our technological hamburger stands seem a *miracle* here —even after they have tasted the meat and listened to the Muzak. We have given up trying to explain ourselves; it's enough to enjoy everything that's around us.

October 31

JEANNINE: We saw the portents of All Saints' Day during the last few days of October, but didn't recognize them. In New Orleans the signs were always chrysanthemums; they appeared in dime stores, grocery stores, on stands along the streets just before the first of November. In the cemeteries, families gathered to whitewash the beautiful high tombs for All Departed Souls who would surely be pleased by the candles and chrysanthemums placed on their graves. In Horta the sign was chestnuts—great woven baskets of them, brown and shining in the doorways of the little shops. In some stores an entire wheelbarrow full had been dumped in a corner, a small mountain of chestnuts sprawling over the floor. We asked Peter about them.

"They are for eating on the Dia de Todos Santos," he replied.

"Oh, do you celebrate Halloween?" the children asked.

"No, I don't know what that is."

"Hey!" Melissa suggested, "we should have a Halloween party at the Café Sport to show everybody what American Halloween is like! We could treat all the people who have been so nice to us."

"That's a good idea," agreed Matthew. "Could we do that Peter?"

"Sure, why not? What is it like?"

We described Halloween, our enthusiasm snowballing as we planned the event which became the best Halloween party of our lives. Matthew described it in his log.

October 31

MATTHEW: When we got to the Café, it was very crowded. We lit the jack-o'-lanterns we had carved, passed out the popcorn and let people guess who we were. I was a pirate with a black eye patch and watch cap. Melissa was a gypsy with a long skirt and gold earrings. Dad was the captain with white bell bottoms and an engineer's cap. Mom was just plain dressed up. I guess she went as first mate. We hung the paper chains on the ceiling and decided it was time to initiate everyone. Out came the paper streamers.

The Azorians had a certain style for this. They blew into the center of the roll and the tape came spurting out at the victim. Then they let the streamer unwind around him. There were streamers all over the floor after the last person had been initiated. Then Dad told me to come in the back room, where he had a candle and was blackening a plate. I knew what he was up to so I blackened my hands on the plate. He got his cameras ready and went out to take pictures of the party. Then I came out and announced that I wanted a special portrait of Othon. I told him I wanted to make the picture perfect and proceeded to move his head around with my blackened hand (which he couldn't see). By this time everyone was screaming with laughter. We finally showed him a mirror and he turned redder than a ripe tomato. All he could say was, "Who's going to wash my face?" and then he would start laughing again.

I sat down and immediately got bombarded by a flying wad of streamers. Another one fell in my lap. With the third missile I discovered the launchsite. I immediately pronounced war! I got the materials and started manufacturing ammunition. This enemy was very hostile. He launched another attack at someone to my rear. I had an ally. The war went on and soon John, the pilot, and his wife joined the battle. Another power had entered the skirmish. The ammunition was refined and improved and the shots got more accurate. Some stray missiles hit neutral powers and started them into action. The casualties were high but reinforcements just kept coming. Soon a man came in with a wide-range destruction weapon. Green paper dots cannonballed into the air and destroyed reservoirs of beer. Before long everyone was involved. The air was full of flack. The war had a quick ending when the surrounding area was sapped of materials to make ammunition.

While we recovered from the devastation, people sang. Mom played her guitar and sang some English songs, and then a great big guy who looked like a prizefighter started playing the trumpet loudly. Peter looked a little strained then; I think he was worried about the family who lived above the café.

So we all went outside for fireworks. Green, blue and red glowing dots in the sky fell into the water making loud bangs. It was around twelve o'clock and a few people were getting drunk so Peter had to close up the wasteland. One drunk man followed me everywhere saying "Goodbye!" fifty times. I had to climb over chairs to escape him. I turned around and there he was, "Goodbye, goodbye, goodbye!" I finally sneaked outside and waited for Mom and Dad and Melissa. What a party!!!!!

November 2

JEANNINE: We understood more about the chestnuts when we went to José's house (the engineer of *Perola*) the next day to celebrate Dia de Todos Santos. He had slaughtered a pig, an event which probably happened once a year for his family. Several cousins and neighbors had gathered to help with the process of cooking and preserving the pork. The women were in back of the kitchen sitting at great tubs, making *mucella,* a highly prized blood sausage made by stuffing the intestines of the pig with a sloppy mixture of blood, onions, seasonings and pork fat (a combination remarkably resembling the original contents of the bulging membranes).

We had been a little concerned that the visit might be awkward because of language problems, but it was surprising how much communication went on. Matthew and Melissa had brought a gift of chocolate for José's son, and some games to play. The two boys became engrossed in making a model airplane. There was real warmth between Matt and José. They each recognized in the other a competence, a manliness, an enjoyment of work that required no words.

The chestnuts were dessert, a large steaming bowl of them, to polish off a delicious meal. We sat for a long time, peeling the chestnuts, popping them into our mouths, sipping red Pico wine. There was another bowl of chestnuts on a sideboard. Did they think we could go through that many chestnuts? Several knocks at the door resolved the question. It was children doing the Azorian version of "trick or treat." Young José went smiling to the door carrying the big bowl to his friends.

On the street, as we returned home, we saw other groups of children happily knocking on doors—a ritual different enough from our own to be intriguing and novel, similar enough to evoke feelings of kinship and common tradition. We were warmed by the Pico wine and a sense of unity with humanity—a reassurance of the traditions held in common, like hospitality and caring for strangers, which bind *Homo sapiens* into one unique tribe. How would we ever be able to pull ourselves away from this nourishing little island?

We refused to be weaned, although we knew the time had come to break away. (It seems to be a common syndrome, judging by other voyage accounts we have read: after a long crossing sailors remain unreasonably long in their first port, making all kinds of dazed, irrational excuses for their prolonged stays.) Actually we had another good reason for staying. Matt was waiting for whales to be sighted so he could go out with the fishermen and photograph a whale hunt.

November 10

MATT: I decided that if I ever wanted to see the great beasts of the ocean at close hand I would have to join a whaling expedition like those which originated at our doorstep every few days. I expressed this wish to Peter, the master expediter, who had been so helpful with repairing and resupplying *Aquarius;* Peter immediately arranged it. It was not so difficult as I had imagined. From the Port captain I obtained a paper, a sort of contract, known locally as the "Death Warrant," which Peter translated for me and I signed. It described the manifold dangers of whaling and I agreed that I understood them all and was prepared to die or be maimed for life without holding the Port captain or anyone but myself responsible for my folly. This accomplished, the whale hunters were informed of my due certification and they agreed to take me along on the next hunt. I can't understand why. If I were an Azorian whaler I would never agree to allow an American photographer with no knowledge of Portuguese or whales underfoot on an enterprise that is manifestly all business and some danger. But they did and I am grateful to them. Except for the price of the few revenue stamps I attached to the Death Warrant, no money changed hands and no promises were made. I was told to be ready to leave on five minutes' notice any morning between six and ten. I made up a camera kit of long lenses and high-speed Ektachrome and a personal survival kit of food, dry socks, foul-weather gear and brandy. I stowed the kits aboard *Aquarius* and went back to my daily routine, which was now enhanced with a certain tense expectation.

Whaling has taken a special form here. Americans, as everyone probably knows, were pelagic whalers, they ranged the seven seas on hunting safaris that could last as long as five years in ships that were floating factories, fully equipped to process hundreds of whales and survive any contingency. Each voyage was a major undertaking in finance, ship chandlery, seamanship and nautical daring.

By instinct and tradition the men of the Azores were small boat men with neither the resources nor the inclination to mount long, hazardous expeditions. Their home waters already abounded in schools of sperm whale, so they perfected techniques of open-boat whaling learned from the Americans, and operated from shore stations instead.

Every morning, as soon as there is enough light to illuminate a spout, dozens of lookouts climb to their posts in lonely huts on ridge tops and cliff heads around the islands. For hours they sweep the sea with powerful spyglasses straining to catch the elusive tracery of spouts that betrays a school of sperm whale. If they have seen nothing by ten or eleven in the morning they return to their villages and their every-day jobs, for the hour is now too advanced to make a foray ten or more miles offshore, to fix and kill a whale before darkness. If whales are sighted the lookout will signal a shore station by telephone or radio.

Whale hunters are rather like volunteer firemen. There is not enough money in whaling to justify paying them to sit around the whalehouse playing cards and polishing the brass, so most of them work at regular jobs keeping an ear cocked for the signal (a rocket arcing lazily over the town) that will transform them from shopkeepers into big-game hunters.

It was several days before the rocket came and then I didn't actually hear it; my ear wasn't tuned to that dry pop among the many harbor sounds. What I did hear was the powerful diesel of the whaling launch, *Walkiria,* being warmed up, and in a matter of minutes I reported myself breathlessly to the helmsman, who indicated with a nod and a grunt that I should go aboard. Most of the gear was already stowed. Some tubs of line came aboard to supplement those carried in the whaleboats, the engine roared, the moorings were cast off, and we were away. A smaller launch had already left minutes ahead of us.

Walkiria was built long and narrow for speed. She could make eighteen knots under full power or could throttle back and tow a whale. I guessed she would roll like a witch in a seaway—and I was right. We were out of the harbor and heading north up the Fayal Channel before I could collect my wits. I found myself feverishly loading film, cleaning lenses, talking to myself, planning strategy. The launchmen were in a rage of excitement too. They shouted furiously at each other over the roar of the engine. The radioman was below in the tiny forecastle screaming Portuguese into his radio. The radio screamed back at him in Broken Static. The noise was so bad I couldn't imagine, even if the radio had spoken Portuguese, how communication could be possible. *Walkiria* pounded briskly along the spectacular coastline taking sheets of spray over her bows while I huddled behind the pilothouse or joined the helmsman in its shelter.

We continued onward for perhaps an hour, past the bluff of Ponta da Ribeirinna with its fine old lighthouse, then northwest for a spell as the precipitous coastline changed direction. I wandered in my mind, dreaming of whales, and when I returned the launch had caught up with its predecessor and both were stopped and rolling heavily in the swell a short distance off a small fishing village that nestled at the base of a high rocky cliff. Now I saw the whaleboats that had come out to meet us—two of them so hidden in the valleys of the swells that I didn't notice them at first. They put lines aboard the launches and the men from one of the boats clambered aboard our launch, leaving three behind to steer the whaleboat, or *canoa,* as it was called. The *canoa* was a lovely craft, long and graceful in the ends, maybe thirty-eight feet overall, very strong but lightly built with clean sweeping lines that would give great speed when the gaff-rigged mainsail and jib were set. The sails lay along the center of the boat now, furled together with the mast, and the whole affair was arranged so it could be set in a moment. When the wind was favorable, sailing was the fastest and most silent means of coming up on a whale. There were oars stowed alongside the mast, and paddles too; and in the bottom, two tubs like the one on the launch with line laid into them in meticulous coils. A snag here could mean disaster. The *canoa* was guided by a long steering oar or a rudder when undersail. The entire craft was freshly painted; white on the outside, pink within, the gunwales red and the top strake yellow, everything shipshape and orderly. And rightly so. A piece of gear out of place might spell the difference between success and failure; or between life and death.

Now we were off again—off on a wild sleighride, with the

launch playing Prancer to the whaleboat scudding along behind. We headed directly out from the island, pointing north. The helmsman seemed to smell whales for he never changed course or slackened his furious pace. Occasionally the radioman would duck into the forepeak to question his apparatus and relay messages from a lookout high on the island behind us.

My teeth began to chatter and I crawled into the engine room for warmth. The noise was tremendous, an overpowering torrent tearing at the outer dimensions of sound. More time passed and abruptly the engine relented. On deck in the ringing silence, men looked tensely in all directions. The helmsman left his post and climbed to the crosstrees of the stubby radio mast. No whales. Another short run, another pause, all eyes straining outward. Then from the helmsman an explosive shout, *"Baleia!"* Whales! He gripped my shoulder, the first direct acknowledgment of my presence aboard, and pointed out into the blinding water at a spout I couldn't see.

Another short run, a pause and this time the *canoa* was drawn alongside, plunging and twisting in the uncertain sea, seemingly ready at any moment to shatter her bows against the launch. The men boarded her one by one, each clutching his little bundle of food and clothing, each negotiating the angry chasm with practiced ease.

The boatheader, master of the whaling boat, took charge now, standing erect in the stern and directing the raising of the sail—an upright man with a ready smile and formidable mustaches. It was he, the *mestre,* who would divine the moment for going in on the whale, and guide the *canoa* down that narrow pathway close to the body and behind the periphery of the whale's vision; guide it into that circle of danger where the harpooner would have a fair shot. It was he who would call the cadence *(forca!)* for the quick reversed strokes of the oars by which the men might claw free from the fury of the whale's upended flukes after the harpoon had struck. He would plan strategy and guide the boat through the difficult hours from harpooning to kill. I looked across the water at the harpooner sitting in the bow. He was a young man, strong and daring. The *mestre* looked twice his age, seasoned in the heat of a thousand encounters. He was talking quietly to his men and they seemed different now—like hunters. The boat gave them an identity they lacked on the launch. The *canoa* squared away and moved off. The stalking began.

"*Bloz!*" (Portuguese for Nantucket's "Thar she blows"). The launchman pointed urgently off the port bow and this time I saw it, a misty curtain of spouts rising from the water, indistinct but unmistakable. I felt a chill, an ancient warning: *Leviathans in the water.* Biblical fish—immensely larger and more powerful than any of us and our puny machines.

The sail was raised; the *canoa* moved off toward the whales at a good clip. One man stood on the gunwale holding onto the weather shrouds and leaning far out to windward to prevent the narrow boat from capsizing. The others crowded up on the windward side also. With its large high-peaked gaff mainsail and full-cut jib the *canoa* seemed over-canvased, but she made a brave sight in the sparkling water and I uncorked my 500-mm lens to get closer to her, for our launch was holding back to avoid frightening the whales or interfering with the hunt.

The school of whales was swimming quietly in an easterly direction, about half a dozen of them, their humps barely visible in the roil of the sea. I would lose them for minutes at a time, assume they had sounded, and then a chorus of spouts would come from a little further along their track. The *canoa* was almost on them and I could read tension in the stance of the boatheader as he braced in his station at the stern, leaning forward, staring intently ahead; the harpooner was also standing now, his left thigh braced into a notch cut in the thwart. I waited for him to raise the harpoon and throw; I was braced for it also, jammed up against the front of the pilothouse with the 500-mm lens cradled in my hand against the roll of the launch. But the throw never came. The school sounded, right under their bow, it appeared. A flash of flukes and they were gone.

Now the waiting began. The men in the *canoa* appeared completely relaxed, smoking, talking, some eating from their sacks. The sail flapped idly. Aboard the launch it was the same. The wait might grow long—as much as half an hour.

When sperm whales surface and are undisturbed they may stay up for some time, swimming along in company, playing together, even appearing to blow in concert. This is why they can be hunted from open boats. They take their leisure on the surface long enough for an oar- or sail-driven craft to approach closely; and they are normally not aggressive, even when harpooned, but an injured whale can do great damage with his sounding flukes. It is not unusual for a whaleboat to be upset or stove in during one of these encounters, and on rare occasions a whale will turn on a boat and deliberately attack it. Then the carnage can be terrible.

"*Bloz!*" The whales surfaced about half a mile ahead of the *canoa,* which was already hauling her sheets and starting to move. Another approach was made but also unsuccessfully; the whales sounded again before the iron could be thrown. Another wait, another approach, and this time the harpooner's arm darted forward. A triumphant shout from the launchman, a quick image of upraised flukes in my lens and the drama moved underwater. In the whaleboat the danger now was from the hissing, snapping line as it dissolved in coils from the line tub, stretched back taut and smoking around the loggerhead (two oarsmen threw water on the coils to keep the line from burning), and whipped forward along the boat's centerline to disappear over the bow chocks with a whine that caused the whole craft to sing its frequency. The work of dropping mast and sails went on about and around this deadly snake. A snarl in the line tub now would wreak havoc in the boat and lose the whale; a loose coil catching an arm or leg would snatch the owner from the boat and down to his death before anyone could make a saving move.

There was no stopping the first mad plunge of the whale. The line had to run free until the whale bottomed-out. Then the work of reclaiming line began. It was slow, laborious, backbreaking. Standing along the length of the boat, the men straddled the rope, seven backs bent over pulling together, regaining the lost ground handhold by handhold; and the whale remained underwater, nursing his hurt, anonymous, mysterious.

Abruptly he surfaced and took off through the waves, towing the *canoa* and its men behind him like a toy on a string. It must be a wild ride, thrashing over the waves hitched to a sperm whale; in square-rigger days they called it the Nantucket Sleigh Ride. It stopped as abruptly as it began. And now the *mestre* was beckoning to us, shouting, urging us close with wide sweeps of his arm. We swung past him heading toward the whale, and I realized with a shock that our quarry was not alone. The other whales had not scattered as I had expected; the school was staying with the injured one—swimming alongside, perhaps helping him, certainly sharing his distress and giving him courage by their presence, entirely heedless of their own danger. It was such a *human* reaction, the whales' expression of solidarity and concern for their injured fellow, and I was strongly moved by it. For the first time I sensed the presence of a social group with its own rules and morality, perhaps not so different from ours.

The task of the launch now was to play quarterhorse to this herd of leviathans, to cut them out and drive them away from the wounded brother so they couldn't interfere with the chase. We roared back and forth, chasing whales as though they were steers, cutting the injured whale out from the group (they kept circling back to stay with him), and eventually driving them all away.

During the chase I got my first look at a whale close up. What did I see? Not much. A sperm whale swimming on the surface is still ninety-eight percent submerged. I could hardly see flukes at all, the only part available for inspection was the whale's back from nose to hump, twenty or thirty feet of black oily skin moving fast through the water, the whole whale rocking ponderously forward and back as he swam like a huge animated log, nose to hump, hump to nose.

Now the hunt moved into the second stage, the object of which was to tire the whale sufficiently so the *canoa* could move in and lance him. A harpoon rarely hurts a whale, it is only a hook at the end of a leash. Killing is done with a lance, a stout wooden shaft about ten feet long armed with a steel head that is diamond-shaped and razor sharp. If the harpooner is daring and skillful, his lance will penetrate deeply and accurately enough to sever an artery. Then the whale bleeds to death and the hunt is over. The boatheader will try to improve his chances by guiding the bow of the boat right up against the whale, "wood and blackskin," they say. Then the harpooner, leaning out over the bow, will thrust the lance home with both hands and may actually *churn* it up and down trying for a vital spot. This is the worst moment for man and whale, comparable in danger to the matador going in over the horns with his sword at the climax of a bullfight. A variation requires going at the whale head to head *(cabeca com cabeca)* down the narrow slot of blindness directly in front of the animal where his fields of vision fail to merge. More commonly, though, the *canoa* will not reach the whale before the harpooner, sensing that the animal is about to sound, launches his lance from a distance. It is a skillful harpooner indeed who can kill on his first throw— many tries are usually needed, many moments of danger. In modern whaling killing is done from a safe distance using explosive projectiles. Years ago the Azorians themselves experimented with lances carrying an explosive charge but abandoned them as unsatisfactory, and returned to the older, more dangerous practice.

But the kill was still hours away, the whale still fresh, and the business of wearing him down dragged on through the afternoon, until I could only marvel at the endurance of the men and the whale. (It was a cycle repeated many times:

whale sounds, stealing line from the *canoa;* whale lies quiescent somewhere below while the men regain the line by yards and inches; whale surfaces and begins his run, towing the boat behind; whale lies exhausted while the whalers ply their oars, seeking to get close enough for a lancing; whale takes fright and sounds again.) Little by little his endurance ebbed and finally the boat was able to approach. *"Forca! forca!"* The men strained at their oars, the shaft flew to its mark and the whale gave a great lunge and sounded again. When he reappeared his spout came up bright red with his own blood. "The red flag," whalemen call it. He spouted again, great gouts of blood. I knew the whale's hours were numbered and it chilled and sickened me. I had been able until now to hold my feelings at bay, to follow the changing fortunes of the hunt with interest and excitement, but no longer. I wished now with every incredible crimson fountain for some Intervention to save the whale—a hand to cut the line, a bolt of lightning to sunder the whaleboat. But there were no miracles, the hunt went on, only not as I expected. The wound seemed to scour up some desperate energy in the whale. He sounded, the whaleboat lost ground and when he blew again the red flag seemed a shade less bright. Was he out of blood? Dying? Healing? I couldn't tell, but instead of ending quickly the hunt dragged on weary hours more, the incredible endurance and courage of the whale beyond my belief, the determination of the men equally so. Why wasn't he drowning in his own blood? The red flag came again and again, staining the sea all around us with his life blood. The animal seemed barely able to swim now, no longer sounding, but somehow keeping ahead of his tormentors. His agony numbed me to the passage of time and the increasing chill of the ocean. I waited only for the end, myself dead from hours on my feet.

The sun was crimson on the horizon when I heard a hail from the whaleboat. I looked and the boat was still, the men sitting quietly on their thwarts, the fierceness somehow gone out of them. What did it mean? I looked at the whale. He was swimming away. Then I understood. The whale had won. The *mestre* had given the order for the line to be cut. In these wintry months of uncertain weather and frigid nights it was not safe to pursue the whale beyond darkness. They had given up. I looked at the whale again, distant now, swimming slowly. Magnificent animal! Would he live? I couldn't tell but I believed he would, believed it strongly. He'd won the right.

The remainder can be described simply. The second *canoa* had killed their whale. We rendezvoused with them miles away at dusk. The other launch took both *canoas* in tow and headed for the fishing village. *Walkiria* was harnessed to the anonymous black monster they had left behind and we began the long slow homeward tow around the opposite side of the island. Night and monotony closed in on us. I packed my cameras and my spent film away and tucked myself into a warm corner of the wheelhouse, musing on the strange creature I had come to admire and wonder about so much in the course of the afternoon.

Was he intelligent, I wondered? I'd recently been reading *The Mind of the Dolphin,* a book by John Lilly, the scientist who'd had such success communicating with the bottle-nosed dolphin. Lilly believed whales were intelligent, perhaps vastly more so than men. Throughout nature, he argued, there existed a general correlation between brain size and intelligence. The dolphins with the biggest brains were the brightest. The bottle-nose, about equal in brain size to humans, appeared to have a similar intellectual capacity, although directed toward very different ends. But the volume of the sperm whale's brain, Lilly argued, was six times that of man. Was he not six times brighter? Possibly so. The idea staggered me.

A light flared briefly in the dark cabin as the launchman lit another cigarette. I looked at his tense and weathered face peering intently into the night. How did *he* feel about the creatures he hunted so fiercely? Did he ever admire the courage of a wounded whale, ever consider the impulse (was it "instinct" or "intelligence"?) that drew a community of sperm whales to the side of an injured brother? Or were whales just so much meat to him, like the anonymous mass we were dragging through the night so laboriously by a chain through its fluke?

Sperm whales have become an endangered species, and they owe that special distinction to the fleets of mechanized factory ships that even now hunt them without mercy in all oceans of the world. By comparison, the open-boat whaling of the Azores is a *handicraft* and I don't know whether it has any effect at all on the sperm whale population. But I did know from what I had witnessed today that the sperm whale is a *remarkable* creature who should not be killed for any reason—a peaceable animal, undoubtedly intelligent, possessed of great courage and feeling for his fellows. I agreed with Lilly that if we destroy this animal, if we remove all possibility of contact with his intelligence, we will lose something very valuable that he may have to teach us, not only about the sea and his own habits (or even his ethics), but about ourselves as well.

We arrived, long hours into the night, in the tiny harbor of Porto Pim, just a stone's throw from Horta, where we left our whale shackled to a buoy. Tomorrow he will be butchered at the whale factory just up the hill, his flesh converted to animal food, his blubber boiled for industrial oil, his bones ground for fertilizer. The whalemen will claim his great teeth, and some of them will find their way eventually to Peter's café to be sold as mementos to tourists like myself. I returned to *Aquarius,* full of wonder and brooding.

15

Harmattan

November 27

JEANNINE: Our ambivalence about departure continued but the weather brought the issue to resolution. Ten consecutive days of cold and wintery North Atlantic bluster served to jolt us back to reality. Peter began tactfully to suggest that perhaps we had better think about waiting until spring to make our run to the Canaries. We'd been here almost fifty days—had we dallied too long?

The barometer had settled to a dismal low and we were almost despairing that it would ever rise again to a height reasonable for a safe dash to the south. But it finally lifted and we were assured by the United States Air Force Weather Station on the island of Terceira that it would remain high for eight or ten days with no low pressure systems anywhere in the Atlantic to the east and south of us. It was time to go back to sea. Matthew wrote an account of departure day:

November 27

MATTHEW: I got up and was told to hurry and get dressed—there was work to be done. We were going to try and leave this sunny day. Mom was busy wrapping Christmas presents for relatives in America and cleaning up the room. We had four packages and eight letters and a gift of macramé coasters I had made to give Peter. We said goodbye to the *senhora* and she was sad, like saying goodbye to her own family.

It was noon when we finally got to the post office. We were supposed to have been at the boat at nine o'clock to help Dad get ready. Mom stood in line to get the stamps. I watched a fly eating the glue people use for sticking on their stamps. He just sat there eating and eating and eating. He never seemed to get stuck. The stamps cost about fifteen dollars. I pasted them on. The fly stopped eating the glue, flipped over on its back, wiggled its legs a few times and died. Now I know why there aren't many post office flies.

We loaded the things from our room into a taxi, drove to the dock, unpacked everything and left Melissa on guard. I rowed out to *Aquarius* to help Dad bring her in to the dock while Mom went by taxi to buy some ice. We really worked for a few hours stowing everything away. We scrubbed the decks; we cleaned the icebox; we filled the water tanks; then we went up to Peter's to say our goodbyes. The fishermen were telling us to stay until summer when the weather would be better.

Peter and a lot of friends came down to the dock to see us off. The departure was all very seamanlike and orderly. We passed the light on the seawall at five-fifteen (our usual departure time) and suddenly there were all our friends again —they had jumped in cars to race to the end of the seawall. They were shouting and waving their hats. The last thing I saw was Henrique's white handkerchief waving slowly back and forth.

The seas were calm and we were on a broad reach with a nice breeze. Dad let out some fierce howls just to release the tension of all that hectic preparation. As the sun went down it lit the top of Pico and we could see for the first time that Pico's Pike was covered with snow!

On this leg of the trip, because Phil had left us, Melissa and I had to take night watches. I had one from 2200 to 2400;

Mom and Dad had theirs from 2400 to 0600, and Melissa had hers from 0600 to 0800. On my first watch the wind was steadily picking up, and I was constantly getting hit by squalls. It was only a taste of what was yet to come.

November 29

MATT: I am tired this morning—tired and apprehensive. The weather has been favorable, as the U.S. Air Force prophet at Terceira foretold, and the barometer remains high —all good signs; but even in good weather the winds blow like fury at this time of year and we are taking a beating. Henrique's warning about the lateness of the season rings in my ears. I shudder to think what it will be like if the weather turns really bad.

It began well enough. We footed out of Horta in a moderate northerly breeze, all delighted to be at sea again and *Aquarius* lively in the easy swells of Fayal Channel. Jeannine brewed hot chocolate in the galley and we watched Horta come alight behind us in the darkening sky. The twinkle on our stern guided us for hours until the horizon swallowed it and left burning only the memories of our many happy days there.

By 2100, off point São Mateus on Pico's southern shore the wind died entirely and I thought we would spend the night flopping about in the lee of the island; but soon it revived from the northwest and we ran before it making a brisk six knots. The Pico porpoises came out to bid us farewell and staged a brilliant phosphorescent lightshow in our honor, cutting swaths around the boat until *Aquarius* glowed with their acrobatics. We settled down to a night of uneasy watchkeeping. Running dead before the wind is difficult work for the helmsman in any kind of breeze and we had a hatful.

By morning of the 28th the wind had backed to the west and intensified, and I settled into my familiar-but-curious state of post-departure lassitude. Energy fled, muscles went on strike, will and resolution took the day off. I slumped in the cockpit thrashing feebly in a quagmire of indecision. A succession of squalls was attacking us from the west. With the genoa still up, *Aquarius* was pressed to the maximum, yet I dallied all morning inventing reasons to put off the few moments of heavy energy required by a change of headsails. This squall would certainly pass ahead of us, that one we'd probably outrun. When a squall did strike us, I resorted to the oldest of lazy-sailor devices, the "fisherman's reef"— slacking off the mainsheet until the flapping mainsail spilled most of its wind. Finally indecision became more agonizing than action. I made the change to working jib and tied a reef in the main for good measure. I lost the topping lift up the mast in the process, and the loose end, encouraged by the roll of the boat, tied itself into the rigging with the most intricate knots. I was too drained to go aloft and untangle the line; I went below instead to lie on my bunk and wish for the services of Martin Alonso Pinzon, that doughty voyager who intervened on behalf of another sailor in these same waters seventy-five years ago. The story is interesting:

Captain Joshua Slocum, the first man in history to circumnavigate the globe singlehanded, left Horta on July 24, 1895, according to his account, *Sailing Alone Around the World.* He was bound for Gibraltar in his thirty-six-foot sloop, *Spray.* On the third day out he partook injudiciously of a near-lethal combination of Pico cheese and Pico plums given him by the kindly natives. The onset of paralyzing cramps coincided with the beginnings of a strong gale. Slocum reefed as best he could, then threw himself on his cabin floor in great pain:

> How long I lay there I could not tell, for I became delirious. When I came to, as I thought, from my swoon, I realized that the sloop was plunging into a heavy sea, and looking out of the companionway, to my amazement I saw a tall man at the helm. His rigid hand, grasping the spokes of the wheel, held them as in a vise. One may imagine my astonishment. His rig

was that of a foreign sailor, and the large red cap he wore was cockbilled over his left ear, and all was set off with shaggy black whiskers. He would have been taken for a pirate in any part of the world. While I gazed upon his threatening aspect I forgot the storm, and wondered if he had come to cut my throat. This he seemed to divine. "Señor," said he, doffing his cap, "I have come to do you no harm." And a smile, the faintest in the world, but still a smile, played on his face, which seemed not unkind when he spoke. "I have come to do you no harm. I have sailed free," he said, "but was never worse than a *contrabandista*. I am one of Columbus's crew," he continued. "I am the pilot of the *Pinta* come to aid you. Lie quiet, señor captain," he added, "and I will guide your ship tonight. You have a *calentura,* but you will be all right tomorrow." I thought what a very devil he was to carry sail. Again, as if he read my mind, he exclaimed: "Yonder is the *Pinta* ahead; we must overtake her. Give her sail; give her sail! *Vale, vale, muy vale!*" Biting off a large quid of black twist he said:

"You did wrong, Captain, to mix cheese with plums. White cheese is never safe unless you know whence it comes. *Quien sabe,* it may have been from *leche de Capra* and becoming capricious—"

"Avast there!" I cried. "I have no mind for moralizing."

. . . Great seas were boarding the *Spray,* but in my fevered brain I thought they were boats falling on deck, that careless draymen were throwing from wagons on the pier to which I imagined the *Spray* was now moored, and without fenders to breast her off. "You'll smash your boats!" I called out again and again, as the seas crashed on the cabin over my head. "You'll smash your boats, but you can't hurt the *Spray.* She is strong," I cried.

I found, when my pains and *calentura* had gone, that the deck, now as white as a shark's tooth from seas washing over it, had been swept of everything movable. To my astonishment, I saw now at broad day that the *Spray* was still heading as I had left her, and was going like a racehorse. Columbus himself could not have held her more exactly on her course. The sloop had made ninety miles in the night through a rough sea. I felt grateful to the old pilot, but I marveled some that he had not taken in the jib.

I sympathized with Slocum. The combination of Pico cheese and Pico wine that I had imbibed on the fishing boat *Perola* had given me a day of cramps and diarrhea such as I never care to repeat. But I wish I had Slocum's luck. We could use an experienced pilot on this bark.

November 30

MATT: Methuselah has developed respiratory complications, predictable in an old man, I suppose. He has difficulty breathing and coughs a lot. I spent the morning at his bedside tearing down his carburetor. It was clogged with phlegm, rust, gunk, and viscous humors, and gave me quite a time. He's better now, since his purgative, but not perfect. I have to watch his fuel filter like a hawk. I promised him a new one if he got us to the Canaries and it seemed to raise the old man's spirits no end. It's a tribute to Methuselah that he has kept going at all. The sea air is bad for his lungs, his fuel tank's a bit decrepit and rust-prone, and I've noticed his blood pressure has been dropping steadily ever since we left Bermuda—a general weakening of the main and the camshaft bearings is my diagnosis. Oddly enough, none of Methuselah's maladies, short of a total cardiac arrest, has the power to disturb me. I've played his games, I know his tricks, he's lost the ability to surprise. I'm quite fatalistic about the old man. He'll make it or he won't, and if he doesn't, I'll bury him in some foreign junkyard, say a prayer over his rusty remains, and figure out another way to get us home.

December 1

MATT: Today the cabin looks like an icicle cave. I should really say *beefcicle* cave, because the long festoons

hanging from the grab rails overhead represent the early
stages of beef jerky, or pemmican, the dried meat that was
a staple in the diet of American Indians, Pilgrims, early
explorer types—and Matthew during our Atlantic crossing.
On the day we left the Azores Jeannine bought nine pounds
of tender boneless beef in the market. This was cut into long
thin strips and dipped in boiling sea water to seal and cook
the outer surface while the meat dried to an antique and
ageless mahogany. It dangles in our faces as it dries, swinging
above the boiling pots on our swinging stove. Fortunately
there are no flies at sea. I'm keeping my mouth shut, but I
confess to a certain jerky skepticism. I remember the rolls of
wet toilet paper that festooned our grab rails for so long
during the crossing, their dampness renewed periodically by
dashes of salt spray through the hatchway.

Last night Jeannine and I spent several hours tearing
the boat apart trying to locate the source of a heavy pounding that is beginning to worry me greatly. It seems to come
from deep in the forward section of the keel, a heavy periodic crash as if a great weight were shifting with the roll of
the boat. Yet I know from the architect's drawings that our
keel is frozen solid in cement. We have torn up every foot
of floorboard from amidships clear to the stem without being able to locate the source. The whole boat shudders
when the blow falls, and I only hope we don't tear a plate
loose before we reach Las Palmas.

The passage so far has been extremely rough, uncomfortable, and uneventful. For each of the last three days we have
clocked an unvarying one hundred ten miles. We are running
closehauled, wind northeast, and the boat has been steeply
heeled for so long I think I am developing a permanent
abridgement of my starboard leg. The vane gear tends the
boat day and night and there is little to do but lie in a bunk
and wonder why we chose such an exceedingly uncomfortable means of crossing the ocean.

December 4

MATTHEW: WOW! What a trip! We had bad weather all the way. The sea didn't give us one second of peace. We spent seven days below deck under reefed main and storm jib. There was nothing to do. The boat was rolling furiously and everything was flying around. I went into a sort of interrupted state of suspended animation. I was always sleeping. The time was always speeding up or slowing down. Once in a while I would get up to eat but not often. The boat was pure chaos. All the foul-weather gear was dropped everywhere. All the dishes were dirty. No one cared. Every time I tried to get up seasickness forced me down again.

For the first time we had leaks! Now I know why people like dry boats. The water was coming in through a fitting on the foredeck that had worn out its waterproof seal. It was perpetually dripping right where my head rested or tried to rest. I had a real Chinese water torture; any unsteady rhythm will drive me crazy. Dad put a patch around the hole, but this only slowed the leak.

Yesterday morning Dad and I set out to fix the leak. Dad went on deck to hold the fitting while I tightened it from below. The bolt snapped! Oh! What a trip! We tried several times to repair it, but finally Dad had to lash the substay, which the fitting held, to a cleat on the foredeck. We now had a wounded substay, a gaping hole in the deck the size of a nickel, and heavy winds.

Dad stuck a cork in the hole. Surprisingly, it stopped the leak altogether until today, when we had another stroke of bad luck. The sea was playing tricks on us. In the late afternoon the wind died down until it was almost calm. We were really fooled by it. We waited two hours thinking it would start blowing again. We consulted the barometer to make sure we weren't in the eye of a low-pressure system, but it was steady. As soon as Dad shook the reef out of the main and put up the genoa, the wind picked up to gale force again. How mean can the sea be?

As Dad was stomping around the deck putting the reefs back in and changing back to storm jib, he kicked out that very precious cork that kept the water out. From then on I just put a towel under the hole and slept on the floor.

December 4

MATT: This weather is a complete mystification. There has not been an overcast moment since we left Horta. Without exception the barometer has been steady and high, yet the wind blows like fury all the time. It has been blowing for days, and is now very gradually increasing and shifting eastward. The sky is extraordinary—completely clear of clouds (the same condition preceded our gale, but with falling barometer) and tinted a dull brownish gray with a hard metallic glint from the horizon to about 30 degrees upward; beyond, it gradually shades into bright blue directly overhead. Although there is nothing on the horizon to check my perception against, I sense that visibility is greatly reduced.

As the wind veers it is forcing us more and more westward of our intended course to Las Palmas on the island of Grand Canary. This afternoon Jeannine and I gave up trying for Grand Canary altogether and set a course for the island of La Palma, the northwesternmost of the Canary group, which we should be able to fetch without having to beat into this miserable wind. We can lay up there until the weather moderates.

The change means we should make a landfall much sooner, between two and four tomorrow morning if my navigation is accurate. But navigation has not been a simple matter these last few days. Around five this afternoon I decided to go on deck for a sight—the last before our landfall and therefore a vitally important one. *Aquarius* was plunging and twisting like a log in a millrace as she tried to punch her way into waves which broke every few moments with solid force against the bow, sending solid sheets of spray across the boat. I emerged from the cabin swathed toe to parka-top in heavy seaboots and oilskins, my sextant wrapped in a plastic bag against the spray. My progress from cabin to afterdeck was somewhat slow and lumbering and I snapped a safety line to a stanchion as I clambered across the web of steering lines crisscrossing the cockpit. The afterdeck was canted almost 40 degrees and pitching violently, but it was the only corner of the boat I could wedge myself into securely enough to leave both hands occasionally free. I braced a toe under the vane gear support, wedged a shin against the backstay; with my butt on the after-rail and one hand clutching it, I was fairly secure except for those prayerful moments when I had to let go to adjust the micrometer screw on the sextant. At those times I feared being pitched off the deck and losing the sextant in the sea.

To measure the angle of the sun above the horizon, one must actually *see* the horizon. All I could see were angry waves and, sometimes, when *Aquarius* teetered on top of one, a glimpse here and there of what *might* be a horizon line.

I flashed an image of Captain Nemo, Man of Iron, standing on the bridge of the *Nautilus,* sextant fixed in his vice-like grip. *Bloody ridiculous,* I thought, *no sane person would try for a sight in these conditions.* My only hope for accuracy, if indeed there was any hope, lay in attempting a series of sights that I could plot later on a graph. I tried this with Jeannine recording the chronometer and stopwatch from below while I cursed and fiddled on the afterdeck, waiting for *Aquarius* to rise to a wave, hoping for a lull in the spray, whipping back the plastic to expose the scope and mirrors of the sextant, swinging it with one hand, letting go my grip on the after-rail to nudge the micrometer drum, wondering if what I had glimpsed was an actual sun balanced for a fleeting moment on a tangible horizon. After five approximations I drained the salt water from my precious sextant and escaped below to plot each altitude against its Greenwich time on an improvised graph. To my astonishment four of the plots lay neatly along a straight line; only one wayward sight languished in Outer Mongolia. I took real satisfaction in washing and drying and oiling the sextant. Our position was reasonably certain; we'd make landfall tomorrow.

December 5

MATT: What a night! I turned in about eleven-thirty exhausted and determined to catch a few hours sleep before we sighted La Palma. Jeannine promised to call if anything poked above the horizon. The children, rebelling entirely against the dampness of the forepeak, had taken over the main cabin bunks, so I crawled into their rabbit warren. It was like bunking down inside a piledriver; the pitching was absolutely brutal in the forward end of the boat. As *Aquarius* rose to a wave I would soar aloft, float briefly as the wave rolled under us and the bunk dropped away, then nosedive sharply to a shuddering stop. Crunch! Blood rushing to the head, body weight increasing by multiple-G's as the bow found water again. In the course of such unrehearsed flying, actual sleep was impossible, but I did manage, tired as I was, to doze a little. About one o'clock a strong intuition caused me to crawl out of my damp little dice box and go on deck. Over the last hour I had been aware of a distinct increase in the pressure of the wind and sea, together with an uncomfortable sense of that indistinct island, somewhere off ahead of us, its rocky coastline drawing steadily nearer.

"What about La Palma," I asked. "Seen anything yet?"

"No sign at all," Jeannine reassured me.

Just to quiet my forebodings I peered into the gloom and froth ahead. A dim but unmistakable shape loomed hugely out of the night. Christ! La Palma for sure, jagged, volcanic, towering, and apparently about to run us down.

"Put the helm over," I shouted. "No, wait. Let's try to figure out how close that thing really is." A sober inspection of the chart revealed that La Palma heaved itself up to a volcanic cone nearly eight thousand feet high on a base scarcely fifteen miles wide. On that scale, the island towering over us was not so close as I feared—perhaps twelve or fifteen miles off—but the wind was now well above gale force, probably nine on the Beaufort scale, and for the first time an occasional wave was beginning to break on board. *Aquarius* had proven herself a stiff and able boat in gale conditions. She could keep going with the best of them, but I could feel now that she was hard-pressed, and I knew the sea would only get more tumultuous as we moved nearer land and the bottom shoaled. A prudent sailor, I thought, would probably strip off all canvas and lie ahull, drifting slowly to leeward and waiting for the wind to subside. But how long would that take? The wind had been blowing and building for a week now.

"What are we going to do?" Jeannine shouted. "We can't get into a harbor in this stuff and I don't think we can keep going much longer."

"Let's try pressing on into the lee of the island," I suggested. "We've never tried sheltering that way but the land is high and it should take the edge off the wind. If we like what we find, we can heave-to and wait for better weather. If not we can run off west before the gale. There's plenty of sea room between us and New York."

Jeannine grinned. "You're crazy if you think I'm going to let myself be blown back across the Atlantic with you. I'll get off right here and swim ashore."

We unharnessed *Aquarius* from the steering vane and slacked the mainsheet so the boat would run off more. She picked up more speed than I cared for, the ride getting wilder and wilder as we slewed down the side of one wave and up another. Jeannine and I took up our accustomed crisis-stations: her strong and confident hand on the helm, my doubting eyes peering into the gloom ahead, a lump in my gut for the increasing seas, the closeness of the shore, and what we would find ahead.

We continued so for nearly two hours, the island looming darker and more mysterious, the seas becoming more chaotic. I had begun to question how much longer we could maintain control of the boat when we both felt a slight but unmistakable drop in the wind.

"Hurrah! We've made it!" Jeannine shouted. She was enjoying this engagement, and some credit was due the seasick pills we had discovered in Horta.

"Maybe," I cautioned, "but don't count your calms too soon."

We sailed on into the wind shadow of the island with the blow dying steadily around us. Half an hour later we sat bemused, becalmed, and slightly terrified by the suddenness of our release, the sails flapping idly, *Aquarius* rolling uneasily in an oily swell, not a breath of air stirring anywhere. The only reminder of the tumult we had left so recently was an occasional freak wave that came frothing out of the darkness, angry and strange in the eerie silence all around. We sat nervously for another half hour, feeling as if we had passed through a time lock, trying to make ourselves believe it, the memory of yesterday's false lull fueling our paranoia. But the night remained benign, the stars shone brightly overhead, little wavelets slapped at *Aquarius*'s hull, little eddies of distrust dissolved in our minds. Around three-thirty, accepting our good fortune in a rush, we rousted out the children to tend the boat and fell into our bunks below, exhausted and reprieved.

MATTHEW: It was creepy out in the cockpit alone. Waves would break behind us that sounded as though they were breaking on rocks, and around six A.M. a huge fish or something jumped out of the water, causing me to shorten my watch by one hour. It is very scary to be on a small boat in a big smooth ocean and have something jump out of the water. It makes me think of sea serpents.

In the morning we sailed over toward a little town called Tezacorte that we could see on the coast. There, drifting with no sails, we did a major cleaning up job. Everything was Aquarius Dry. (That is, a little damp.) All the pillows and blankets came on deck to dry out. Foul-weather gear was put away. The galley was cleaned. The boat looked like a boat again. Melissa and I made lunch while Mom and Dad slept. They decided to go in closer to anchor while it was still light. After we had anchored a fisherman named Tomas came in his boat and said he would take us ashore in the morning. That night I slept in peace.

December 8

MATT: *Rap! Rap! Rap!* I poked my sleepy head out the companionway. It was six, and Tomas was pounding cheerfully on the side of the boat. I smiled a greeting and before I could protest, Tomas had dumped on our bridge deck a basketful of tiny mackerel, wet and gleaming from his morning nets. He's done the same each morning we've been here and cheerfully turns away all offers of payment; I think he's adopted us as his own. I have a growing respect and affection for fishermen. They have been our staunchest friends both here and in the Azores.

The quiet life of this coastline, the warm sun and placid waters, seem like Eden after the trials of our recent passage. Yet the gale continues. It's difficult to believe in gales here in the profound shelter of the mountains rising behind Tezacorte, but we hear of it from Tomas, who brings us daily weather reports, and we see it in the color of the sky.

We won't give up this pleasant vacation until the howling subsides, but at least we have been able to identify the weather that was the agent of so much discomfort. It is of the genus *harmattan,* but it has no blood relationship to those cyclonic winds revolving around low-pressure systems that we learned so much about in the Atlantic. The harmattan is a periodic hot wind that blows straight out of the desert interior of North Africa, mostly during the winter months. It has no subtleties; it always blows like hell from the east, carrying as its distinguishing mark a fine emulsion of dust that gives the atmosphere a hard copper glint. Now I understand why the barometer had always remained high and why I cursed unjustly the prestidigitator of the Air Force in Terceira who had predicted no gales.

December 15

MATT: Our six-day layover at Tezacorte has ended. Last week after the harmattan retired to plague the oases of the Sahara, we hauled anchor and proceeded south around the wedge-like extremity of La Palma and then north again along her eastern shore to the island's single harbor and principal city, Santa Cruz. It was a lovely trip along a coastline of pine forests, fields and pastureland alternating with the raw scars of recent lava flows that dripped from the island's ridge like black icing on a devil's cake. At the water's edge the lava had frozen in fantastic forms—fairyland grottoes that invited our exploration.

A mile south of the harbor entrance, just as my ear was tuning to a hesitant note in Methuselah's throbbing, three black-and-gray forms surfaced in unison and wheeled swiftly beyond our bow, moving like porpoises with an aggressive, liquid energy. They were gone in a moment, but their bold markings were unmistakable and I identified them from a book in our library: killer whales. The name is misleading. They are dolphins, not whales, and while they attack other sea creatures, even whales, they have never been known to harm a man. What treasures and surprises the sea holds for us! A giant turtle thrashing in a storm, a convoy of sperm whales protecting a wounded brother—each encounter fills us with wonder, and yet we have only scratched the surface. The sea is the last great wilderness, the last to resist man's encroachments. But how long can it prevail? Our destiny seems to be to tame the sea or to destroy it. Or do they amount to the same thing?

December 19

MATT: It is Saturday morning. *Aquarius* rides quietly
on double anchors in a small harbor in a small city on a small
island. All is very peaceful in Santa Cruz and we are looking
forward to spending Christmas in this friendly place.

Matthew and Melissa are just coming awake in the forepeak. Matthew likes to wake up gradually. He lies very quietly, wide awake and giggling occasionally but not moving
very much. In a few minutes he will have a full head of steam
up and be bustling around the boat, confronting me with
some fully conceived plan for his day's activity. Melissa is
lying on her bunk reading. Occasionally I hear her singing
—a nonsensical but very happy song. Both children read a
great deal now, one of the plus benefits of being a long time
away from civilization's electronic distractions. They read
not only children's books but a lot of adult books too: science
fiction, Jules Verne, Jack London, even Orwell's *Animal
Farm.*

Last night there was a small social gathering aboard
Aquarius: Roger, a young Englishman, and his friend, Prue,
who live on a tiny yacht anchored nearby, and a retired
couple, also English, living on a very beautifully made ketch.
Both boats will be leaving after Christmas along a southern
route for the Barbados in the West Indies, some fifteen hundred miles to the west. We sat around drinking a brew I had
prepared according to a special Canarian recipe. An inexpensive local rum is steeped for about a week in mint and anise.
The herbs seem to take the rough edge off the rum. At any
rate it is very good and it stimulated some fine music. Roger
and Jeannine played guitars, Melissa and I played our flutes.
We sang some Christmas songs, American Folk, British
Rock and a few others. Very nice to be snug in a small cabin
with good people.

Our guests departed carefully; getting to shore by Zodiac
can be a comic procedure in this harbor. We commute to a
landing stage cut in some very unfriendly volcanic rocks

about two hundred yards away. As we approach it, the landing is either awash or, at low tide, about eye level above us; and due to the surge it is usually plunging or rearing a couple of additional feet. If the surge is particularly nasty we may find ourselves triumphantly riding the top of a wave right onto the landing stage like Cleopatra on her barge. But disaster usually follows, the wave is sure to slosh into the dinghy, wetting ankle and ass and demolishing whatever dignity we have tried to bring with us for the business ashore. On festive evenings it is rather amusing to watch Jeannine in her only dress-up costume leaping for the shore in an ankle-length skirt.

I have noticed that all boat people, whatever their differences, are very light-footed and agile, like fast-stepping mountain goats when it comes to negotiating that ever-precarious, rapidly fluctuating space between dinghy and shore. Shore people, probably because of their stable environment, are usually very stiff, clumsy and distressed when attempting the opposite migration. The transfer point is unavoidable, like an initiation ceremony, and it certainly cuts down on one's visitors.

Spread out above the landing stage along the rocks is a very fancy, very private club in which we have honorary membership. The Club Nautico is a yacht club; it has two swimming pools, a bar, and the town's most exclusive clientele, but no yachts whatsoever. Almost every Spanish seaside town boasts a Club Nautico, and few of them have any active sailors. Perhaps in recognition of this deficiency, they open hospitable doors to all visiting yachtsmen, and through them pass a multitude of scruffy, impoverished voyagers like ourselves.

At the opposite end of the harbor (and the social scale), lives a busy community of fishing folk who have a great deal of practical experience with the sea. Here a fleet of dories is drawn up on the little pebble beach near the inner turn of the harbor; a bit farther beyond lies a small but busy boatyard with several fishing boats in various stages of overhaul. Riding at moorings just a short distance off is a fleet of a dozen or more of these boats; and along the beach by the harbor wall is set a row of tiny one-room cabins which fishermen and sometimes their families inhabit. Just over the wall the morning's catch is spread out on the sidewalk and sold to housewives; and across the street is the Bar Atlantico, where, when the catch is good, the fishermen carouse. No world could be more self-contained, constantly changing or consistently interesting.

The town beyond looks much more Mediterranean than Horta did. Santa Cruz has the same cobbled streets, but the shops are filled with manufactured goods from all over the world and there is a commercial bustle, more dirt and heavier traffic. By contrast Horta looked provincial. I think the difference is partly due to different philosophies of taxation and commerce in Spain and Portugal. Portugal seems to live off her possessions; customs are a major source of revenue. Thus, imported goods are scarce and extraordinarily expensive in Horta, and people tend to buy little and live from their own resources. The tariffs were so universal a few years ago that even goods transferred from one island of the Azores to another had to pass through customs and pay duty. But Santa Cruz and all ports of the Canaries are duty-free zones; and as a result, business is booming.

It's astonishing how laws and taxation affect even the physical appearance of the two countries. One reason for Horta's Old-World look is the almost complete absence of commercial signs. Businesses marked by a sign are taxed at higher rates, so none display them and the location of goods and services depends on local knowledge. The stranger is told, "Go to the third door on the left beyond such-and-such a corner."

In La Palma I was struck by how ugly most of the cement buildings looked. Almost all were unpainted—none of those warm Mediterranean pastels. The tax rate on a building in the Canaries increases once it is completed; thus if it has never been painted it is still (and perpetually) "under construction."

Christmas 1970

MATT: Christmas came by surprise. Trying to haul *Aquarius* had been our early December preoccupation, along with a lot of minor repairs and alterations, and if the season of yule and holly had not crept up on us entirely unnoticed, it was no more than a week off before we began to realize there was plenty of preparation ahead if Christmas was to be a day of cheer and not of homesickness.

Santa Cruz did not lend itself to Christmas shopping as readily as we had expected. There was no lack of goods, but the quality was usually cheap or the price beyond our decidedly limited means. The selection was also limited by our own special problems. With a boat so small, any sizable present would upset the carefully structured ecology of our space. Stuffed giraffes were out, also pool tables, toboggans and dancing bears. What remained? Above all, a folding bicycle, the ideal gift for everyone. A bike would free us from dependency on buses and taxis, and considerably enlarge the scope of our shore-going explorations. Not least, it would serve as an ideal safety valve for excessive youthful energy: "Why don't you stop your bumbling and take a bike ride?" Best of all, it would fit on the boat. (Jeannine developed a special technique for burying it in the hanging locker and was thereupon appointed Folder-of-the-Bicycle, for life.) Peugeot makes a lovely folding bike with two-speed gears, but it was impossible to find one in the shops of Santa Cruz. We persisted nevertheless, and after some disappointments and many excursions, a merchant located a used one that we could afford. I restored it to mechanical perfection and salted it away in the tool room of the Club Nautico for unveiling on Christmas morning.

The rest was not difficult. A dress and boots to make

Melissa feel like a growing-up female, a harmonica and air-plane models for Matthew. For Jeannine (and all of us) I installed two large mirrors in the main cabin and on the door in the forepeak. It was amazing how much larger the boat felt. On the day before Christmas we decorated *Aquarius*. A green paper Christmas tree adorned with yarn pompoms was erected against the cabin table that folded underside-up against the forepeak door. The table leg became the tree-trunk. The kids made chains of popcorn and paper to hang from the grab rails. Jeannine sewed giant stockings from red flag bunting and decorated their cuffs with shocking pink fan-dance feathers from Grandma's Bag of Tricks. We were ready.

The churches of Santa Cruz celebrate midnight Mass each night during the Christmas season, and afterward people go through the streets of the town singing—each church a different night. On Christmas eve we took Matthew and Melissa to Mass in the old stone cathedral in the center of town. The candle-lit interior of the church was packed with people when we arrived; and the smell of the incense, the chanting, the echoes of the bells, and the glowing sea of faces amid the rich sonorities of the cathedral aroused an ancient response in me. I've always had a taste for Catholic pomp although I'm a complete non-believer. Maybe the vein of Irish Catholicism runs too deep in my genes for my father's rebellion to have wiped out. I can't think of a better way to welcome Christmas.

The service ended on a modern note. An instrumental choir of twenty or thirty young people—proud, handsome boys and girls—performed church music on guitars, mando-lins, castanets and tomtoms. They were proficient and very Spanish, and they ended with "Michael, Row the Boat Ashore." Out on the plaza, the air brisk and cutting after the closeness of the cathedral, we found not one but two people's choirs in action. One group seemed to bear the sanction of ecclesistical legitimacy; they sang from printed scores, and sang well, but their carefully modulated tones lacked the

spirit we hoped for in carolers. From the edge of the crowd
came news of a second group, more boisterous, less rehearsed, younger in age and spirit, and possessed of an ultimate weapon—a loud and somewhat defiant trumpeter.
Clearly the second group intended to sing the first one down,
and after a lengthy contest the harmonious ones withdrew
and we followed the guerrillas out into the street. They were
on more of a lark than a concert—well-bred teenagers taking
the unaccustomed holiday freedom to be a little gay and
disorderly. It was a nice counterpoise to the solemnity of the
cathedral, and we left them by the towering electric Christmas tree at the harbor's edge, feeling ourselves well settled
into the Yule spirit.

Christmas morning we awoke late and attacked the
lumpy stockings. Matthew presented Jeannine and myself
with fantastic "chest hangings" (I can't call them neckties or
necklaces) that he knotted in macramé with plenty of beads
and feathers interwoven—perfect garb for the weird and
woolly parties we used to attend in New Orleans. I hung
mine on the cabin wall in anticipation of the next weird-and-
woolly-party season. Melissa gave us a dolphin very cleverly
fashioned of matchsticks pasted on a cardboard sea. Then we
paddled over to the Club Nautico and the children discovered their bicycle waiting by the pool. It was a good Christmas.

In New Orleans, Jeannine liked to prepare huge and
informal Thanksgiving feasts for as many of our friends and
homeless transient guests as could fit around a large table in
our backyard. It was fun and seemed to suit the spirit of the
occasion. Now, so far from home, our resources and especially our space were more limited, but we asked Roger, Prue
and Francisco, a fisherman friend, to take Christmas dinner
with us.

Francisco came aboard with a cheery grin and several
cartons of beer. He'd been down at the Atlantico, attending
the Spanish fisherman's equivalent of an office party, and was
well on his way to Yulish cheer. The seven of us jammed the

tiny cabin tucking away ham, French fries, beer, squash, tomato salad, more beer, tinned peaches with tinned cream, and still more beer. Roger told a funny story; Francisco made eloquent speeches in Spanish. There was much laughter and some singing. It was an altogether surpassing meal, and just as we were sinking into that comfortable heaviness which signals the onset of a restful night, we became aware of a sharp and unpleasant change in the weather outside.

The wind, which had blustered all day, was close to howling now, and the instinct of boatmen sent all of us—Roger, Francisco and myself—piling out of the cabin to check the anchor for dragging, but *Aquarius* was riding fine, her twenty-two-pound Danforth snagged solidly in the bottom and 250 feet of ¾-inch nylon taking the strain easily.

"Christ! Look at *BiBi!*" Roger shouted. The thirty-foot ketch anchored fifty yards to the right of us was dragging her anchor. As we watched she snubbed her chain and inched closer to the jagged volcanic rocks at the base of the Club Nautico against which the sea was slamming viciously.

"Ben's gone! His dinghy's drawn up on the rocks." I remembered seeing Ben and Bea, the owners, stepping ashore earlier in the afternoon dressed in their Sunday finest. They'd never make it back in time; it was only a matter of minutes before *BiBi* herself would go ashore.

Ben and Bea were the British pensioners in their sixties whom we had entertained the week before. (For reasons that will become clear, I have changed the name of the yacht and her owners.) Ben had built *BiBi* (if you can bear the procession of B's) in his backyard over a period of six years, and they were finally on their way to the West Indies—the long-dreamed-of retirement voyage. We'd had a very hospitable cup of tea aboard *BiBi* a few days ago and she seemed very soundly built if a bit heavy on the chintz-patterned Formica, but she was planked in plywood and wouldn't take much pounding.

"We've got to get a line on her right away. Jeannine, start tying our docking lines together. Francisco and I will take a line over in Zodiac. He can stay aboard and look after her while I go ashore for the owners."

The pleasant afterglow of Christmas faded in this new emergency. Francisco and I strung the heavy cable from *Aquarius* to a sampson post on *BiBi*'s foredeck. I piled back into the dinghy and managed to make the landing stage and dismount without catastrophe. At the Club Nautico I found only the bartender and a single patron, but they were positive the British couple had driven to a village restaurant in the mountains for dinner. The club member offered his Mercedes and we set off on a fruitless search that covered several mountain restaurants and used up a precious hour and a half during which I could feel the tempo of the wind picking up, minute by minute.

Meanwhile, back at the pass, the settlers were holding off the outlaws with every trick at their disposal. Jeannine and the kids decided they would feel safer on *Aquarius* with the engine running. Our single anchor line was now holding both boats, with the storm building rapidly. (Thank God I had fitted everything heavier and stronger than necessary.) If the anchor let go, nothing could save *BiBi*, but Methuselah might keep *Aquarius* off the rocks. However, Jeannine ground away at the starter in vain. Matthew took over the problem and solved it with characteristic ingenuity. Having discovered we were out of gas, and finding no fuel funnel aboard, he improvised one from cardboard.

Aboard *BiBi*, Francisco was having troubles of his own. With her anchor useless, the English yacht was now completely dependent on our life line, and as the wind veered and gusted, sometimes to near hurricane force, she thrashed and gyrated at the end of the line like the fall guy in a game of crack the whip. Sometimes she rode directly behind *Aquarius*, sometimes pulled sharply off to starboard, sometimes threatened to strike us amidships, and occasionally seemed bent on sailing completely around the harbor. Francisco tried to control her erratic wanderings and prevent a collision with *Aquarius* by hauling on *BiBi*'s stern line, which was still, by some miracle, attached to a ring on the rocks at the Club landing stage. He was beautifully drunk—all five-feet-four of him—wringing wet from the driving rain, and completely equal to the situation. As Melissa described it:

> When the wind came, it came in big puffs that lasted about a minute with a minute in between them. Some gusts pushed us over on our side. Francisco was on *BiBi*. Whenever she came too close, he would pull on the line to shore. He had no raingear on or a sweater so when the big puffs of wind and rain came we could hear him shout, "OOOOOUUUUUUHHHHHH!"

I found the Bs at last, in town, not fifty steps from the harbor; but not before I had inspected every restaurant, café, and hotel bar in Santa Cruz. The couple was just emerging somewhat uncertainly from a small café when we came upon them quite by chance. I was angry now. The storm had been in progress some time, and what skipper would ignore the howling wind and crashing waves without at least a precautionary look at his yacht?

"Get in the car," I ordered. "Your boat's going aground. I've been looking for you almost two hours." As we drove away and I tried to explain the situation, I began to realize they were both outrageously drunk. At the landing stage Ben still hadn't grasped the situation. He seemed befuddled and belligerent by turns.

"Take your hands off my dinghy!" he shouted as I tried to help launch it. We had arrived at *BiBi*'s stern before he noticed Francisco, by now numb with cold, but still faithfully tending the lines.

"What's that bloody Wog doing on my boat?" he roared. "Get off my damn boat or I'll have you arrested!" Fortunately all but his tone of voice was lost on Francisco, who is not slow to defend his good name.

I took him aside. "Better go back to *Aquarius*," I suggested. "Let me try to handle this guy. *Hombre muy loco!*

Muy borracho!" Francisco departed, bestowing a few of Andalusia's choice curses as he went. I tried once again to apprise Ben of the dangers to his boat, tried patiently and step by step, but it was like attempting to reason with a drunken rhino. We made repeated trips to the afterdeck, to the bridgedeck, to the foredeck. Like a sightseeing guide I invited him to observe the proximity of the rocks, the slackness of the anchor chain, the tension of the warp stretched between his boat and mine. He seemed to be dreaming, but suddenly, like a man surfacing from a dream, he focused on the rope.

"What's that damned line doing on my boat?" He blustered. "Cast it off! Cast it off right now!"

I explained that the line was all that stood between him and a full-fledged shipwreck. I even paid out a few yards of it to demonstrate the ineffectiveness of the anchor, but nothing would sink in. I wanted to shout, *Shut up, you bloody fool, and do what I tell you!* But I knew if I gave in to the red knot of rage hardening in my stomach, Ben would only throw me off the boat; and I could visualize only too well the dismal sequence of events that surely would follow: endangered boat skippered by incoherent inebriate leading shortly to shipwreck necessitating risky and difficult rescue operation, in which we would be obliged to play the major role, followed (quite conceivably) by legal charges filed against me for interfering with his boat in the first place. *Ben's impossible,* I thought. *Maybe I can get the message through to Bea and she can translate for the old man.* I cornered Bea and presented my PLAN: that we should haulass across the harbor to the mole where the big ships moored and where *BiBi* could lie in safety until the storm abated.

Then I withdrew while she talked to Ben. It was an uncomfortable position for me, an outsider telling a stranger how to handle his own boat, but I could see no way out of it. For all Ben's belligerence he badly needed my assistance whether he recognized it or not. And I had to give it whether I wanted to or not. They wrangled interminably but at last got the stout Lister diesel fired up and the anchor aboard. We dropped the warps and lurched off into the storm.

It was a strange night to be traveling. The wind came in bursts of overpowering force (velocities of 125 mph were clocked outside the harbor mouth), but between gusts it could be almost dead calm. I think we were shielded from the steady force of the storm by the high land around us, so it could only gather its strength and hit us in punches. They might come from any point of the compass but the worst were generally from the land. They came whistling down the side of the mountain off the rim of the caldera like fury incarnate, and hit our yachts with enough force to lay them almost on their sides. In the darkness it was like trying to prizefight blindfolded; the blows came without warning from any direction and the best we could do was wait and try to react.

I hoped we could take advantage of the calms to tie *BiBi* up in safety, but no ship, not even the *Walloping Window Blind,* ever proceeded more erratically across a harbor. Before we had covered a hundred yards I became aware of a basic flaw in the construction of *BiBi.* It was not possible while standing at her helm to control the forward or reverse motion of the boat. These necessary adjustments had been delegated to the whim of an "engineer" stationed at some lever in the bowels of the yacht. It's an arrangement that works tolerably well on a merchant ship of eight thousand tons or more, a ship with a recognized chain of command, a tradition of naval discipline and the mechanical assistance of telegraphs and speaking tubes. But tonight in the storm with drunken Ben shouting at tipsy Bea, I stood on the foredeck, a coil of docking line in my hopeful hand and sought refuge in prayer.

"Damn it, Bea!" Ben shouted, "I said *forward!* Did you hear me? FORWARD! No, wait, Bea. I've got to slow the damn engine. Where's that damn throttle?"

It was, in truth, a moment of rare existential clarity. I certainly could not foretell with any precision what would happen to us during a single instant of the next ten minutes, and when I realized this and gave myself over to it, the true humor of our predicament became clear and I found myself roaring with mirth. At that moment I don't believe any catastrophe—the loss of the yacht, the destruction of all the boats in the harbor, or my own demise by drowning—could have fazed me in the slightest.

We proceeded on our mission, weaving and wobbling like a tipsy june bug. First we nosed up to a barge tied along the mole and I managed to get a line around a bollard while Ben struggled to untangle his forwards from his reverses. But almost immediately three workmen appeared, shouting and waving us off, and as they did so a great-grandaddy gust struck us an awful blow and laid us over almost flat. Skittering like a chip of wood, *BiBi* began to drift rapidly down on the fleet of fishing boats moored in shallow water at the inner circle of the harbor. Fortunately Ben began to get his brain and his engine into the same gear at the same time and we lunged forward on the wrong course at about six knots, weaving in and around and over the warps of the fishing boats, while I stood at my post on the foredeck wondering if it was worth shouting directions and waiting for our screw to snag an anchor line and either cut a fishing boat adrift or stop our engine for good.

But God was on our side and *BiBi* at length cleared the fishing flotilla and made it to a vacant spot along the mole. Roger and Prue came out to help with the lines. It was three A.M. by the time we had her secured and the spring lines set. I finished translating the message of friendly harbor officials for Ben: *BiBi* could lie there the night but would have to leave by eight; a cargo ship was expected in. Ben was just overhauling his umbrage for fresh duty as I walked away. I never saw him again.

Shortly before eight in the morning, with the gale still howling fiercely, *BiBi* left the mole and made for the harbor mouth. She circled there irresolutely for a half hour then headed out and disappeared in the froth of the gale. We assumed she had made for another port in the Canaries and inquired after her among the yachtsmen we met in later weeks, but she was never heard from. There were reports out of Gibraltar of an air-sea search for a similar yacht, and we wondered if *BiBi* had gone down; but recently friends wrote of seeing her in the West Indies. Neptune, in his infinite wisdom, had elected to spare her.

If this account were varnished fiction instead of unvarnished truth, we'd all have returned to *Aquarius* after disposing of *BiBi* for a hot rum and a good laugh before falling into untroubled sleep. Unfortunately the storm had other plans.

Roger and Prue returned to *Busola,* which had been tied alongside a fishing boat for several weeks following the loss of their main anchor. Francisco was there, trying to sleep on the fishing boat. Jeannine and I retired to our bunks but not to sleep; as long as the storm continued unabated, we thought it prudent to keep anchor watch. We dozed alternately, going on deck frequently to check the anchor line for chaffing and to assure ourselves by sighting buildings lined up on shore that we weren't dragging. The nylon anchor line was so elastic it would stretch ten or fifteen feet in a heavy gust, and I had my hand on the engine switch several times before I realized we were still solidly nailed to the harbor bottom. Once, when a stentorian blast hit us from astern, a big shadow passed several times across the companionway as if a giant hand were shutting out the moon. It was Zodiac, airborne at the end of its painter, flying in graceful arcs back and forth across the after end of the boat. On its first pass it took out our radio antenna whip, but a few minutes later I cornered it and tamed it alongside us by adding a second line to our bow. The lights of the town were all flickering, whole blocks of them blinking in time with the sparking of high-tension wires that were coming together in the wind. As I tied down Zodiac I caught a flash of light in the periphery of my vision that could have been a distress flare, but I discounted it. The giant Christmas tree in the square extinguished itself in a volley of sparks. I wondered how Roger and Prue were doing.

Late in the night I heard a peculiar howling and *Aquarius* was struck by a tremendous blast that laid her almost on her beam ends. I rushed on deck in time to see a funnel of wind cross the harbor and take out a line of storage sheds on the mole. Pieces of boards and tin were sucked high into the air; I think it could only have been a tornado that must have passed very close to us.

At dawn *Busola* and the fishing boat were gone from their mooring, but we were reassured to see the little yacht tied to the same barge that was so nearly the undoing of *BiBi*. The storm had eased enough for us to go to bed and we slept until early afternoon.

We were awakened by a hail from the shore. It was Roger, a very worried Roger, who came aboard to tell a worried tale: As the storm increased through the night, the rafting arrangement between *Busola* and the fishing boat became less and less tenable. The boats began to chew at each other, separating and slamming together in the rough water. The fenders were all carried away and *Busola*'s bulwarks began to go. Roger, Francisco and Prue worked frantically through the night renewing lines and fenders, but they were unable to prevent serious damage. At the height of the storm the fishing boat's mooring broke suddenly and she was driven ashore, carrying *Busola* with her. Roger had foreseen this danger and had a sharp knife ready. He cut the warps in seconds, heaved a small kedge anchor overboard and threw himself below to start the engine. It caught on the first turn (a miracle in itself), but *Busola* was already on the rocks and the engine was too small to push her off. They remained in that position for several hours, pounding with every wave, and trying desperately to free the boat. Roger fired every emergency flare aboard (he lit the first one upside down and almost burned his foot off and half the boat as well), but nobody in this crowded harbor in the middle of this populous

town (including myself) saw their flares or came to the rescue. Eventually they rescued themselves using the kedge
anchor and the engine together to work free of the rocks (a
rising tide may have helped), and made it across the harbor
to the barge.

Roger looked grim and exhausted as he told the story. He
feared the night's damage marked the end of his dreams of
sailing to the West Indies. *Busola* was leaking some, and he
had hardly enough money to provision the boat, let alone
haul her for repairs. (When they sailed a month later they
carried, as their sole provisions, thirty days' supply of tinned
baked beans, and steak and kidney pudding—surely one of
the most eccentric menus ever freighted across the Atlantic!)

I went down in scuba gear to have a look at *Busola* the
next day. Her wooden hull was heavily built with a massive
keel in the best tradition of British cruising yachts. I could
find no damage at all save a few square feet of scraped paint.
The bulwarks were another matter. Most of the stanchions
had been knocked loose along with six or eight feet of the
bulwarks themselves, but a week later all the damage had
been repaired.

16

Mother Dredge

January 10, 1971

MATT: This afternoon we said a sad farewell to Francisco and Santa Cruz; to Roger and Prue and *Busola*. (May their winds be fair and their crossing swift, may steak and kidney pudding attend them well.) We dipped our flag to the Club Nautico and sailed out of the harbor, bound for another Santa Cruz, this one the principal city of the island of Tenerife; and if any part of this voyage qualifies as a milk run, this must be it. On a clear day the dramatic twelve-thousand-foot cone of Teide, Tenerife's volcano, is plainly visible from the seawall; sometimes *only* the cone, floating in mid-air thousands of feet above the sea and fifty miles to the east. If we maintain our course through the night we'll be off Tenerife's northern coast well before dawn tomorrow, it's that simple.

Aquarius seems more vivid under sail this afternoon, her cabin more of a haven, her mahogany warmer and richer, her decks whiter. It happens every time we put to sea and strikes me freshly each time. I mentioned it to Charles Rand, a friend who has joined us for the pleasure of sailing this brief sea and he noticed it too. Since Charles is an enthusiastic helmsman, I don't expect to be doing much work between the jetty lights of Santa Cruz, La Palma, and Santa Cruz, Tenerife.

That suits me fine. For some reason I am feeling buoyant and reflective this evening—spirits bubbling, no seaman's worries to distract me. I'm inclined to sit by myself and let my mind find its own course. I have been feeling extraordinarily fit and happy these last few weeks, as if the trials and achievements of the voyage have begun to come together in some unfathomable way.

I like what is happening to me now, as well as to my family. I am nearly forty, and for the first time my body feels as good as it did twenty years ago when I was swimming for Princeton. The teddy-bear fat is gone; my hands are hard (handling ropes has calloused them so heavily I can't completely double my fists); I *move* better than I used to, and it gives me pleasure once more to look at myself in a mirror. I have body feelings as never before: my skin is alive, it is fun to move, I feel sexy and my body is sensitive to itself. When I eat too much, drink too much, or sleep too much, it tells me so immediately. The discipline of yoga is no longer a chore because there is so much pleasure in the contraction and relaxation of muscles and organs. Above all there's the usefulness. I have *used* my body at sea in activities that, though sometimes disguised, have as their underlying purpose survival. The result is very satisfying and makes me feel extraordinarily alive. I think I know tonight what I was searching for, what we all have been searching for—what the voyage is about. It is very simple: *to feel alive.*

There were many satisfactions in New Orleans, but there was also much in our environment that inhibited the kind of aliveness I feel now. That's what I was trying to express when I told Roy Reed of the *New York Times* that we wanted to substitute *active* for passive experience. That's what bothers me about much of contemporary American life, especially television: in order to feel real aliveness one must participate in life. There must be movement and engagement, not only of the mind but of the body. Either one by itself is not enough.

People can learn a great deal from television. It's pretty

clear that my kids and their contemporaries are more hip to
what's going on in the world than my generation ever was
—better informed, quicker to detect lies and phoniness—and
much of their information comes from television. But the
passive sitting-before-the-tube kind of learning, or sitting-in-
a-classroom learning, can go only so far. Risks must be
taken, pain felt, and work accomplished before understanding becomes incorporated in the individual. I have a personal
theory, which is probably refuted by all kinds of scientific
evidence: I believe that knowledge gained by activity, by
movement in the world, literally becomes a part of the body
structure, in the same way that a sport or physical skill when
it is mastered affects the development of muscles and actually
changes the body. Knowledge thus incorporated really
affects future actions, and maybe explains the difference between knowledge and wisdom: the reason why young men
can be very knowledgeable, but only old men—very special
old men who have expended both their minds and bodies—
are ever really wise.

Men are animals, and like other animals must use their
bodies to learn. If one's body feels alive—if it is not deadened
by fat, inactivity, poor health or the chronic tension that
comes from never releasing in work, play or love—then one's
mind will also feel alive and the human instinct of curiosity
will be freely exercised. That fits in well with the alternating
rhythm of our voyaging life: harbor—sea, harbor—sea, the
yin/yang of action and reflection. Our sea life is very intense;
pleasure/pain is very close to the surface and the demand to
be active in defense of our existence is sometimes an absolute
imperative. To sail well requires judgment, decision, caution,
boldness—the body and the will are strained to perform well.

But we have the reflective side as well, the reactive "yin."
In port, or as I am now, sitting coiled under the cabin lamp
with the boat quiet about me, trying to put words in a notebook, there is time for reflection on our experiences, and that
is becoming very important. I was doubtful at first about
trying to write about this voyage. I dreaded it; and the writ-

ing is still very difficult, but very rewarding too. It is a way of being thoughtful about ourselves and what is happening to us. I think it has added a dimension to almost everything we do; like sailing, it's helping me to feel more alive.

January 11

JEANNINE: At last a really sheltered harbor! The sea wall of our new home, the fishing harbor near Santa Cruz, Tenerife, stretched out parallel to the land, forming a long, skinny and totally protected rectangle, open only on the leeward end. Everything that began at sea would stop at the great wall. Boats lined the two sides of the rectangle, a row of commercial fishing trawlers on the land side flanked by a trim-looking schooner. A fancy motor yacht led the head of the line; two trimarans were anchored in the cul-de-sac, and several small monohulls like *Aquarius* were tied up against an ancient dredge moored fore and aft on the sea-side of the harbor.

We chose the dredge, and birds of our feather. The flock included *Begone,* a smart, well-found steel ketch; *Tapioca,* a graceful little sloop, and *Pollux,* a ferro-cement ketch. The dredge was a temporary perch had taken this covey under her wing, and she accepted us easily as one of her brood.

Peter and Karin of *Begone* helped us tie up. We immediately felt welcome. Within minutes we were aboard their boat, where we met the rest of their crew: Jesper, Karin's nine-year-old son, and Jan, a friend. Matthew, Melissa and Jesper set out to get acquainted with the dredge. It was a natural playground and they clambered over every inch of it, sneaking up and down the bucket train, swinging down off the end of it, exploring dark holds, racing up the stairway to the big wheel, lurking in ambush in recessed corners.

Their manic investigation took them to land, where they found a secret way to get inside the breakwater; into a long dark passageway filled with imagined ghosts, tramps, spiders, snakes and other mortally dangerous creatures. Over the top of the breakwater, via a ladder, they discovered the perfect hide-and-seek ground, acres of huge boulders piled one on top of the other with invisible caves and clammy tunnels underneath. It was late in the afternoon when they returned to *Aquarius* lying quietly aside the unruffled dredge. They were grimy, wet and vastly satisfied with our new nesting place.

Early the next morning Charles and I shouldered our packs and set out by bus for the big market place in Tenerife. It is one of the best markets in the Canaries, and Charles was taking this opportunity to carry a big haul of groceries back to his family on La Palma. It was strange to be in a big city again with tall buildings and heavy traffic, honking taxis and window-shopping pedestrians. We went into the market through huge gates inscribed OUR LADY OF AFRICA, and just inside we were attracted to a table covered with herbs and spices, neatly tied in little bundles. Charles, who is an excellent cook, began nosing through the fresh fragrances to the delight of the little old lady who owned the stand. She explained in Spanish what things were, as we smelled them in order to identify them. It became a game; we would pick up a bundle and try to identify it while she laughed at our sniffings.

"That's verbena, Charles!" I exclaimed. "Lemon verbena! I know because my father has some growing in his garden, and he makes great tea with it."

"So it is!" he confirmed. "I've only seen it dried and crumbly, not green like this. Let's get a couple of bundles."

The old lady beamed. *"Verben,"* she agreed.

We proceeded like this for half an hour, through carnations, pine needles, mint, camomile, basil, sage and quite a few we couldn't fathom. The old lady obviously felt she had scored in this game whenever we couldn't identify the smell. I was marveling at the wonderful sensitivity of her nose when, as I watched her counting out our change, I realized that she was almost totally blind.

Around the corner we came upon a vast assortment of

caged birds, mostly the canaries for which these islands are named. Beside them was a man with a seed business. Some of the seeds were for planting, but most were for feeding to the canaries, which are seen everywhere hanging in little cages in front of shops and houses. Charles started looking for alfalfa seeds, which, when sprouted, are his daughter's favorite food. As we searched we found a small barrel full of round, green . . . we did a double take . . . yes, there was no doubt about it . . . hemp seeds. Plain old ordinary sisal—a whole barrelful (which may account for the extraordinary warblings and trillings produced by these local songbirds).

Finally we located alfalfa and Charles convinced me to buy five pounds, although I had never tried growing the sprouts he and his family were so fond of. (After he told us how to sprout them and keep a jar for every day, we had fresh crunchy greens for salads or sandwiches on the boat, with never a worry about the amoebas or other parasites that are found in abundance among the leafy greens of some countries and are the cause of debilitating dysentery.)

We proceeded around the market, loading up our packs with potatoes, oranges, tangerines, cheeses, salamis, tomatoes, meat, bananas, pineapples, squash, onion—until I could hardly stagger with the load. Eggs on top, wine in a jug, and we were bound for the port, where Charles boarded a passenger ship to return to La Palma. Mellow people are so rare; it seems like we are always saying goodbye to those we want to stay close to. "Goodbye, Charles. Say hello to Roger and Prue when you bump into them!" Feeling lonely, I found a bus and made my way back to Mother Dredge.

And Mother Dredge she was. Her pitted decks became town square and workshop for our little community of boats. Ken and Jim from *Tapioca* came to inspect our vane gear; they were about to cross to the Barbados but lacked self-steering. Ken decided it would be practical to duplicate our vane, using only materials already at hand, a necessity since they were completely penniless. A flurry of measuring, scrounging, and remeasuring resulted in a hopeful beginning:

a slightly used piece of marine plywood was cut for the wind vane, cement in a tin can formed the counterweight, pieces of waterpipe became the bearings. The work was carried on in a corner of the dredge already provided with a workbench and heavy vise, and the male denizens of our community managed to pass by more than once a day to scrutinize Ken's progress and offer imaginative, if not always practical, advice. It was gratifying to see so useful an object take shape out of so little.

The old dredge played host to a host of other crusty characters. Persistent and noisy, these fellows stayed on until they practically had to be pried away. They were known for their cliquishness—in fact we went to sleep at night listening to their noise through our steel hull; they carried on into the late hours like a thousand tiny castanets.

Besides boats and barnacles, the dredge harbored other dwellers—colonies of hydra, anemones, and limpets. Matthew and Melissa have collected specimens of marine life for study throughout the trip, hauling out a magnifying glass when they wanted to examine the tube feet of a star fish, or their microscope when they were curious about some fish eggs. But in this harbor they began to explore the marine world with a new enthusiasm. The dredge yielded any number of fascinating specimens, and in the rocks beyond the breakwater Melissa discovered a whole new world of sea slugs. She came excitedly with the first captives and we improvised an aquarium from an old washtub, which we had to replenish with sea water three or four times a day to keep the inhabitants happy.

With my encouragement, both children began to keep biology notebooks. First they wrote down as many observations as they could list and made detailed drawings of each animal; later they checked in our marine biology book to see what they had missed. Melissa watched sea slugs with intensity for several days. It was she who discovered what they ate and how they ate. She scrutinized them unembarrassedly during copulation, egg laying, and elimination. (Sea slugs are extraordinarily blasé about such things.) She searched carefully for eyes and noted they had none.

Several days later Matthew came chortling up to us. "I found their eyes," he said smugly. We went suspiciously to confirm this because none of us had been able to discern eyes. But sure enough, two of the tiny spots on the head which had appeared identical to all the other freckles, revealed on close examination a unique glint, a brighter aspect than the others. Aha! Someone in there after all! The blobby creatures no longer seemed quite so soulless. Outscooped, Melissa went off grumbling to correct her notebook.

MELISSA: I was walking down the beach one day and all of a sudden I saw a black blob lying in front of me. I poked it and pushed it and it contracted. It was alive! It looked funny. I took it back and put it in a bucket. Then I found a couple more. They were sea slugs.

The next day I went along the beach to collect seaweed because I had found out that the sea slugs eat it. I found five more! We decided to try to keep them alive so we could watch them.

Facts About Sea Slugs

1. They have a head with a small slot in it that is its mouth.
2. They contract when touched.
3. They shoot out white or purple liquid if disturbed.
4. They have ~~no~~ eyes.
5. They pile on each other like elephants.
6. They have ripply fins on their backs that they swim with.
7. In between the fins is a sack with a hard covering containing its insides.
8. Behind the hard sack is a large funnel-like rectum.
9. They also lay eggs in a long fat green or pink thread in heaps on seaweed.
10. Some slugs are a sandy color and a little brown so they can hide in sand or on rocks.
11. Also when disturbed they may roll up and turn hard for self-defense.

12. Some dig down in the sand and cover themselves with it.
13. They move like an inchworm.
14. They have a star-shaped pattern on their hard sack.

I have learned some other things from the book on marine life.

1. A sea slug is a mollusk.
2. Its real name is Sea Hare.
3. The bottom of a sea hare is called the "foot."

February 2

JEANNINE: Across the narrow harbor the graceful schooner *Algu* snuggled alongside a snub-nosed fishing trawler, a young greyhound beside an old St. Bernard. Her name was a sonorous blending of the first initials of her four owners. But it implied a cohesion of their personalities which unfortunately had begun to dissolve during the early months of *Algu*'s maiden cruise from England to the Canaries.

We met Annika and Umberto, first and last (literally) of *Algu,* having a despondent cup of tea with Peter and Karin on *Begone.* A handsome Swedish couple, they dreamed of cruising the world. They had pooled their savings with those of two friends in order to buy the forty-foot, newly built *Algu* and now the two couples were hardly speaking to one another. We asked if it were not possible for the disputes to be resolved—perhaps an intermediary, a U.N. peace force of other sailors could be formed to forge a truce.

"No," Annika said sadly, "it's not just a matter of personalities clashing. On a boat everyone must be dependable. Our contentions arise over responsibility for *Algu.* It's not something we can change by talking."

Umberto agreed. "People are either responsible or they are not. We can't afford to buy their share of the boat, so we will just have to sell her and look for a smaller boat that we can afford by ourselves." They were passionately disappointed, yet not discouraged. They had no doubt that their dream would eventually come true.

We were attracted to them. I was attracted to their optimism and vitality; Matt was attracted to Annika's bikini. In fact, he admitted later, he was so blinded by her beauty that it took him a while to get around to appreciating all that optimism and vitality. I could understand that; I felt the same thing—I just wasn't as honest about it. As I got to know Annika, I realized a little sadly how long it had been since I had been close to another woman, not since I had hugged Holley and Caroline goodbye in New Orleans.

We shared pizza and scones and long conversations in *Algu*'s elegant cabin. We went camping partway up the mountainside of Teide, hiking along logging trails, with Tjabo, their beagle puppy, displaying his joy in very unbeagle-like ways. Annika taught Melissa to count in Swedish as we walked. As we sat in front of a campfire after a long day, Umberto and Tjabo entertained us by singing. Umberto made peculiar high-pitched noises by blowing between his lips until Tjabo, unable to bear it any longer, threw back his head and uttered the most absurd and mournful sounds imaginable. We laughed uproariously until he stopped and looked at us with reproach. It took some consoling and praising to mollify him, but he was not the type to hold a grudge.

A French sailboat arrived and tied up in front of us against the dredge. It was from Nantes, the city my mother was born in, and was owned by a marvelous sixty-seven-year-old doctor who had spent ten years of his life treating lepers in Cameroon. We passed several evenings with him and his *camarade,* Yves, a young Parisian.

The doctor was a durable, lovable, impossible old man who went continuously around the port and to the city on his folding bicycle; and over the sharp volcanic stones of the island on his bare feet. He astonished us with his energy. One day he and Yves came and consulted us about the tides; that afternoon they motored their boat up onto the beach of a nearby fishing village, waited for low tide, cleaned, scraped and painted the entire hull during the night, and by morning had returned to their berth next to us.

The following afternoon he invited us to lunch on his boat—he was fixing *haricots* in the style of a region just south of Nantes. They were delicious, of course, and he laid a magnificent table with white tablecloth and flowers! He also whipped out grilled pork chops and several bottles of very nice wine, grumbling amiably about the Spanish beans which, it seems, took three times as long as French beans to cook in his *cocotte-minute;* and he had nothing at all favorable to say about the way the Spanish laid a table.

He was a doctor of philosophy as well as medicine. By the end of the meal we were discussing the genetic theories of Monod, and a new book of philosophy by that great scientist (obviously a hero to him) in which he declares that there is no God, all of which made the doctor very sad, and strained my French considerably. The talk went on late into the afternoon and when we departed we felt as if we had been entertained in a château instead of a sailboat.

Epic lunches with our harbor friends became one of our chief pleasures: garbanzo bean soup with garlic and cabbage, or fish stew and beer at the Comedor, a nearby cafeteria— they were hefty menus that would flip us right into a soggy siesta if we ate too much. The boat people would start maundering toward the Comedor, shortly after noon. Matthew and Melissa played Frisbee with Jim and Ken as we walked, Annika and Umberto ambled, Tjabo gamboled, and from the opposite side of the harbor a family of six plus two large Dobermans would all descend from their thirty-foot catamaran like a circus act to join the procession.

The cafeteria, run by a hard-working Spanish family, was a gray cinder-block building, impossibly bare when empty, but cheerful enough when full of dockworkers, fishermen and sailboat people. Its charm, Matt said, lay in its total lack of pretense. But the food was good and cheaper than if I did the shopping and prepared it myself. We sat at long tables and broke fresh sourdough bread together, dipping it

unabashedly into our soup. Conversations ranged from discussions of boat gear, to the fishing methods of the big trawlers, to French literature. It was here that Pape first told us about the Gambia River. Pape was a teenaged African boy from Gambia who worked on one of the trawlers that filled the harbor.

"You must go see the Gambia River," he said enthusiastically. "You could take your boat two hundred miles inland. You would see hippos and many small villages, and peanut boats, and baboons."

It was an attractive idea. Why not sail up an African river? Normally we would be forced by geography to put in at harbors along the coast that were well populated, but penetrating the interior by sailing up a river would really put us in contact with village Africa.

"Thanks, Pape. I think we might do that," Matt said thoughtfully.

The conversation brought us back to the object of our voyage—Africa! What were we still doing in the Canaries? Strangely enough everyone else was feeling the same stirrings, as if some instinctive migratory urge were about to put us all to flight again. We didn't realize until the Great Migration began what a unique association this had been. Most of the sailing boats in the harbor were planning to cross the ocean for the first time. Our companions may have been neophytes but they were not dilettantes—they took themselves seriously. If there was tension in the air it cycled rhythmically between apprehension and anticipation; if there was anxiety it buzzed at low frequencies between preparation and procrastination. The dominant tone was vitality, intense and harmonious, setting up sympathetic wavelengths among us, perhaps vibrating through the water, our one common connection. What we had found here in this improbable fishing harbor was a real community, more loving by tens of times than an average group of families in a suburban tract or an urban apartment house might find, and yet totally transient.

To those skippers with their eyes on the Carribean, our harbor was an outpost for trading and outfitting, a jumping-off place. Tenerife was to them what St. Louis had been to the wagon trains of the American frontier. Their ships were the prairie schooners of the great Atlantic plains, going west. *Begone* was the first to leave; she fluttered away from the dredge and took off toward the harbor entrance, bound southwestward across twenty-five hundred miles of ocean to the West Indies. Across the harbor *Algu* tooted a *bon voyage*. The trawler beside her gave an accompanying blast of its foghorn. Melissa rummaged hastily for the voice of *Aquarius* and contributed our own raucous tin-horn honks. Finally the whole flock joined in the cacophonous salute, trumpeting noisily until *Begone* neatly came about beyond the breakwater and disappeared.

Sunday, February 7

MATT: The dredge seems forlorn and lonely this morning. *Begone* has left and the other three yachts that shared the dredge with us all departed yesterday. The old derelict no longer rings with the plans and preparations of soon-to-leave voyagers; the rusty creaking of her mooring cables calls mournfully, all too clearly, in the unaccustomed void: *"Why are you still here? The business of this harbor is arrivals and departures. Do you want to spoil that rhythm by staying too long?"* Relax, Dredge. Tomorrow feels like the day. Soon you'll be shed of us, and soon after that a new generation of expectant voyagers will make your boiler plate ring with their preparations.

Pollux and *Tapioca* were the next to depart. Both yachts left for Barbados together, but I know they will not sail in company—two boats could not be more different. *Tapioca* is a demitasse of a boat, only twenty-six feet of fiberglass and light as a sprite. Ken, her owner, built her for a pittance and that's how she earned her name: tapioca is cheap. It's what poor people eat. But cheap or not, the little boat is groomed with all the burnished mahogany and loving detail that only an owner-craftsman would lavish on his personal boat. *Pollux* is a cement ketch, about forty feet overall and as massive as *Tapioca* is slight. She was also built (poured?) in England, like *Tapioca,* and Terry, her owner-builder, is an American nuclear physicist of international repute, retired now from projects shrouded in government secrecy. *Pollux* is still "in progress," complete in deck and rigging to the last detail, but rough and cement-barn-like below. For Ken the crossing will be a young man's lark, at least he would have you believe that; for Terry it seems more of a quest and an obsession.

I almost missed seeing them off. Using our own practice as a model, I had expected the boats to depart considerably behind schedule, but as I stepped off the bus from Santa Cruz I saw the two sails making for the harbor entrance. I sprinted to the fishing pier and ran its length waving my arms and shouting like a fool, all the emotions I could not permit myself to feel on my own departures crowding through me. Goodbye! Bon Voyage! Take care! Don't slip in the sea. Wear your rubbers and earmuffs. Don't go out when it's squally. Offer libations to Neptune. Please, somebody watch over them. Please!

Tapioca danced ahead, light as a feather, hardly touching the water, tanbark sails winged to port and starboard, dripping russet reflections among the wavelets. Ken and Jim noticed my absurd gyrations. A grin and a casual lift of a hand from Ken. Goodbye and gone.

Pollux plowed along behind, only her genoa up as yet, Polly at the helm, Terry fighting a halyard. The mainsail climbed the mast, caught the following wind and fouled in the rigging. A moment of confusion or maybe panic, then Polly swung the boat head to wind and the main was brought under control. A trifling matter, a tiny flaw in seamanship, but it told me the boat was not theirs yet. They would have to lay claim to her, master all her eccentricities in the days ahead or suffer the consequences. I wished them easy lessons from a benign and indulgent wind. Good luck, *Pollux!* Goodbye, and Godspeed!

The doctor abandoned us a few hours later. Salty old dog, baked dry and durable as leather, tough as nails in that white man's crucible, the Cameroons. I could hardly justify worrying about him. It was difficult to imagine any situation the old man couldn't handle, but if it did come to pass, if he were finally overwhelmed in some ultimate storm, I could picture him going under for the final time, resigning his life with a grin and a shrug.

"Where are you going?" I called.

"I will sail north of the island and I will look at the wind. If it is favorable I will go north to Madeira. If not, I will sail west to La Palma." He grinned at us—his irrepressible gamin's grin—but it changed in a moment to a roar of alarm as Yves, casting off the lines, allowed his intricate and precious vane gear at the stern to drift dangerously close to the dredge. As they slipped away Jeannine ventured the final word. "I love that old man, I really love him, but I wouldn't sail with him for anything."

17

Prophecy's End

February 8,

MATT: Departure day once again. The certainty of it settled on me last night. Those things done, were done. Those things undone would have to remain undone. So be it. Jeannine joyously confirmed it. Today, Africa.

Algu, the beautiful Swedish blonde of a schooner, came over to the dredge yesterday and lay opposite us. We feel the imminence of separation from Annika and Umberto as real pain and we want to be with them as much as possible. They have decided to sail in company with us for a short distance when we leave. We supply each other with many reasons for this: to photograph each other's boats under sail, to check the reception of radio-telephones, but in truth we simply find it difficult to part from one another. Something akin to love has grown up among the four of us during the brief weeks we've been here. We have yet to test it much, but we sense that it is unique and would endure; we are regretful to go our separate ways. It was eleven before I cast my lines from the dredge. I was alone. Some hours earlier Jeannine and the children had taken the bus for Santa Cruz to purchase final provisions and replace some of the rags the children have been wearing for clothes. Of course the first leg is not so arduous: two miles under power to the main harbor for water and fuel, for çargo and family, then out to sea.

Goodbye, old dredge. Goodbye, Your Rustiness, I'll miss you. May you eat from many harbors before obsolence melts you down. *Aquarius* and I chugged out of the harbor behind *Algu*. I looked for some genetically perfect replica of myself to run along the wharf, waving and shouting farewell, but no clone appeared, no one took the slightest interest in our departure. As we left the harbor entrance, my buoyancy vaporized in a cough. Methuselah was trying to choke himself. Damn! My brain, rapidly scanning its Methuselan Data Banks, registered "Carburetor Dirt," it seemed for the hundredth time on the voyage. From the sound of him we'd make the main basin well enough, but I knew I would have to deal with the problem at sea and it would probably cost me time, patience and some anguish. It was not a good omen.

February 8

MATTHEW: "Prepare to cast off lines!" Now *Aquarius* was out of the main harbor, sailing side by side with *Algu*, doing about six knots. Before we left, it was decided that we would try to communicate by radio, but first we took pictures of each other. We called each other on our radios and found that they both worked, which was pleasing because no ships at sea would ever talk to us. Then *Algu* turned back to land. We spent the rest of the day broad-reaching for Africa—with fried chicken for dinner!

February 9

MATTHEW: The day started off in a dead calm. No wind at all, just swells. The jib was down and we were just drifting along. I made my usual chocolate milkshake out of the tons of chocolate and powdered milk we now had on board, and then went outside to see our first full day at sea. When Dad finished his breakfast he got the engine going.

There was something very wrong with the engine; it had no power at all and was always dying and sputtering. Well, we ran the engine·at a low speed for about two or three hours. Then Mom said it was time we had some school. We listened to the news. There was trouble between the Arabs and the Jews so we looked up Israel and Egypt in our world atlas. We had a biology lesson in reproduction and I asked for a handwriting lesson. My handwriting is very poor because I am left-handed. We also wrote in the log. We have not been very good about that. As a reward for school we treated ourselves to a piece of chocolate.

After school I made a fitting for the bottom step of the companionway so that I could use it for a typing table. In the evening Mom decided to make some cakes. She picked a *(yum yum)* chocolate cake mix with *(yum yum yum)* chocolate icing. In about an hour she and Melissa had the batter in the oven cooking. Our oven is a collapsible one and doesn't work very well because when you put it on the stove the burner is under only one side. This made one half of the cake cook faster than the other.

Just as the cakes were almost done, Dad shouted: "Dolphins!" We all came running out and sure enough, there were maybe fifty or sixty of them, but they were small. They darted through the water just under the bows. One of them actually hit the boat with its dorsal fin. Suddenly I saw something fantastic. As a large swell passed us a dolphin leaped out of it and, as his tail came down, he flopped it over his head and made a loud "crack." Then they were all doing it! Doing half somersaults in the water.

After a while I went inside to see how the cakes were doing. Mom was taking one out of the pan. She got it out in three pieces and also found it was burned on the bottom. Melissa made the icing, which was supposed to sit for twenty minutes, but after half an hour it was still very soft and gooey. I decided to go to bed. In another half hour Melissa came in and announced that we were going to have runny icing on our cake. It was runny but it was good. One cake disappeared in about fifteen minutes. After the cake I went back to bed again. We all slept well. I think I have finally learned to ignore the little noises of the boat.

February 10

MATTHEW: The morning started off with a good wind from behind and we were all hoping that the whole trip would be this good. Dad decided we had finally found the trade winds. The only time we had had steady winds was on the run from Florida to Bermuda. About noon Dad decided to clean the carburetor. Carburetors are hard to clean, but have you ever tried to clean one at sea? It's a mess. After he got the carburetor out, he opened it up. Out fell rust, dirt, water, and everything else you could imagine. He got some clean gas, soaked all the little parts and then scrubbed all the big ones. With a wire he opened a few holes that had been totally clogged up. At last he had found the trouble with the engine. About three o'clock he had all the parts cleaned and everything ready to put together. He mumbled to himself, "Now let me see, I think this bolt might go over here—or, maybe over there. How come there are two washers for this one hole? Oh no!" He dropped one of the washers into the bilge. He got down on his hands and knees with a flashlight. After a few minutes he screamed, "There it is! Hooray!" Soon he had the washer in his hand. He felt like kissing it. Then he started fiddling again. "I just don't know where this washer goes. Maybe here. No, that's too big. Aaaaah! I've found the place. Oh! I'm soooo stupid!"

He had dropped that washer in the bilge again! Down he went again on hands and knees looking with the flashlight. He saw nothing. He couldn't be so lucky twice. Without that washer we would have no engine and without the engine we would have no electricity. He saw it! No, it was just some junk.

"There it is," he shouted, "only I can't reach it." He tried a pair of pliers. How lucky! He got it! After that he put all the floorboards back so nothing could fall in. He picked up another piece of the carburetor and found the place where the washer went. In a little while it was together and installed. Ready to run. He started the engine up. It caught and then died several times. It was obvious that the carburetor had not been the problem. When the engine did finally run, it ran with a high-pitched whine, a whine that meant something terribly wrong. That dumb engine might have to be overhauled, but we couldn't do that without mailing away for parts. From that day on, we started saving our lights and only using them when necessary.

February 11

MATT: For the first time on this voyage we are running almost due south with the coast of Africa slanting obliquely in toward us from the northeast. By comparison with previous sailing this is almost like traveling on an expressway. We are smack in the middle of the main shipping route that follows the west coast of Africa north to Europe. I'm told it's the busiest shipping lane in the world since the closing of the Suez Canal, and I believe it. In the North Atlantic we were lucky to sight six ships a week. Now we frequently have six in view at once, and keeping out of their paths requires a different order of vigilance and raises some new problems. For example, it is no longer prudent to run at night without lights, but with Methuselah acting so poorly, electrical power is at an all-time premium. I figure what vitality Methuselah has left could be worth a lot to us if we get in trouble entering Port Etienne, Mauritania. I've heard plenty about the vicious swell on Africa's west coast and the danger of getting caught in it and driven ashore. When that time comes, I'll want some power in reserve, so we jolly Methuselah along and compromise with power requirements by burning only a masthead light at night, switching on running lights only when a ship is near enough for them to be effective. For the cabin we have an oil lamp.

We found use for our lights this evening. About 2000 in murky darkness I raised the lights of a large ship dead ahead. She appeared to be closing rapidly, but her light configuration was confusing. I looked in vain for the two masthead lights carried fore and aft by all merchant ships to indicate their direction of travel; and I had to assume she was bearing directly down on us. I jumped below and threw all the switches I could find until *Aquarius* was lit like a Christmas tree, but as I was preparing to alter course the approaching ship swung suddenly broadside to us about half a mile off, and hove to. I could just make out her silhouette, showing like ebony on coal, and I realized with a sudden and distinctly unpleasant chill that she was in fact a ship-of-war—a cruiser perhaps, certainly larger than a destroyer, my memory observed, recalling those wooden ship models I used to play with as a child. But what in hell was she doing here? *Aquarius* seemed too small and vulnerable for such murky encounters.

Now came the flashing of an Aldis lamp on her bridge: CT . . . CT . . . CT . . . , the light insisted in Morse, "I wish to communicate with you." CT . . . CT . . . CT . . . Stage fright replaced the crawly feeling. We'd been fooling with Morse since the middle of the Atlantic, but this was the first opportunity to use it. I fumbled for the signal light jammed in a cockpit locker and finally flashed back: T . . . T . . . T . . . T . . . , indicating I was ready (I hoped) to receive their message. My T's instantly released a flood of flashing, the Aldis fairly rattling with communication. I, too, was rattled, too much so to make words out of all the dotting and dashing, but I did shout the letters to Jeannine, who was wide awake by now: W . . . H . . . A . . . T . . . N . . . A . . . M . . . E . . . "They want to know who we are," Jeannine translated. "But what do they mean? Are we Herrons or Aquarians?"

Aquarians, I was sure, and I grasped the lamp and blinked back: Y . . . A . . . C . . . T . . . A . . . Q . . . U

...A...R...I...U...S... The ship apparently forgave
my dropping of h's (maybe it was accustomed to Cockney)
for it moved off into the night before I could finish blinking
out my own query, the gist of which was, "Who the hell are
you?"

February 12

MATTHEW: I woke up to find the wind very strong. It
had swung around until it was coming almost directly at us.
We were heeled over very far. Dad said we were in for
another storm.

It got worse and worse as the day went on. Dad put a reef
in the main and then changed the jib. The wind and the
clouds were rushing toward the center of a low to the north
of us; the sky looked like a quiltwork in some places. Mom
had been seasick almost the whole trip so far and this wasn't
helping her any. It's funny but I haven't been seasick at all.
I didn't even feel queasy. The storm got worse and worse,
and finally Dad put another reef in the main. When it got
dark Dad suddenly spotted a ship right in front of us so he
ordered, "Five-minute lookouts tonight." I took watch that
night.

February 12

MATT: Jeannine and I turned out late this afternoon to
tie a second reef in the mainsail. The wind was piping up to
force seven with a big sea running. *Aquarius* slammed into
it, making little headway, burying her lee rail; it was time to
take the pressure off. It's strange, though reassuring, that
we've heard nothing during this heavy weather from that
troll with the sledgehammer who tried to pound our keel off
in the harmattan north of La Palma. His disappearance is a
complete mystery. After arriving in the Canaries we turned
the boat inside out, trying to find the source of that pounding,

but nothing turned up. I even wrote urgent letters to the builder. I guess we'll have to add "one poltergeist" to our crew list.

To begin the reefings Jeannine unhooked the tiller from the vane gear, bringing the boat close to the wind and taking the pressure off the mainsail. I snugged in the topping lift and lowered the main to the last row of reef points—the storm reef. (By God, we've used that one a lot!) I secured the luff and leach cringles by their pendants and began tying in the reef points. Through the operation Jeannine kept the sail full and drawing, meeting each sea exactly, as it tried to come aboard, and regulating the amount of wind in the sail with a fine touch of the helm—pressure enough to keep the sail taut for a smooth reef, not so much that my work became difficult. I grinned at her from my perch on the cabin top as I tied in the last reef point. "We're getting to be pros at this. Remember what an exercise in frustration and panic reefing used to be?"

"Yes, I've noticed everything's been easier lately. No more struggles with halyards or spinnaker poles. No more torn sails. Could it be that we're getting experienced?"

"Don't say it," I cautioned. "Old Father Neptune will come up with something new and nifty to keep us humble."

Aquarius was sailing easier now—less pounding, much less heeling. We went below, well pleased with the exercise; maybe we *are* getting experienced.

February 13

MATTHEW: When I got up the weather was still bad. Everything was like the day before only the barometer was very slowly rising. Most of the day was spent napping and reading. Toward late afternoon the weather started getting calmer and calmer. Soon both reefs were out of the main and the genny was up. By evening the barometer was high and there was not a breath of wind. Everyone was overjoyed— Mom the most because her seasickness started to diminish.

We cooked a wonderful dinner that night. Mom and I made French fries, fried chicken and a wonderful salad with alfalfa sprouts in it.

You raise the sprouts like a crop in jars. I am the alfalfa farmer and this is how I do it. I use five mayonnaise jars and on the first day I fill one jar with about an inch of water and stir in two spoonfuls of alfalfa seeds. I let them soak overnight. On the second day I start another jar the same way, pour the water out of the first jar and rinse the seeds with fresh water. I do this for five days, starting a new jar each day and rinsing the old ones in fresh water to prevent mold. I keep all the plants in darkness so they think they are underground and will grow fast. On the last day I bring the jar that is finished out in sunlight and the sprouts turn green. We eat the contents of that jar (plain or in salad) and start a new batch of seeds in it. This way we always have sprouts and they are delicious—our only fresh greens when we are at sea.

After dinner we took an astronomy lesson from Bowditch. I was surprised how much I learned. We started at Orion and made a circle around the sky and back to Orion again. That way we could easily find each star that we learned. Part of the circle was made up of the Gemini twins (Castor and Pollux) and the Seven Sisters.

The water was full of phosphorescence. If you shone a light in the water, the area seemed to glow after you turned the beam off. Some glows were very big too. I think they must have been squids because they seemed to move. We also saw places where all at once the water would light up like there was a shark down there. Sometimes it was so bright we could see the light reflected off the sails. We were very scared and would keep away from the edge of the boat.

February 14

MATTHEW: There was still no wind this morning but Dad said we might pick up the trades later in the afternoon.

After my chocolate-milk breakfast I decided to make gigly twirls. My definition of a gigly twirl is anything attached to a string that spins in the wind. First I made a small pinwheel, which I hoisted it up the flag halyard. Then I made a paper helicopter and found that if I held it close to my face while it was spinning, the light reflected off the sides would almost hypnotize me. I put three or four of those up for telltales (on a sailboat, telltales tell you which way the wind is blowing).

Later the wind started to pick up from behind us as Dad had predicted. It kept getting stronger and stronger. We hoisted sail and started off again for Africa. There were no clouds in the sky at all, just bright blue; it looked like the harmattan. In the evening we sighted the aero beacon at Port Etienne. The wind was heavy from behind and it was very difficult to steer. We didn't like to come into a port in the dark so we hove-to for the night.

February 14

MATT: "Cruising has two main pleasures. One is to go out into wider waters from a sheltered place. The other is to go into a sheltered place from wider waters"—the observation of Howard Bloomenfield in *Sailing to the Sun.* At the moment we have enjoyed our fill of wider waters and are very intent on the sheltered places. It really seemed a defect of generosity on the part of Old Father Neptune to send us that last gale. We were already sufficiently impressed with the majesty of O.F.N.'s works, and could well have done without that final demonstration. Especially Jeannine. The magic pills that shielded her so effectively from seasickness during the passage to the Canaries have not been quite so successful lately. When the gale departed we all waited for Jeannine to return to her normal equilibrium, but that did not happen. The night and morning of calm were more like a breath of air than a rescue, and this evening, with the trade winds whipping up a lively sea, she seems more tired than ever. I think she is sick with more than *mal de mer,* but the motion makes every affliction worse, as we learned from Phil. The best cure right now would be that sheltered place, but it seems we are not going to achieve Africa so easily.

The first sign of African shores came about three this afternoon when we began passing through a fleet of trawlers, indicating that we were well inside the hundred-fathom curve. My 1600 running fix put us about thirty-five miles north-northeast of Cape Blanc, and about eighteen miles offshore. We continued southward at a furious pace, running before the trades at about six knots with the Canary Current adding possibly another knot and a half. At dusk we picked up the loom of the aero beacon from Fort Etienne airport arcing across the horizon. It was the first tangible evidence of that abstraction, Africa, which we've been struggling toward for so long. "We'll be in port tonight," I promised optimistically.

We plowed on into shoaler but not sheltered waters, practically surfing as the waves got steeper and began to crest. Still no sign of the Cape Blanc light—only the ghost of the aero beacon drawing slowly abeam; but our handsome sailing was rapidly turning into an uncontrollable sleigh ride. *Aquarius* was carrying all the sail she possessed and showing signs of broaching as her stern lifted to wave after wave. I didn't like to think about the broken gear and shredded canvas an uncontrolled broach and the resulting jibe would bring down on us. (We had fallen into the common trap of downwind sailors: a wind blowing in the same direction the boat is traveling never seems as strong as it actually is, and there is always a temptation to carry sail way beyond the limits of safety or sanity.) My fears, however, were racing far beyond our immediate problems. What were the waves like in the darkness ahead? If they continued heaping up at their present rate they would be breaking before long and we could be in serious trouble. In the absolute darkness I had no way of judging what might lie ahead, but we were about to get our first taste of West Africa's notorious coastal swell. In my fantasies I pictured us overwhelmed and rolled ashore in great breaking combers.

My charts brought no comfort either. They pictured Cape Blanc as a long and pendulous peninsula that dangled due south from the outthrust belly of Spanish Sahara. From its southern tip dripped a pestilence of shoals and sunken wrecks. We would have to negotiate this unfamiliar labyrinth in absolute darkness, rising winds and unpredictable seas. Once inside the shoals, we would have to beat a further fifteen miles north along the landward reach of the peninsula before we gained the shelter of Port Etienne. It was too much. To attempt the Cape tonight would be purest madness. The prudent sailor would heave-to and wait for daylight, when, presumably, the entrance to Port Etienne could be negotiated more easily.

We got the pole off the genoa, fought the sail to the deck and brought *Aquarius* head-to-wind so the main could be reefed down to storm dimensions. I hanked on the storm jib and we hove-to on starboard tack, reaching slowly out to sea. These operations, simple as I write them, consumed twenty or thirty minutes of the most violent effort. We finished drained and weary, depressed as much by having to relinquish our African landfall as by our foredeck gyrations.

Africa faded behind as we picked our way westward through the fleets of trawlers. The cabin seemed snug and friendly in the warm glow of the oil lamp, but only the watchkeeper stayed up to enjoy it. Port Etienne would have to wait another day.

February 15

MATT: We slept long and late. It was nearly noon and we had passed from the zone of trawlers into the shipping lanes before I summoned the resolution to reverse our course and head back toward Port Etienne. A noon latitude put us on a line about ten miles north of the Cape, but I had no idea how far off the coast we had sailed during the night. A family consultation ensued. The question was whether to make another attempt on Port Etienne or forget Mauritania altogether and turn south to run before the trades as far as Dakar. After some discussion we decided that skipping Mauritania would violate the intentions of our voyage and deprive us of our only opportunity to see the desert. Besides, after eight hard days at sea we longed to ride quietly at anchor in a secure harbor. (How easy that seemed!)

The wind was still strong and we made slow progress eastward under reefed main and working jib. A 1730 running fix put us about twenty-eight miles west of the Cape Blanc beacon in virtually the same discouraging situation as the night before—darkness imminent and all the hazards of the Cape untried. Should we repeat yesterday's tactics and heave-to a *second* night? There *must* be a better way. We were beginning to feel like Yo-Yos.

I studied the charts, and my growing concern for Jeannine's well-being made me a little less fearful of the African coast. North of Cape Blanc along the western side of the peninsula there stretched a series of shallow coves—no more than scallops in the coastline, most of them. They were entirely unprotected from the sea but the northernmost cove, tucked into the lee of a bump known as False Cape Blanco, ought to provide shelter from the trades. Perhaps we could anchor there in comfort and safety so long as the wind held constant. I took a bearing of the wind and confirmed it.

We trimmed the sheets and laid a course for the cove. The going was tedious. *Aquarius*'s working jib is not an efficient sail for beating to windward, especially with the Canary Current sweeping us steadily south of our course. For every mile gained we paid a heavy tax in leeway, and we tacked again and again as I repeatedly misjudged our progress. Sometimes the chop took so much speed off her that *Aquarius* came almost to a halt, but when I eased off and she picked up speed we sagged to leeward so much I despaired of ever gaining the cove.

We ground on and on, hour after hour. The children went to sleep; Jeannine lay below on her bunk. When I ordained another tack, she would come up and take the helm while I wrestled with the sheets—then flat below again. She looked white and peaked, and I felt a kind of desperation to gain that haven. Far across the water at the edge of the cove I could make out the lights of a military outpost. They stood in stiff formation along the shoreline, lighting up the buildings with a harsh sodium glare—inhuman, forbidding. *Aquarius* humped along like a stricken whale, straining toward the cove, which seemed to recede before us like a magic castle in a children's fairy tale. To compound our difficulties the starboard winch began to break up. It let go with a clatter as I was winding in the last few inches of jib sheet, wrenching the handle from my hand and flinging it overboard. With no spare winch handle aboard we had to luff up every time we came about while I strained to sweat the sheet in by hand.

We pressed grimly on, gaining advantage inch by inch. The shore lights spread out, the land began to take shape, the waves lost their antagonism as we entered at last the arm of the cove. At two in the morning, utterly spent, we dropped anchor in two fathoms of placid water about a hundred yards off the beach. Africa was ours.

Jeannine woke the children, who came on deck for a look at the elusive continent. There was not much to see—a few dim sand dunes, the low dark line of the beach, not a sprig of vegetation anywhere.

"Let's celebrate," Matthew said. "What can we have?"

"Well, there's no champagne," Jeannine said, "but we do have a bit of ice left in the box and I put a can of peaches on it this morning. What about the custard Matthew made this afternoon?"

With the sand blowing over us from the beach, we prepared a victory feast: iced peaches and lemon custard. Even our Azores champagne couldn't compare with it. Then we folded out the double bed and lay down to sleep.

February 16

MATTHEW: The next morning I woke up to find a beach on our afterdeck. Everything was covered with fine dirt. The air was thick with it. That morning I had my first look at a desert. Everything was light brown as far as I could see. There was only the military post and a small village up the coast.

We declared the sixteenth a sleeping day. The sailing had really been difficult. The wind was still blowing hard and was still out of the northeast, but there were no big waves in our cove so it was comfortable inside. In the afternoon the wind suddenly shifted to a sea breeze, and we were no longer safe where we were.

February 16

MATT: At 1500 the wind shifted as swiftly and precisely as if some hand had thrown a switch, and our snug harbor was snug no more. Within minutes the wind was bearing directly in off the reaches of the sea, churning up a nasty chop in the shallow waters where we lay. There was no choice: we had to get out, and fast. We abandoned our lazy plans for another night in the little cove, made sail, raised the anchor and in no more than ten minutes were frothing our way south along the coast toward Cape Blanc.

The sailing was glorious, wind almost astern and fresh. Once moving I couldn't regret our unceremonious eviction; I was tempted to stay with the wind all the way to Dakar, but we had an appointment with Port Etienne that was beginning to take on the character of an obsession.

As we passed the Cape I cast the log to get an accurate measure of our speed: six and a half knots. We were aimed at a sea buoy that terminated the long arm of shoals extending six miles southward from the Cape, but I was afraid we would miss the buoy altogether in the low-density sandstorm that seemed to be a permanent feature of Cape Blanc weather. Once clear of the shoals, the channel doubled north

until it reached the Cape again—on the inside of the shoals
this time—and continued still further north along the eastern
shore of the peninsula, ten miles, until it gained the protection of Cansado Bay scalloped out of the inner reaches of the
peninsula with Port Etienne tucked in the back of its throat.
Going south around the shoals was a mistake and a serious
one, although I had no inkling of it at the time. With the
engine available on an "emergency-only" basis, and our handling of jib sheets seriously hampered by a broken winch, the
stiff beat northward once we rounded the buoy was nothing
to take lightly—especially with the afternoon rapidly wearing itself out. I was piloting by the rules, following the big-
ship channel for absolute safety. What I should have done
was slip across the shoals just south of the Cape where my
chart showed a least depth of almost four fathoms, thereby
cutting out nearly fifteen miles of hard sailing and putting us
within striking distance of Port Etienne while there was still
light. Even if the chart were inaccurate and the water shal-
lower, we probably could have made it easily, exercising
caution and our depth sounder. But I was chary of shoals and
chose the longer and apparently safer path. It nearly proved
our undoing.

   With a following wind we covered the six miles to the
buoy in barely three quarters of an hour. But now began the
long and tedious beat northward hour after weary hour until
at last we found ourselves under the headlands of the Cape
once more, inside the shoals this time, perhaps a mile and a
half east of the point where I had so confidently cast the log
more than four hours earlier. It was dark now. We were bone
tired from the endless and inefficient tacking. The wind, so
briefly deflected to the west by the afternoon seabreezes, was
back in its unholy groove again, howling down the inside
reach of the Cape from the northeast; raising a vicious chop
in the shallow waters of the bay where I had counted on
smooth going.

   Once past the lighthouse, blinking on the high bluffs of
the Cape, I spread my charts for another look at our situa-

tion. Port Etienne still promised the most convincing shelter from the wind but the path lay due north right in the teeth of the trades for ten punishing miles. Beating back and forth, in our crippled condition, we would cover at least twice that distance, and my best estimate put us in the port at about three in the morning. It was too much—too hard on the boat, too impossible for all of us. Find something better, Jeannine suggested. About three miles north of the Cape the chart noted a loading facility for iron-ore ships that made an enclosure with the shore, its open end toward the south. The pier was L-shaped and might prove a haven from the wind; the bight between it and the shore showed a hopeful two fathoms of water.

"Shall we try for it?" I asked Jeannine. "It's just plunked there on an exposed coastline and might offer no shelter at all. I don't trust it; it's hard to tell what we're letting ourselves in for."

"Let's go close and take a look. Anything is better than this."

"Okay. I just hope the goddam engine works. I have a feeling we're going to need it."

It was very cold. Jeannine looked like a space explorer in her oilskins ballooned out with wool sweaters. I wiped a dash of spray from my beard. "I thought Africa was known as the Tropical Garden of Mankind. Where in hell are those balmy zephyrs? This one's a gale trying to pass for a trade wind."

"Listen, Matt, what do you see over there? It's too confusing."

With no moon to give shape to things, the lights on the dock were meaningless points of no-reference in the all-over blackness. They could be a hundred yards away or a hundred miles; they told us nothing. It was like trying to make sense from one of those "Connect the Numbers" puzzles without drawing in any of the lines.

"We're going to be right on top of all that stuff before we have any idea what it is," I said. "We'd better get ready to move fast." Time for Methuselah. I had no intention of charging into that inky enigma without an engine to back us up. But would it back us up? I opened the cockpit locker to expose the engine controls. They were soaking with salt spray. Every time I touched the starter button I got full benefit of twelve volts, shorting direct from battery to me. Somehow the engine started, though, and I nursed it along, bending the choke control wire to hold it half closed. The engine held its own, limping along half choked, with the throttle wide open. Through the din I could hear the starter motor whining in time with the engine. I guessed the switch had shorted and the starter would probably run until it burned out. What the hell, we needed the engine right now worse than the starter. Let it burn.

The camera speeded up, frames flickering faster, time and events accepting the tempo of the wind and the seas. We held course until we were almost on the dock, then got the sails down and Matthew and Melissa furled them from the wind—every week of practice saving us seconds now. *Aquarius* bucked and pitched like a stallion. I cut the lashings of the anchor so it could be dropped in a moment—our only insurance if the engine failed.

We were close enough now to sort out the lines and shadows of the pier. It was hardly a pier at all—just a gaunt steel superstructure for supertankers that loomed above us like a giant centipede in a footbath—everything silent, blank, depopulated, motionless in a violent world of wind and thrashing water.

At the water line not a shred of accommodation for a small craft—no fenders, no docks, nothing except the forbidding steel pilings towering out of the water. The scale did not favor our puniness—in the land of elephants we were gnats.

Was the captain cool in his hour of crisis? No, he was half mad with panic; but doing the best he could with what little brain remained unparalyzed. What to do? Docking here was impossible. Nothing to tie to, we'd be pulverized against the pilings. If not here, then *where?* "Jeannine, what do you think we should do? It's no good docking here. On the other hand—"

"For Christ's sake! Don't *ask* me what to do, *tell* me! We can *debate* later."

"Okay, okay! Hard to port—NO, HARD TO STARBOARD!" The names of directions deserted me as they always do when I need them most (something about mixed dominance), but Jeannine understood. She keeps her head in a crisis even if she shouts and curses like a banshee to relieve her feelings.

Aquarius veered madly away from the pier, but I was no closer to a solution than before. Should we try to anchor here in all this froth and risk being driven into the pier if the holding ground was poor? Should we try to get behind the pier and hope we could tie up without going aground? Either choice offered more uncertainties than advantages. Okay, Hamlet, *choose!*

"Let's try for the backside of the pier, Jeannine." We lurched south along the structure, past the elongated immensity of a bulk-cargo ship, the wind lending us more speed than I liked. Then past a trawler, tied stern-to at the end of the pier, swinging tight around her bow, the sea an absolute chaos of quarreling waves, Methuselah barely delivering the power to maintain control, but making it somehow.

Inside, a shade calmer. Only a shade of a shade—the pilings offering scant shelter from the wind and waves that coursed through them. Underneath us, one and a half fathoms if the chart was right. Ahead I could make out tiny fishing boats (if they anchored there, why not us?) but before we had gone more than a few feet the engine quit. I was at the controls in a second, energy and resolution boiling in me now, but Methuselah was dead and repeated rounds of the starter failed to spark him to life. No way left now to move *Aquarius* by our will. I scuttled to the foredeck, quick as a fox, and dropped the anchor.

Then we relaxed, slightly, and watched to see what *Aquarius* would do. She didn't do much of anything at first, just drifted about in a kind of messy limbo, nagged at but not bullied by wind, waves, and current. The bulk-cargo carrier, lying against the opposite side of the pier, effectively cut the wind in half, but the structure itself seemed to make the waves more irritable; and a countercurrent, sneaking up the shoreline against the wind, held us in a kind of uneasy suspension. We did not fall back and lie firmly against our anchor, setting it solidly in the bottom as all proper boats ought to do. We circled it uneasily like a dog sniffing a porcupine, and I could never tell whether it was holding or dragging or indeed if it was down there at all. But after a few queasy swings, some buttress in the balance of forces gave way, and we began first to drift, and then resolutely to bash and pound against the pilings of the pier. All four of us went to work with every bumper, boat hook and bare hand trying to hold our seven tons of *Aquarius* off those girders.

MATTHEW: It wasn't really a dock, just a steel superstructure. With such big swells and heavy wind if we had gotten our bow under it, it would have crushed the pulpit or even dismasted us. We made a frantic scramble for bumpers lashed to the cabin top. I dived for a big tire and just managed to hang it between the boat and a piling before we hit. But I wasn't so lucky the next time. The swells were carrying us all over the place and I kept missing with the tire and we kept banging into the iron I-beams of the pier. Melissa was in a panic. The boat was carried in circles by the tide and wind, missing the dock by inches. I heard the engine start and run just long enough to get us away from the dock and then die again.

Now we were in real trouble. The anchor rope which had wound around the keel as we went in circles was now also wound up in the prop. We were stuck. We couldn't pull in or let out on the anchor line or use the engine, and we were drifting into the dock for the third time. This time when we hit Mom jumped off with a line.

JEANNINE: With the anchor line wound around the keel we had no way to control the boat. The superstructure still threatened us within the scope of our line and we swung toward it once again. The children were ready with tires as the bow crunched against the steel pilings. We would keep battering them all night unless we could rig a second line to pull us against our anchor in another direction.

The refueling trawler lay at an angle to the dock. I shouted to Matt: "If we could get a line to that trawler we might be able to pull ourselves off the dock."

"That seems worth trying!" he answered. "We're in real trouble!" We leaped to fend off again as we blundered into the steel, the bumpers flattening like balloons.

I gathered up the longest docking line I could find, whipped it around a cleat on the afterdeck and balanced myself on the bulwarks outside the life lines. When *Aquarius* lunged again at the dock, I jumped off onto one of the steel crossbars and clung to the upright. The girders were greasy with iron-ore dust. I climbed, my arms and legs confidently remembering all the tomboy tree-climbing of my childhood. The task was more difficult than it had appeared, but somehow, thinking like a child, concentrating on the goal rather than getting panicky about slipping, I made it twenty feet to the top and ducked under a guard rail to the narrow walkway beside the fuel pipes. My hands, which had been playing out rope, suddenly stopped—there was no more. *Aquarius* was pulling away from the dock, pulling me with her. I tried to bend the line around the guard rail, but I was at the bitter end—the ever-so-bitter-end. I couldn't wrap it around; I could hardly hold onto it. "Matt! I don't have enough line!"

As I struggled, a turbaned Mauritanian came down the walkway. I asked in French if he could help me. *"Bien sûr! Un moment."* He continued on and never came back.

I snubbed the line against the rail as hard as I could and held on. The tension eased a fraction as *Aquarius* rode up on a wave and I took in an inch or two of slack, then held on again. Little by little I gained enough to make a whole turn around the rail. Just when I had enough to think about making a bowline the whole line went slack. "Good Lord," I thought, "she's broken away! I didn't take enough time with that cleat on the afterdeck!"

"Haul in!" Matt shouted. "I've given you more line at this end!"

I hauled. There was enough to get me to the trawler. I made my way with the line to the top of a kind of circular cement tower at the end of the dock. Here dockworkers handled the fuel lines and controlled the flow of gasoline and oil to the trawler. To my dismay I discovered that access to the trawler lay across a gangplank about eighteen inches wide and fifteen feet long. I flashed back to my childhood. A man I hero-worshiped was leading me across a narrow dam near a power plant. A trickle of water going over the top increased the illusion of danger. It was a long drop down if I fell, but I knew it was not difficult if I just walked steadfastly straight ahead. I was frightened, but I wanted more than anything for this man to admire me. My stubbornness walked me right across that dam, and I was proud. The gangway was like the dam—no rail, except this time there was space to both sides, and my motivation was a little different.

I walked across.

Communication with the trawler's crew was difficult. For one thing they were Italian; for another, we held different viewpoints. In my mind there was a crisis going on; in theirs it was time to arrange the nets for the morning's fishing. In the end they helped me graciously, and we succeeded in tying the line and drawing *Aquarius* off the dock.

I had accomplished my mission, but my thinking had gone no further than this point. How was I going to get back on the boat? I went back to the platform where we could call to each other.

"I'm going under to untangle the anchor line!" Matt shouted. "We can't depend on it to hold the way it is." Was he serious, going down in pitch darkness into that freezing

water, under seven tons of bucking-steel bronco, to untangle
a line he couldn't even see? He was. In the dim lights from
the trawler I could see his white skin and red bathing suit on
the afterdeck—and then he was over the side.

I was helpless; my job was over. I had to depend on the
kids to monitor his safety line and haul him in if anything
happened. Okay then, they could do it. My enforced role as
observer left me nothing to do but think. I couldn't tell what
was happening; I wasn't even close enough to tell when he
came up for air. So I fantasized about what to do if something
happened that Matthew and Melissa couldn't handle. I
would have to jump fifteen or twenty feet down into darkness
and swim about fifty yards. I could get to him if I had to, but
what if the plunging stern caught him a full blow on the head
as he was coming up for air? What if the cold and exertion
did him in? (We once had a dear friend, strong and healthy,
who died of cold and exertion in a sailing accident just five
miles from downtown New Orleans.)

Thoughts of death come when one is feeling helpless, not
when trying to survive. Were the kids listening for him to
come up for air? Would they know what to do if he didn't?
Would they be strong enough to help him? We had to rely
on them now as never before. What an ironic arrival in
Africa! Was this test to be the undoing of our voyage of
testing?

*It does not further one to cross the great water. Going
through to the end brings misfortune.* The *I Ching*'s ominous
forebodings leaped to mind. These words had alarmed us
when we first consulted the book for advice about the crossing. Were we experiencing their fulfillment now? Was this
how going through to the end brings misfortune?

MATT: I watched Jeannine scramble up twenty feet of slippery iron in her seaboots with a rope looped over one shoulder. Jesus! She's some woman! There are men who like their
women fragile, but I'll still take this gutsy, independent

broad for a wife any day—you could found a dynasty, fly to the moon with her. The Germans have a word I like better than "wife": *Lebensgenossin,* companion in life. It's not a bad word for marriage either, at least for the kind we try for: no pedestals, no prisons called "kitchen," or "office," only two persons standing separately, sharing equally, but bonded together by love.

With Jeannine ashore and that warp tied solidly to the trawler, our outlook was somewhat improved. Now, possibly, we could control *Aquarius* where she lay, slung between the anchor and the stern lines, and prevent any further damaging rendezvous with the pilings. It was a temporary solution at best, but the *only* one I could think of and it might serve until conditions moderated and we could improvise something better.

So far we had been lucky. Aside from a few dents, *Aquarius* had apparently suffered no serious damage through all the follies of the evening. But the ability to pull in or slack off the anchor line was critical to our mooring plan, and when I uncleated that line on the foredeck I found it *already slack,* and leading, not forward to the anchor, but aft, loosely, to some underwater snarl on the underbody of the boat—our unfortunate new anchor cleat. I tried to clear the line from deck, but it was locked solid somewhere in the water, and there was no way at all to control the anchor, no way to be sure if it was set or dragging, no way to ensure that the snarl would not come loose suddenly in the night and set us drifting, no way to release the anchor in a hurry if we needed to. I had no choice but to go underwater and try to clear the blockage.

The captain faced a chilling prospect. Did he experience bravery as he stood on the plunging deck at midnight? No, not bravery, exactly. Well then, fear? Not exactly fear either (*reluctance* was closer), but the captain did come to a definite understanding that life had suddenly become very *open-ended.* A hundred possibilities awaited in the water, a hundred outcomes. Until experienced, it couldn't be known which were real, which imaginary.

I stripped and found trunks, a face mask, a knife (vision of entangling, drowning, in the anchor rope), and a safety harness (vision of stern plunging, clobbering head). I handed the life line to Matthew: "If you don't hear from me, pull like hell."

JUMP!

Cold! Spikes in my ears, muscles contracting, piss freezing. Cold penetrating everywhere. No defense against it, none except speed. Skin, my vulnerable organ; skin leaking warmth like a radiator, leaking energy, leaking life over every cell and follicle of its surface. How much can I stand? How long in the cold before there's no warmth left to wind the chemical springs that drive the body? Got to spend warmth to get the job done. Okay, skin. There's warmth to spend; adrenalin to redeem for warmth.

I felt for the rope (eyes no good here), groping, twisting, gulping. What's this? Tangle around the prop. A good place to begin. Stern pounding theatrically overhead. You can't hurt me, *Aquarius.* Your steel ass is a paper tiger. All I need is a hand against it, one hand over my head and you can't hurt me. We move together in this fluid medium: you dive, I dive. Four, maybe five underwater gropings (brain not recording sequences very well), and the first tangle came loose. Up and blowing like a porpoise.

Now the keel. Cold intense. How are we doing, body? No sensation of chill now; enemy closing in, all-out attack over every inch of skin. Jaw stiff. Ears starting to ache, ACHE! Enough juice left for a gambol 'round the boat, Captain? No choice. *If I don't go, no one will.* Go!

I dived and started around, tracking along the rope: as deep as the keel, as far as the bow. Barnacles cutting my hands; little stabs of salt pain reporting back. Hand on the steel. Familiar old bottom! Iron bastard! I know every inch of you, every inch scraped and painted a dozen times. Under the rudder, another snag. Then, the rope unexplainably free in my hands. Churning, churning for the surface, fist above my head all the way (no sense taking a knock now). "I've got it! I've got it!"

MATTHEW: He gave us the life line and said, "Haul me out if I don't come up!" We waited a long time, once in a while hearing a gasp to reassure us. While he was down I cleaned the cockpit, it seemed like every rope in the boat was filling the cockpit! There *was* no cockpit! Down in the galley Melissa made tea to warm Dad when he came out. I followed him as he swam around the boat, holding the line and watching to be sure he was all right.

Finally Dad shot up, shouting, "I got it!" and waving the rope in his hand. Things were starting to look better.

MATT: Jesus! Hot tea and a dry towel! Long live Melissa! She stood over the little swinging stove, adjusting the flame, commanding its obedience, singing to herself and fussing over me—happy and serene. I haven't seen her so sure, so competent, so utterly lovely and graceful during the whole trip.

It struck me how wrong I had been to feel so very alone fumbling below in the icy murk. Melissa was at work up here ensuring my survival with the brewing of tea; Matthew and Jeannine were looking after me and the boat from opposite ends of the same rope—a harmony of cooperating opposites.

I looked at Matthew and Melissa. My God, what simply super incredible, uncommon kids they were! They might complain when the sun was hot, or school boring, but when the chips were down both kids were in there pitching like adults. I felt the tears dripping into my teacup.

My *blessed* teacup! I couldn't believe how cold I was. I held the scalding cup in my icy hands and felt nothing; there was more sensation of warmth from the steam rising off the surface of the tea. By now I was in wool pants and sweater, my teeth chattering like castanets, every muscle shaking uncontrollably, my brain shaking in its case, the cup dancing an athetoid dance in my convulsing hands.

I struggled into oilskins, but no amount of clothing seemed to quell the trembling. I was as cold as if still in the water. I couldn't go to bed now, the shaking would surely kill me; the only alternative was to keep active, go back to work. I vibrated up the companionway. Jeannine on the trawler and Matthew on the afterdeck were completing the final arrangement of lines. *Aquarius* was safe. We eased close to the trawler so Jeannine could jump aboard, then labored another hour to reduce the chaos of ropes and gear. I was sweating at the end, a blessed sweat of abundant warmth; and there was a glow among the four of us as we brought the work to completion.

I thought of the *I Ching,* so wisely tempering its warning with advice: *To avoid conflict everything must be taken carefully into consideration in the very beginning. If, in a group, the spiritual trends of the individuals harmonize, the cause of conflict is removed in advance.*

I tried to remember back to the beginning of this day. It seemed a hundred years since we'd snatched our anchor from that sandy cove—almost as long gone as that dim afternoon when we departed New Orleans. We could never go back to that day, either. Too many testings in between. We're different now, veterans and comrades as well as parents and children; and our harmony has overcome much conflict. I know there's more water ahead—the whole coast of West Africa, in fact, lies before us. But the doubts and fears we began with are gone. We've made it to Africa. Tomorrow we'll step ashore for the first time; step into a whole new world of adventures. But for now at least, the voyage of *Aquarius* has reached a sheltered place, safe in the arms of Africa.

Epilogue

Ancient Chinese sages were not literal men. Uncharted by any Admiralty, Great Water surrounds us all. Its horizons are only seen by sailors who set out upon a crossing.

Afterword:
How to Get There

STRANGER ON THE DOCK: (After several minutes' silent inspection) Uh. That's a nice boat you've got there, Mister. Taking some kind of cruise somewhere or something?

THE CAPTAIN: (Busy painting hatch cover) Well, yes. As a matter of fact I'm sailing to West Africa.

STRANGER: *West Africa!* You must be kidding. That's some voyage. Are you alone?

CAPTAIN: No, I'm taking my family—wife and two kids.

STRANGER: You're taking your *family* all the way to Africa on *that* boat? It's a little small, isn't it? Aren't you afraid?

CAPTAIN: It's not really so dangerous. She's a good boat, big enough for where we're going, and I think we've worked out most of the difficulties. . . .

STRANGER: (Wistfully) Must be wonderful to have the freedom to do something like that. Uh. What line of work are you in? (Meaning, where does the money come from?)

CAPTAIN: I'm a photographer; and my wife and I write. We're hoping to support outselves by doing articles as we go.

STRANGER: Boy, that's really the perfect combination. I certainly envy you—always wanted to do something like that myself, but in my position I can't even think about it. Got a wife and family to support.

CAPTAIN: I've got a family too.

STRANGER: Yes, but that's different. With your job you've got it made. You're not tied down; you can go where you please. I've got to be at the office every morning. I've got a boss to keep happy. Only three weeks off in the summer. Besides, the wife is afraid of the water. Must be nice though, not to have all those obligations. Sure wish I had your luck! (Stranger moves off to ogle adjoining yacht.)

(Fade-out)

MATT: We choose our own fates. At twenty-six I quit a job with a large, benevolent corporation because it seemed a trap to me—an opulent trap, to be sure, all plushed out with Christmas bonuses, stock options, credit unions, pension plans, and burial benefits; but freedom seemed more important to me than security. It still does. There have been actions I've regretted, but the decision to strike out on my own is not one of them, and I am reminded of how right it was every time a dockside sightseer compliments the boat and remarks wistfully at how "lucky" I am to be so free.

Wistful strangers on the dock are not rare in this world. Almost every American harbor we entered produced a few. In some the procession seemed endless, my disclaimers and explications a nightly ritual. It's surprising how many American males long to play Jack London and run away to sea. Well, why not? Voyaging is one of the very few occupations remaining in this modern world whereby a man can go where he pleases, do what he wishes, be what he will. The life is certainly attractive, yet pitifully few of the dockside dreamers ever realize their Great Ambition. What's the problem? Is breaking away all that difficult? I suppose it must be, or more would succeed.

I'm sympathetic. I've stood on the dock myself, looking at the lovely ladies rocking in their slips. (Every one of them whispered, "Sail away!") And somewhat later I stood on my own foredeck and experienced the not-so-romantic reality of that gossamer dream. Now that the reader has followed our erratic track across five thousand miles of ocean, I will presume to stand in the center of this stage and address some remarks to him (the male reader especially, but by no means exclusively) on the subject of voyaging, and how to get there.

Let us begin by disposing of one large misconception. Money is not the problem, not for most Americans at least. Our economy has grown so astonishingly wealthy that virtually any determined citizen of moderate means can gather the wherewithal for a sound boat, well-fitted for sea. *Aquarius* cost no more than the price of your average, run-of-the-mill luxury automobile. We invested about three thousand in stocking the boat and fitting her out for sea—after that, expenses were minimal. During the eighteen months of the complete voyage the four of us lived on less than seventy dollars a week. That figure included all living expenses and incidentals, and all maintenance to the boat (we hauled her twice). To be sure, we were careful with money; there was never very much of it, but we weren't parsimonious. We ate out from time to time, we took taxis when convenient, and we sent multitudes of cables to our agent in New York. Experienced cruising people have estimated that a family should be able to live on their boat and travel for no more than a thousand dollars a person per year. That's impossibly cheap by American standards, but for cruising abroad it is feasible; we did it on less.

All well and good, but most families can't put their hands on $500.00 in ready cash, let alone the few thousands required to cast off the lines and sail away. If voyaging is your dream then, how is it made real?

The California boatyard where *Aquarius* came to rest after her travels is home to more than twenty couples at various stages of building the dream boat in which they plan to explore the world. Most, but not all of them, are young; some have children; none is wealthy. They work at all manner of jobs, from school teaching to building maintenance and night watching; and they save their pennies, not for some far-off retirement dream, but for the immediate, step-by-step boat construction that they carry forward every day. The boats are not luxury yachts by any means, but most are soundly constructed and comfortably fitted for living afloat; there's no sign of skimping on materials, workmanship or aesthetic embellishments. The boatyard couples manage handsomely on very little, and they do so because (here's the catch) *nothing* is more important to them than finishing the boat—their passport to a new way of life. They have established their priorities to make this happen: they drive old cars, own no real estate, accept no long-term job commitments, and they shun beauty parlors, haberdasheries and insurance brokers. As a group they strike me as happy and self-reliant. They seem to have found a kind of security in their own energy and purpose, one that takes the place for them of the financial and institutional security most Americans work for.

Building one's own boat is certainly an impressive project, but not necessarily the easiest or even the best way to get to sea. I would recommend it only to the man who derives his chief satisfaction from the work itself—work that can easily eat up seven or eight years. I've seen many a would-be voyager run aground on an overly ambitious construction project. The coast of California is littered with the melancholy hulks of their half-completed hulls—great upside-down cement whales, beached and abandoned because the builder's dream ran down, bereft of money, energy or belief. On the other hand, buying a used boat can be a good deal cheaper and just as satisfactory as building your own if you proceed carefully. Certainly it is a lot faster.

Keeping afloat financially once the voyage has begun is another problem. Those of us who don't have a large garden of cash growing quietly in some financial greenhouse must earn as we go, and it helps to have a marketable skill—preferably one that is independent of place, like writing, or suited to short-term employment, since no one wants to sit in the same harbor forever. I think it is an advantage in a highly developed country like the United States to know a basic handwork skill like carpentry or engine mechanics. Skilled craftsmen are relatively rare; the pay is good and the demand steady. If I were young and fancy free, I would be tempted to search for a fairly large boat, say forty-five feet (however old and shabby), which could be converted into comfortable living quarters for myself and maybe a companion, with room for a large workshop well-stocked with tools and supplies. A basic knowledge of marine diesels and a stock of spare parts would not hurt at all. It should be possible for a good craftsman to take such a boat anywhere that yachtsmen congregate and earn a good living in relatively few working hours repairing the yachts. The Caribbean, the Canary Islands, the Mediterranean—all would be fair game. The prices and the quality of work usually offered in such places are scandalous.

In less-developed countries different skills are an advantage. Here skilled craftsmen in the basic trades are plentiful and accustomed to working for very little, but a specialized technical ability in a field like electronics may be in great demand. I know several cruising people who find work wherever they sail repairing radar sets for large ships, or working on marine radios, lorans, and the like. Doctors and nurses seldom have difficulty finding temporary hospital jobs in foreign countries, and one good friend of ours, an architect (unlikely cruising occupation), sailed to Lisbon, where he found an interesting and profitable year of work as a city planner! Most important is to remain flexible and resourceful. Anything is possible. Families have supported themselves towing plankton-sampling nets across oceans, or measuring water temperature and salinity for scientific institutions. An Australian we heard of in Africa lived by collecting sea shells, which he shipped home to an agent for resale in curio shops.

So much for money, the least of difficulties, but the one we all feel compelled to talk about first. Obstacles of the mind actually sidetrack far more voyagers than does money, and are much harder to talk about. So let me set down on the blackboard five oversimplified precepts for avoiding the mental obstacles that inhibit launchings. Like all lecturers, I will leave out more than I cover.

Understand your motives. That sounds simple enough. It was suggested by the *I Ching,* which advises in a hundred different guises, that a man know himself and establish the proper relationship to all the forces that surround him before undertaking any momentous enterprise. Let me ask you: Why do you want to make this crazy voyage? Have you really thought about it, or have you accepted the first convenient rationalization that walked down the highway of your mind? Is it adventure you seek? Notoriety? Spiritual awareness? A more vigorous image of yourself? Do you want to get away from your present life? Do you want to get away from your present *wife?* (Or husband?) Until you have honestly answered these questions (and a hundred more) you may find it difficult to muster the single-mindedness you will certainly need to launch your voyage.

Set realistic goals. Why is it that almost every would-be voyager I ever met planned to sail *around* the world? Is circularity that intriguing? Columbus tried it, Magellan did it, Slocum did it alone, Chichester did it fast. *Why do it again?* Surely we have enough proof that the world is round, especially as it abounds in fascinating places, underexplored and ripe for visiting, that don't require three years of one's life and an obsession with circularity.

Those same folks who want to get east by sailing west usually plan to do it in a ninety-foot schooner and expect to depart in two months' time. What fantasy! It's my opinion that more voyages come to grief on reality reef than any other, and it needn't be—there are so many better ways. Read books, look at charts, study weather patterns and sailing routes, talk to experienced voyagers, examine yourself— *then* make plans.

Be simple. A lavish yacht is not a good cruising boat. It is expensive to maintain and its complex amenities will refuse to function after a few weeks at sea. Not least, it will offend the sensibilities of people in less fortunate countries you visit —people who might otherwise become your friends and teachers. Personal simplicity is an advantage too. The less you require for material happiness and the more you delight in such readily available entertainments as the shape of clouds, the glitter of stars, the taste of the wind, the happier you will be with what cruising offers. Simplicity saves.

Proceed in small steps. A man I once knew bought an old boat in Florida intending to sail up the coast to New York. He was a child of the Flower Revolution and he viewed the sea as a beautiful natural wonderland that would preserve him safe from all harm so long as he locked into its many moods at a cosmic level of awareness. He therefore prepared for the voyage, which was his first, by laying in an ample store of organic stimulants—and very little else. He eventually arrived at his destination, I am happy to report, and immediately put the boat up for sale, describing the trip as the most harrowing experience of his life. ("Every time I turned around, Man, something new was trying to do me in!")

If you have had no experience afloat, or have only cruised in sheltered waters, don't try a world voyage the first time you venture beyond the breakwater. Get someone to invite you out for a sail. Rent a boat to see if you like it. Buy a small boat for your first experiences. Try a weekend sail to an offshore island, *but leave the folding aluminum lawn chairs at home.* (You'll never know whether hardship is your cup of tea until you try it—in graduated doses.) As you gain experience you'll know better what you want to do, and will make better decisions.

There's a lot to learn. I found that the amount of new information and seamanship skills I had to master in order to voyage safely was the equivalent of learning a whole new profession. It was a challenge that absorbed me entirely for the first six months of our voyage, and I was not inexperienced at the beginning. People who jump off the deep end unprepared, do so at their peril—the ocean is not forgiving of mistakes. I have just finished reading the account of a man and his wife who spent eight years building their dream yacht, and then lost it on the coast of Baja, California, only six days into the great retirement voyage. The weather that drove them ashore was not particularly serious, but they were physically and emotionally unprepared for it—they'd given all their time to building and almost none to seamanship.

Don't underestimate yourself. I was thirty-nine when we began to think seriously about a voyage to Africa; I was just beginning to deal with the idea of getting older. My first thought was how much easier it would be for us, financially, to go in ten years' time, but I reasoned that if we delayed until all was perfect, I would no longer be young and the voyage would be too difficult. Since crossing the Atlantic by sail was an entry I wanted to leave in the ledger of my life, the time to begin was right away. We went, and I know now that I underestimated myself. There is more in me than I had calculated—at least twenty years of voyages if I want them. Knowing this, I am, in one sense, more youthful now at forty-one than I was when the voyage began.

We have within us reserves we can't even recognize until they are tested. Believe in them. Don't underestimate yourself.

There is another problem, a very important one, which, for good reasons, I have not mentioned before: the relationship of men and women, and the special strains sometimes imposed thereon by boats. I am not the best authority on this subject; and so I leave you now, with many thanks for your kind attention, and appreciation of your occasional scattered applause, in favor of a more qualified observer.

JEANNINE: "The wife" is probably *the* number-one boat problem. You can read all the articles you want about yacht design, stowage, engines, or life rafts, but the real question for many dreamers is: "Will she go with me?"

First of all, don't sell her short. Don't assume what her attitude will be before you know, she might surprise you. And don't use her as your excuse if you really don't have the gumption to go yourself.

A lot of women do balk at boats, and the major reason, I think, is plain old ordinary fear. For the most part, they have led sheltered unrisky lives, depending on someone else to take care of them. They can't see themselves as functioning, important members of a crew, and having had no experience that boats can be fun and safe, they assume that boats are not fun and are unsafe. Perhaps they have never even learned to swim and are really afraid of the water.

If you want to introduce a fearful woman friend to boats, take her one step at a time. Someone who is afraid believes that she is not capable of handling a situation. The best way to get rid of that fear is to slowly teach her that she *can* handle the situation. Assume from the beginning that she will want to *participate* in the sailing. If she is just a passenger, her feelings of helplessness will increase rather than diminish. Explain the principles of sailing little by little so she understands that the boat is *supposed* to heel over, that the keel is heavy so that the boat will not go all the way over, and that it's all right if the lee rail goes under once in a while. If she is afraid of water, take her to a pool and teach her to swim, or at least to tread water. Get her to wear a life jacket in the water so she knows she *will* float. And don't scare her with a rough day the first time she steps aboard.

Some women forget how to use their bodies after they leave junior high school. Melissa's swim coach told me once that boys and girls progress equally well until the age of twelve or thirteen. Then the boys continue to improve while the girls' abilities decline. Girls are not encouraged to be athletic; they are confined in tight skirts and high heels. They forget how to move, jump, climb over, balance or run. I bite my tongue when I see a woman awkwardly climbing aboard a boat. Why should she have to hold a man's hand and be helped aboard? Society has convinced her to go through life as a cripple. (If you mothers think it's too late to reform *your* bodies, at least see to it that your daughters don't accept a state of being crippled as a condition of womanhood!) But maybe she's not afraid. Maybe she just enjoys comfort—the Pussycat Syndrome (it's nicer to sit by the fire and be stroked).

"Why should I leave my warm cosy house and go out in the elements?" That's a question many women ask. My answer to them is, you can't find out by reading a book. You have to go out in the elements and see for yourself. Perhaps you feel it's just too much trouble to live on a boat. That all depends on how you tackle it. A one-pot one-dish meal of good rich stew is appreciated as much as a five-course French meal when you are on a boat. At sea garbage goes over the side (no more smelly cans). Laundry is minimal and there is no ironing. But things balance out: while you may not have floors to wax on a boat, you do have to touch up the varnish and scrape the bottom once in a while! Maintaining a boat household is probably easier than maintaining a land household and usually it's a responsibility shared by the whole crew.

Comfort is important, but some women carry it to absurdity. A friend of mine once told me, "You know, it's a cute boat and all that, but Jeannine, I could never *live* on something like this! Where would I shave my legs?" (That lady will require rather more clever tutoring than I can include in these brief admonitions.)

There is something very fascinating and tempting about a boat to most men. Going off on a sailboat somehow epitomizes independence and manliness. This attraction can be hard for a woman to understand. In essence her man is saying, "I've met another woman. She's gorgeous and sexy and I love her! My friends are envious. *She can be mine!* She fulfills my dreams. Just being with her makes me feel wonderful. Will you accept her presence in my life?"

If you find yourself in the role of a jealous wife, it's important to face honestly what the boat represents. Do you have a good relationship with your husband? If the answer is yes, then you don't need to be jealous. He loves you more than he loves any boat. But take it seriously when boats first start turning his head, it could mean a serious affair.

Suppose your marriage is a little precarious. Better take a long look at yourself and ask what that boat has that you don't have. Maybe he's bored with sitting by the fire with his Pussycat. Bitching isn't going to bring him home from the yacht harbor if he is really happier there. Being with you has to be more attractive.

Of course it could be that he is running away from himself. If you think that's the case, talk about it with him. A real lack of success in everyday life is not apt to disappear magically on a sailboat. He needs to recognize what he's doing and be assured that you believe in him. But if he's running away from *you,* don't blame the boat, FIX THE RELATIONSHIP! If he becomes fanatical about boats, consumed by them, chances are it's bigger than both of you. Better write Dear Abby.

If he's just having a fling, relax and let him enjoy it. (Why not be in favor of anything that makes him feel powerful and manly? Don't you want him to be in favor of anything that makes you feel powerful and womanly?)

The actual situation is probably the one we started with —that is, he would like more than anything to have you share his new love with him, but doesn't quite know how to introduce you. And now the move is yours. Why not? Love is grand—even boat-love. There are thousands of women who enjoy sailing as much as men do, even more. A boat isn't a man's domain—it's anyone's trip. You need some physical strength, some mechanical ability, some fortitude (maybe some seasick pills), that's all. Women have sailed across oceans in small boats *alone!* I know a beautiful woman who makes a business of delivering yachts. She is a most capable and professional sea-person.

Many women think that when a woman engages in some activity that requires physical skill or effort, she inevitably sheds her femininity and becomes dirty and rough. Her hands may become rough, it's true. And we are all besieged by the sell that soft hands are equated with femininity— BOSH!

Joy and contentment are the best hand creams in the world. A happy, alive person is the most attractive person, male *or* female. Accomplishing a difficult thing together with someone you love is the best mortar for a relationship (the strongest mortar always contains a few straws—the last straw, the straw that broke the camel's back, etc.). When you manage to pull through something tough, you really *admire* each other. After all, you can't really look back on a weekend at Disneyland and say, "We *did* it! TOGETHER!"

Rigging
and
Deck
Arrangements

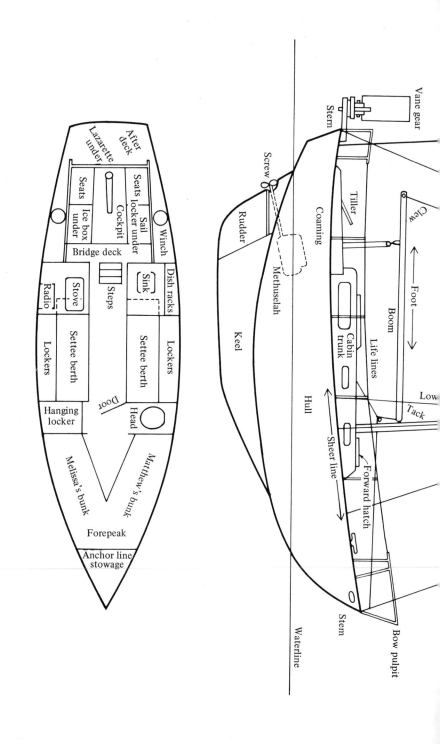

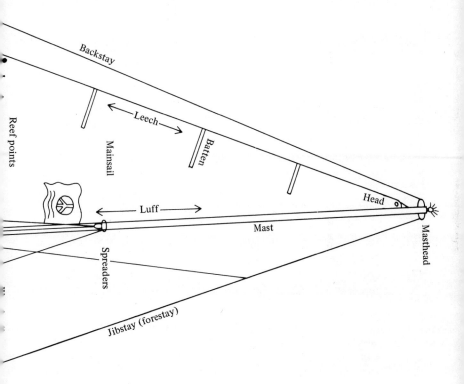

antenna

Backstay

Leech

Reef points

Mainsail

Batten

Luff

Head

Mast

Masthead

Spreaders

Jibstay (forestay)

Aquarius

Designed: Al Mason
(modified: Jerry St. Jacques)

Glossary

A FEW KIND WORDS FOR NAUTICALESE: We entered the world of small boats with scant respect for the nomenclature of seafaring. Our Nauticalese-speaking friends sounded overblown and preposterous to us, the words obscure and archaic. Why learn such a complicated paraphernalia of terms when all we wanted to do was take our little sloop a-sailing? Plain English in simple sentences would do as well, we reasoned.

We are wiser now. We have learned there *is* a purpose to the foliage of exotic terminology that overgrows every vessel, but it is best appreciated on a stormy night when absolutely everything has gone wrong at once. Consider the difficulty of passing orders to the foredeck in plain English when all is confusion and the wind tries to sweep half the words away: "You there! Mayberry! Pick up that rope on the right of you there, the one that's attached to the loose end of the sail. No, not *that* rope, the one that is on *my* right as I face the front of the boat. Okay, Mayberry, now bring the rope back toward the rear of the boat and push the end of it through that pulley contraption, the one nearest the behind end of the boat. . . ."

How much simpler, sweeter, and less ambiguous is: "Reeve the starboard jib sheet through the after sheet block." That is the true and practical reason for Nauticalese.

For readers unversed in sea matters we have compiled this

332

short glossary as a guide to the book; for those who intend venturing upon the water we have this advice: learn the old words. Use them. Your seamanship will improve amazingly, and as you continue the practice of Nauticalese you will recognize that the words themselves are lovely. And by speaking them you help keep alive a proud and honorable tradition.

Aft: Toward the stern; behind.

After-rail: Guard rail or pulpit around the stern of the boat.

Back the jib, to: To pull the clew of the jib to windward so the bow of the boat is forced away from the wind.

Baggywrinkle: Chaffing gear made from old rope and wound around shrouds and other rigging to keep sails from wearing against them.

Beat, to: To tack to windward, to sail hard on the wind.

Bail: A steel hoop to which halyards and other lines may be attached when not in use.

Batten: A flexible wooden strip inserted in a pocket sewn in the leech of a sail to prevent curling and flapping.

Bilge: The space in a vessel beneath the floorboards; the curve of the hull where the bottom merges with the side.

Bimini cover: A cockpit awning for protection from the sun. Well-thought-of in Bimini and other tropical places.

Binnacle: The housing for a compass.

Block: A pulley.

Boat hook: A pole with a hook on the end used for picking up a mooring line, fending off, and a thousand other purposes.

Bollard: A post, usually on a pier or quay, to which mooring lines are made fast.

Boom: A horizontal spar for extending the foot of a sail.

Boom preventer: A line rigged to prevent an accidental gybe when running before the wind. On *Aquarius* the preventer is stretched between the end of the boom and a cleat on the foredeck.

Bosun's chair: A sling or seat attached to a halyard in order to haul a person up the mast.

Bottom error: Meaning obscure, possibly a navigational error due to currents, drift, dreaming, etc.

Bow: The entire front part of a vessel from the mid-section forward.

Broach, to: To lose control when running downwind, usually on the face of an overtaking wave, so that the boat swings broadside to the wind and waves.

Bulwark: Solid barrier at the edge of the deck to prevent people and gear from being washed overboard.

Chaffing gear: Any protection against wearing or chaffing, for example, a wrapping around a rope where it rubs, a covering for shrouds where they touch sails, etc.

Chain plate: A metal strap that attaches a shroud to the side of a hull and distributes its load.

Cheek block: A block bolted to a mast or boom in such manner that the spar forms its inner face or cheek.

Chronometer: Any accurate timepiece used for navigation.

Cleat: A fitting to which a rope may be secured.

Clew: The lower after corner of a fore-and-aft sail to which the sheet is usually attached.

Close-hauled: Sailing as nearly into the wind (as "close") as possible. For *Aquarius* about 45 to 50 degrees off the true direction of the wind.

Coaming: The side of the cockpit extending above deck level and giving some protection from sea and spray.

Counter: A type of stern that extends aft of the rudder post and terminates in a small, flat endplate.

Cringle: An eyelet at the edge of a sail through which a line can be reeved as an aid to reefing. (A luff cringle would be an eyelet at the luff of a sail.)

Dead reckoning: Determining position at sea by estimating the course and distance run from the last known position. A good navigator tries to maintain a continuous D.R. position as a check on celestial navigation and an aid in an emergency.

Depth sounder (echo sounder): An electronic device which measures the depth of water under the keel by reflected echo.

Dinghy: A small boat for commuting between yacht and shore, and for a thousand other purposes. *Aquarius* carried an inflatable rubber dinghy known as a "Zodiac," which doubled as a life raft.

Downwind: To leeward of a particular point. To run downwind is to run with the wind.

Eye of the wind: The direction from which the wind is blowing.

Winds are named by the direction from which they come (a "west" wind blows *from* the west); currents by the direction in which they flow (a westerly current sets *toward* the west).

Fairing: Any putty or filler used to "make fair" or fill out uneven spots in a hull.

Foot: The lower edge of a sail.

Forestay: A wire rope connecting the masthead with the bow, to which the headsails are hanked.

Genoa: A large triangular headsail used in light to moderate airs.

Gimbal: A pivoting device for keeping a compass, lamp, stove, or whatever, level against the movements of a vessel at sea.

Greenwich Mean Time: Local time at the meridian of Greenwich, England. Used as an international time standard in navigation.

Grommet: A metal eyelet in a sail or awning.

Gudgeon: A metal eye attached to the after end of the keel into which the bottom pivot of the rudder stock is set.

Gybe, to: While running, to bring the wind from one quarter to the other so that the boom swings across. Gybing is the opposite of tacking in that the stern rather than the bow passes through the eye of the wind. An unexpected gybe "all standing" in which the boom swings uncontrolled from one extreme to the other can do sudden and violent damage to a boat's rig.

Handbearing compass: A hand-held compass with a sighting device for taking the bearing of any distant object.

Halyard: A rope used for hoisting a sail or flag.

Hank, to: To attach the luff of a headsail to a stay by means of a clip called a hank.

Hard on the wind: Sailing close-hauled.

Hatch: An opening in the deck provided with a cover.

Head: The top corner of a sail; a marine toilet.

Heave to, to: To trim the sails and helm in such a manner that the vessel lies almost stationary.

Heel, to: Lay over, or list.

Helm: The tiller or wheel used for steering.

Jib: A triangular headsail. A working jib is smaller than a genoa and can be set in heavier airs.

Jibstay: See Forestay.

Jerry can: A narrow flat-sided fuel can.

Kedge anchor: An auxiliary anchor, usually smaller than the main one, used to haul or "kedge" a vessel off when she has gone aground.

Keel: The fore-and-aft structural member on which the hull is built.

Lazarette: A stowage space in the stern.

Leech: The aftermost part of a sail.

Leeward: The side opposite to that on which the wind is blowing.

Line: A rope with a purpose. On a vessel most ropes used to do work are called lines.

Loom: Something seen indistinctly at a distance. The glow of a light on the horizon before the actual light can be seen.

Lubber line: The mark on a compass bowl which is aligned with the vessel's head and therefore indicates its bearing.

Luff: The part of the sail along its forward edge. To luff is to turn the head of a vessel into the wind so the luff flaps idly.

Mainsail: The fore-and-aft sail set on the aft side of the mainmast.

Masthead: The top of the mast.

Noon position: A vessel's position at true noon when the sun is at the apex of its travel. Widely used in navigation because latitude at noon is very easy to figure.

Occulting light: A navigation light whose visible periods are equal to or greater than its periods of darkness, that is, a light recognized by its periods of darkness rather than its flashes of light.

Pendant: A short hanging rope or wire, for example, the pendant at the tack of a headsail, which raises it above the level of the pulpit.

Port: The left-hand side of a vessel when facing forward.

Preventer: Any line or rigging backing up or limiting the movement of spars, cables or the like.

Pulpit: A barrier of steel tubing at the stem and/or stern of a boat which provides a secure place where a man can perform work without danger of being washed overboard.

Reef, to: To reduce the area of a sail by tying or rolling up part of it.

Reefing gear: Any tackle used in reefing.

Rigging: Sheets, halyards, topping lifts and the like—all the ropes for hoisting, trimming and controling the sails—are called running rigging. The stays and shrouds, which support the mast and are permanently fixed in place, are known as stand-ing rigging.

Rudder: A flat, movable board hinged vertically at the stern of a vessel that is used for steering.

Run off, to: To run downwind, often before a gale or storm.

Sextant: A reflecting instrument for measuring angles of celestial bodies above the horizon. The principal instrument used in celestial navigation.

Shackle: A metal U-shaped fitting with an eye in each of its arms through which a pin is screwed in the manner of a crossbar.

Sheet: A rope for trimming a sail, secured either to its clew or boom.

Sheer, sheerline: The curve of a vessel's gunwale seen in the vertical plane.

Shroud: A wire rope giving sideways support to a mast.

Snapshackle: A shackle that has a hinged bar instead of a screw pin for quick release.

Spar: Any mast, boom, pole or the like for supporting or extending a sail.

Spinnaker: A large, light headsail for running or reaching in light airs.

Starboard: The right-hand side of a vessel when facing forward.

Stay: A wire rope giving fore-and-aft support to a mast.

Substay: A short stay parallel to the jibstay but running from spreader to foredeck.

Stern: The rear part of a vessel from the mid-section aft.

Swing compass, to: To swing the head of the vessel to all points of the compass in turn when checking or adjusting the compass.

Tack: The lower forward corner of a fore-and-aft sail; also a point of sailing as close to the wind as a vessel will go with advan-tage. To tack is to sail to windward in a zigzag manner, first on one tack, then on the other.

Tang: A metal fitting screwed or bolted to a mast for the attach-ment of rigging.

Taffrail: The rail around the stern, usually on a large ship.

Tiller: A wooden bar secured to the rudder head for steering.

Topping lift: A rope supporting the outboard end of the boom.

Vane gear (self-steering vane): A mechanical device for steering a vessel that is guided by the direction of the wind without the aid of a helmsman.

Warp: A strong rope attached to an anchor or dock.

Warp in, to: To move a boat by hauling on a line attached to an anchor or dock; to bring alongside a dock.

Winch: A winding device consisting of a drum on an axle, a ratchet, and a crank used to gain mechanical advantage when hauling on a rope.

Windward: The side of the boat closest to the wind.

Matt and Jeannine Herron met and were married when they were teaching at Friends' schools in Jordan in the 1950s. Since returning to this country, Matt has been a magazine photographer and writer and Jeannine has done graduate work at Tulane and Stanford. Matt organized the Southern Documentary Project, a team of photographers who recorded the civil rights struggle in Mississippi, and Jeannine was a co-founder and program director of the Child Development Group of Mississippi, the largest head-start program in the South. She recently finished her doctorate in anatomy at Tulane and is now doing neurological research in the organization of cognitive processes in the brain. Both Matthew and Melissa attend school in Palo Alto; Matthew is addicted to computers and radio-controlled airplanes and Melissa has a passion for horses. Both the younger Herrons won prizes in the *Yachting, Jr.* 1972 writing contest and in *Boy's Life* with stories about *Aquarius*.